HOMEMADE
Noodles and Cars

ARLENE CURNS

ISBN 978-1-64458-907-6 (paperback)
ISBN 978-1-64492-524-9 (hardcover)
ISBN 978-1-64458-908-3 (digital)

Christian Faith Publishing, Inc.
832 Park Avenue
Meadville, PA 16335
www.christianfaithpublishing.com

Printed in the United States of America

For God so loved the world that he gave his
one and only Son, that whoever believes in
Him shall not perish but have eternal life.
                                        —John 3:16

If you declare with your mouth "Jesus is
Lord" and believe in your heart that God
raised him from the dead, you will be saved.
                                        —Romans 10:9

Everyone who calls on the name
of the Lord shall be saved.
                                        —Romans 10:13

One of my fondest memories is watching my mother roll out the dough for homemade noodles. I didn't know she was trying to stretch her food budget to feed a family of seven, only that they were so delicious.

She would roll the dough out in large circles and let them dry overnight on the kitchen table. The next day, she would cut the dough in strips, stack them up in layers of five, and cut them into noodles. She would stir them into a pot of boiling broth, and soon we had a wonderful dinner.

My mother learned how to make noodles from her mother, my grandmother. Yes, Grandma made noodles too.

The cars—well actually, I was involved with cars before I was even born. But I'm getting ahead of myself.

So pull up a chair, pour yourself a cup of tea, and I will tell you the story of my ordinary days. It begins with Grandma and Grandpa Yats.

1

I thought grandpas were supposed to be soft teddy bears, yet there it was—printed in black and white, presented before a judge. The divorce papers for my Grandma and Grandpa Yats clearly stated that he had hit her in the face with his fist. The divorce was granted. That was way back in 1917 when getting a divorce was a bit of a scandal.

My maternal grandfather was born in Wabash, Indiana, in 1865, just as the Civil War was ending. He was the youngest of six boys, and his mother named him George.

The Yats farm was forty acres of rich soil where they grew corn and wheat that they either sold or bartered for other goods. Cows, pigs, and chickens supplemented their needs, and occasionally, they were able to spare some of them to sell. Their wood stove called for lots of logs to be split. It was a good place to raise their large family of active boys. The boys attended a one-room schoolhouse. Between school and all the chores involved with farming, it kept them busy and out of trouble as they grew into young men.

Their farm was on the outskirts of Wabash, but still close enough for the boys to walk into town. There was a train that made a stop at Wabash, and like most boys, the Yats boys were fascinated by the train. Most of the activity in town centered on the train depot; everyone congregated there to hear the latest news. The train helped in the development of the town, but it wasn't the train that brought

Wabash its greatest claim to fame. When George was fifteen years old, Wabash became the first city in the world to become lighted with electricity. What an extraordinary event! It was celebrated all over the world. If I had guessed what the first city was to have electricity, I would have said "New York" or "Chicago" or even "Paris." But no, it was Wabash, a reasonably small city of 3,800 people.

The city council had agreed to do a two-week trial to see if the lights would be effective. Four 3,000 candlepower lamps had been suspended from the top of the courthouse. Two wires ran from those lamps to the courthouse basement where they were connected to a threshing machine that provided power. On a balmy spring evening in 1880, the switch was turned on, and the courthouse lit up to the wild cheers of the townspeople.

After the two-week test, everyone was thoroughly impressed, and the city council voted unanimously to have it installed citywide, an area of one mile in diameter. The cost for the complete apparatus was $1,800. The engineer's salary to operate it was $400 per year.

Comparisons showed that it would be the least expensive light system in the world. The cost for the entire city was $800 a year, and by not using the electrical system on nights when there was a full moon, they could save even more. Just imagine any city today turning the lights off on moonlit nights to save a few dollars.

Even though George was the youngest, he had his share of chores to do just like his dad and brothers. He made up his mind very early in life that farming was not his destiny. Getting up at daybreak and working until sunset seven days a week didn't appeal to him. He wanted to live in a city and have his own business, something like that of Mr. Stacey, who owned the general store in town, or Mr. McDougal who owned the hardware.

When George was seventeen years old, he left the security of home and family to make his own way. His brothers were content with farming as a living, and the older boys had farms of their own now—two of them adjoining the family homestead property. George's mother was uneasy about her youngest son leaving, but he was determined.

With a small nest egg in his pocket, George set out on his own. He visited a few towns before finally settling down in St. Louis, Michigan. St. Louis was actually a smaller community than Wabash, but George liked the town. He was excited just to be off the farm and actually living in a city even if it was smaller.

St. Louis, located near the center of Michigan, was often called the "Middle of the Mitten." By the time George arrived there, mineral springs were discovered, and St. Louis had become a destination for people seeking health benefits, so he felt sure the city would be growing.

George took a room in Barry's Boarding House and soon got a job working at Koppel's Restaurant. He was industrious and serious, working hard to get ahead. He saved everything he could, eating all his meals at the boarding house where they were included with the cost of his room. He allowed himself a single luxury—a bicycle—for fun and quick transportation around town.

George had lived in St. Louis two years when he met a young lady who stole his heart away. She was only fourteen years old when they met. Her name was Katherine Ann Sloan, and she lived on a farm in the nearby village of Alma.

George was attracted to "Katie" the first time he saw her. She had beautiful blue eyes and auburn hair cascading down to her tiny waist. A blue satin ribbon was twined playfully through her hair. She was wearing a blue dress that made her eyes look even bluer, if that was possible. Katie had tiny feet, and she was wearing her favorite white button-up boots.

Katie was smitten with George too. And to Katie, he was just enough older than her to be romantic. And he lived in the city!

They had a long distance romance with George pedaling his bicycle over the bumpy dirt roads to court Katie. They started talking about marriage early in their courtship, but Katie's parents thought she was too young and tried to discourage them. "Just wait a while longer," they pleaded. She begged them and kept saying, "Grandma Sloan got married when she was sixteen, and that turned out fine." That was true, and there was little they could say in return except that they loved her and wished she would wait a while. Her parents' plea that if it was true love, it would still be there later on didn't make any difference to Katie and George

There was a silly little song that was very popular then,

Ka-Ka-Ka-Katie, Beautiful Katie,
You're the only ga-ga-ga-girl that I adore.
When the ma-moon shines o'er the ca-ca-cowshed,
I'll be waiting at the ka-ka-ka-kitchen door.

That's what he called her—beautiful Katie. They were married the next year. Katie's parents, impressed with George's work ethic, gave into the pleading and gave their blessing for Katie and George to marry.

The wedding took place in the side yard of the farm where Katie lived. They stood beneath a rose arbor laden with gorgeous pink roses. Katie wore a white lace gown with a tiered ruffled skirt. A circle of plaited white roses crowned her auburn hair. Her wedding bouquet was composed of white roses too intermingled with dainty baby's breath. Streamers of white satin ribbon played in the gentle breeze. The toes of her white boots peeked out the bottom of her wedding dress.

George was wearing his only suit, a dark blue, complete with vest. He had purchased a white shirt with French cuffs and wore a light blue tie and gold cuff links with matching tie tack. His black shoes were polished to a high gloss.

They gazed tenderly at each other as they repeated their vows, their love for each other clearly showing on their faces. They had the whole world ahead of them and were ready to conquer it. George was twenty. Katie was fifteen.

CHAPTER 2

George and Katie were so in love. He absolutely loved Katie, and she adored him. She looked up to him—a man of the world. They started married life very simply. Katie brought a metal trunk bound with leather straps that held her belongings and moved into his room at Barry's Boarding House.

George continued working at Koppel's restaurant, and Katie took a job helping Elizabeth Barry with the cooking and cleaning. They took their meals at the boarding house, and occasionally, George was able to take her to Koppel's for a night out. He bought Katie a bicycle, and they enjoyed pedaling around the countryside.

They were saving everything they could so George would be able to realize his dream of owning his own business. He believed that being the owner of a business was the way to accumulate wealth—not working for someone else.

On their first wedding anniversary, George took Katie to the Park Hotel for dinner. She put on her prettiest dress, styled her hair in the latest fashion, and wore her new hat! A frivolous purchase, but George had relented when Katie admired it in the shop window. It was a pretty broad-brimmed straw in lavender, banded with a violet ribbon of silk, and accented with a matching cabbage rose. With her auburn hair, it was stunning. Katie, only sixteen years old, was a vision of loveliness. Her eyes were sparkling, and George was so proud of her and thrilled to be able to make her happy.

As soon as they were able, George and Katie moved out of the boarding house. They rented a small home, and George left the restaurant to go to work for a steel company where the wages were higher. Katie helped grow their nest egg by taking in laundry and ironing.

They had been married four years when Katie became pregnant. She was overjoyed. George was happy about the baby but could envision his dream of having his own business evaporate. With a baby on the way and all the things they need, it would cost a lot of money.

They had $200 in their little "buy a business" fund. George made a decision to see what he could buy with that sum of money. After all, it was a good starter sum. Maybe he could purchase a restaurant, since he had some experience along those lines.

He came home one day so excited! He had heard of a business for sale in Owosso. The owner would accept the sum of $200 as a down payment, and George could pay the remainder in small payments. He was so excited sharing all this with Katie. "Now is the time to do it with the baby coming," he exclaimed. Katie was so happy for him that his dream would come true. She was thrilled too to think they would have their own business and so happy about the baby she was carrying. Her joy burst like a bubble when he told her what the business was. A saloon!

George bought the business in spite of Katie's protest. He was the man of the house, and he would make the decisions. George was fiercely ambitious and determined to do everything in his power to make his business successful.

Katie delivered a beautiful, healthy baby boy, who they named Clarence. George was so proud of their baby boy and was eager to share congratulatory cigars with all his friends. Katie spent her days playing with the baby and caring for his many needs while continuing to take in laundry and ironing from her established customers.

George was very successful with his business, and soon, they were able to move from the house they rented and buy their first home. It was a pretty home—a two story with four bedrooms—on a tree-lined street with a wide grass boulevard down the center.

Their home was painted pale yellow with white trim. Rose bushes on white trellises climbed up either side of their broad porch. Stately oak and maple trees shaded the home. It looked so peaceful and tranquil. It seemed to be a home filled with happiness—a handsome young couple, owners of a business, and a darling baby boy.

Katie had two more children. Edna was born three years after Clarence, and two years later, my mother, Hazel, was born.

Their children were beautiful, perfect in every way. Clarence was a handsome little boy with blue eyes and light brown hair worn in a short cut. Edna and Hazel were as different as night and day. Edna had dark brown eyes, brunette hair, and an olive complexion where Hazel had blue eyes, blonde hair, and a porcelain complexion. They all had one thing in common—they adored their mother.

Everything should have been perfect in their home, plenty of money from their business and three adorable children. But George had started drinking, and things slowly began to change.

Katie would have dinner on the table at their regular dinner hour, and George wouldn't come home. When he arrived home later, under the influence of alcohol, he was surly, belligerent, and angry. Over time, he began shouting and calling Katie horrible names. It was so hurtful to Katie and very upsetting for the children.

The children tried to stay out of the way when their dad was home. They had been cautioned by Katie to be quiet and not to get Dad upset. What was happening to the man she had married and loved so much? Katie was raised in a Christian home, and she had never heard her father use such language. She was ashamed to tell her parents what was happening because they had tried to talk her out of getting married so young. Now, Katie was only twenty-five and had three children. There was nothing she could do except keep praying for George and trusting Jesus to change his heart. She wanted so much to make this marriage work.

The Yats children
My mother, Hazel (center) with Edna and Clarence

Owosso was a quiet little town—a wonderful place to raise children. School took up most of Clarence's, Edna's and Hazel's time, and there was an abundance of fun things to fill their play time. All three had bicycles. There was a glider in the backyard where Edna and Hazel liked to sit in the shade to read their books. They had a miniature tea set and had tea parties, sipping from the little cups and munching on make-believe cookies. Their mother taught them how to sew and helped them make doll clothes.

Clarence played ball with neighborhood friends. They used to toss a baseball or football around on the boulevard that ran down the center of their street. The Yats kids didn't bring their friends to their house when their dad was home, but he was working most of the time.

As they grew older, they loved going to the roller rink. They also looked forward to the annual Shiawassee County Fair that was held at McCurdy Park in Corunna, the county seat. The fair was a lot of fun and lasted for a whole week. Just the trolley ride to get there was a summer adventure.

Concerts in the gazebo at the park were fun too. All the kids would bring their bikes to ride around, and some played games like hide-and-seek or tag. The best concert of the summer was on the fourth of July because it ended with a huge fireworks display.

One of the most exciting things that ever happened in Owosso was the day in 1909 when Carrie Nation came to town. Carrie Nation was a hatchet-wielding temperance leader who traveled the country and was famous for smashing saloons. George exclaimed that "she better not set foot in my place." His saloon was in a prime location to be noticed, right on the corner of Main and Washington streets in downtown Owosso.

Carrie Nation's arrival in Owosso was to be a momentous event for the town, and everybody was talking about it. The members of the Women's Christian Temperance Union (WCTU) had passed out flyers urging everyone to attend. A lot of people brought picnic lunches to the park where she was going to speak, and many were waving American flags. It seemed everyone in town was there except George.

When Carrie arrived on that Saturday in the summer of 1909, she was wearing a black dress with a white lace collar. She was in her early sixties and had toured America for years in a countrywide crusade against tobacco and alcohol. She was one of the most well-known people in the United States. She had been arrested and jailed thirty-three times for breaking up saloons with her hatchet.

In one of her lectures, Mrs. Nation stated that she would smash the tobacco evil first. She was quoted as saying, "I have received the most abuse in my experience from the rank-smelling, stinking tobacco users." She admonished the girls in the crowd never to marry a man who is so dirty he will defile his mouth with the weed and so senseless he will spend his money for it.

She also had little use for the politicians who supported saloons. "If you men of political parties don't turn your backs on the saloons and become prohibitionists, you will go to hell as sure as there is a hell."

Carrie Nation was well-received in Owosso that day, with the ladies of the local WCTU showing great appreciation. She didn't come inside George's saloon, or she would have met a formidable foe in George Yats. He had a temper equal to hers and was not going to let her through his saloon door with her famous hatchet. He very likely would have run her out of town, but when she finished speaking and had partaken of the picnic lunch provided, she left town.

The next year, on April 4, 1910, Shiawassee County voted overwhelmingly to go "dry."

CHAPTER 4

My mother, Hazel, in white dress, with Edna

It isn't known if Carrie Nation's visit to Owosso was the cause of Shiawassee County voting to go "dry," but Shiawassee County included Owosso, so George's saloon was out of business. He could no longer sell liquor. The lucrative business that he had built up had to be closed.

George was so frustrated and angry. All he had worked for so hard was gone. He was grouchier than ever at home, taking his anger out on Katie and the children. Life in the Yats household wasn't as pleasant as it would appear to others.

Nothing Katie could do pleased George. She tried her hardest to be a peacemaker, but the hurtful words only escalated, making it more difficult to be around George.

George went back to work for the steel company again—heavy, hard labor. When he came home at night, Katie would say, "You must be tired," or "How did your day go?" which only got her a grunt in reply. It really was understandable that George was angry about losing his business, but it wasn't Katie's fault, or the children, but they got the brunt of his frustration.

Katie secured a position at Reliance H&S doing ironing and also took in laundry at their home to supplement their income.

Their eldest child, Clarence, was doing well in the barber trade and was well-respected around town. He had been courting a young lady, Agnes Riley; and in 1910, the same year George lost his business, Clarence and Agnes got married. They bought a house on Main Street in Owosso and immediately set up housekeeping.

Being the only son, Clarence felt a certain amount of guilt leaving home. He had often intervened as his mother's protector from his father's outbursts of temper.

Edna too, who was eighteen years old now, had fallen in love with a young man—an actor. Oh! It was so romantic! Al Leybourne had been in town for a week, appearing in a comedy skit at the theater downtown. He met Edna at the soda counter of the drug store next door to the theater. They had two dates while he was in town, and since he had moved on to his next acting engagement, he sent her a penny postcard every day.

Their relationship quickly went from having an ice cream sundae together and long afternoon walks to exchanging letters. By the time Al made a return appearance to the theater downtown, they were writing romantic letters about getting married. When he came back to Owosso, he gave her an engagement ring.

All of Edna's girlfriends were envious. She was engaged to marry Alexander Leybourne from Camden, New Jersey! A real-life actor who traveled the country appearing onstage! After their marriage, they would travel the country together, and Edna would appear onstage with him as his costar at theaters and opera houses.

Edna and Al had only known each other three months when they set the wedding date. It seemed like a dream come true to Edna. She was happy to escape the small town of Owosso, Michigan, and travel the country with her new husband and being his partner onstage—so glamorous. She was very excited. They set the date for July 10, 1910, just seven months after her brother had gotten married. Older brother, Clarence, and his bride of seven months, Agnes, stood up with them at their wedding.

A newspaper article shared the news of the joyous event,

Leybourne-Yats Wedding

A quiet wedding took place at six o'clock Monday evening at the home of Mr. and Mrs. George N. Yats, when their daughter, Miss Edna, was united in marriage to Alexander Leybourne of Camden, New Jersey. The couple was attended by Mr. and Mrs. Clarence Yats, the former a brother of the bride. Rev. G. W. Jennings performed the ceremony in the presence of a small number of relatives.

Following the ceremony the guests were served a delicious wedding supper.

Mr. and Mrs. Leybourne left on the evening train for Manistee where they will spend the balance of the summer, after which they will make their home in Camden, New Jersey.

Their many friends extend congratulations and best wishes for future happiness.

Hazel was happy for her brother and sister, but she missed them so much. She had been so close to Edna. Being best of friends and with only two years separating their age, they did everything together, shared everything, and withheld no secrets. They used to stay awake half the night talking. And now, she had moved away. Camden, New Jersey, could have been half a world away as far as Hazel was concerned.

The marriages of Clarence and Edna left Hazel at home with parents who did not get along. Hazel loved her mother with all her heart, and Katie returned that love tenfold. Hazel loved her father too and treated him with respect, but George continued to be combative. Katie had decided long ago that she would stay with him until the children were all grown-up and gone from their home.

So much had taken place in that year—George's business closing up and Clarence and Edna both getting married. It was mind-boggling to Katie.

Hazel was fifteen years old and still attending school. She missed having Edna to talk to. Clarence and Agnes just lived a few blocks away. She could see them any time. But New Jersey was so far away. Her loneliness was tempered somewhat by the letters she received from Edna. She was enjoying married life, traveling, and being onstage. Al said that she was a natural at acting, and he was proud to have her as his partner. Edna mailed Hazel several photos of her and Al onstage in costume, all sent from various cities around the country. To a fifteen-year-old, they were living a fairy-tale adventure.

George's belligerent behavior continued to escalate. He was spending his wages on his own pleasures and not contributing to the household needs. Katie's earnings from her two jobs wasn't sufficient either. Hazel completed the tenth grade and dropped out of school to get work.

She was hired at the Owosso Casket Company in the sewing department, a skill her mother had taught her. She sewed the beautiful silk, satin, and velvet liners that were put inside the coffins. She could do all the elegant stitches required—shirring, pleating, and intricate gathers.

Hazel wasn't old enough to be working, so her supervisor told her that if the inspectors dropped by, she should get up from her machine and walk around as though she was a visitor or go to the lunch room to avoid having them find a minor at one of the machines.

My mother with lady who
worked for their family

Hazel enjoyed the sewing, was happy to make new friends with the other girls working there, and glad to be helping with the expenses at home. With the added income, things calmed down a bit.

Working helped Hazel, giving her self-confidence and self-worth. She enjoyed having lunch with her new friends and sharing all the news. They were always anxious to hear news of Edna and her travels. They all thought she had such a glamorous lifestyle.

Hazel came to work one day with the most exciting news! Edna was going to have a baby! "What about being on stage? You can't do that if you're with child," they exclaimed. It was a problem that was being discussed at the Yats household too.

Edna and Al decided it would be best if she came home and stayed with her parents until she had the baby. It would be difficult to be separated, but too hard for Edna to travel, and she couldn't continue being onstage. Al would have to find another partner.

So Edna came home to Owosso. Edna and Al had only been married a year, and she missed him tremendously. Al mailed postcards to Edna daily from the cities he traveled to, but she longed to be with him. She looked forward to the time when they could be together again. It would be hard traveling with a newborn, but they would manage somehow.

Six months later, Edna delivered a beautiful, healthy baby boy. She named him Robert. Even though they had wired Al that Edna was in labor and the baby could come any time, Al didn't respond and was not present at his son's birth.

Grandma Yats, Al Leybourne and Edna at Opera House
where Al and Edna were appearing, on stage

Edna was devastated because Al didn't come to be with her when their baby was born. He didn't come for two weeks. She was having post-baby blues and cried over every little thing. Edna wanted to be with Al, but knew it was impossible for a while.

Edna's father, George, didn't approve of Al's traveling all over the country. He thought he should settle down near them in Owosso and make a home with Edna. Al loved the limelight of being onstage and wasn't about to agree to any change. It was the only lifestyle he knew. He was eager to get back to his stage commitments. Besides that, he wasn't comfortable in their home. There wasn't any place for him and Edna to have privacy.

Al stayed with Edna four days and left for Philadelphia. Edna was weeping, pleading with him to stay.

"You knew how it would be when we got married," he said. "You didn't go into it blind. I have to be working to support you and the baby."

"But I thought I would be with you," cried Edna.

"You will be soon," Al promised.

He departed early the next morning on the train, leaving Edna behind, tears coursing down her cheeks.

Hazel was overjoyed to have Edna back home with them. She'd missed her sister so much. She couldn't wait to get home from work to play with the baby. He was such a darling and so good-natured. After all, he had his mother, Grandma Katie, and Hazel all wanting to cuddle him and rock him. His need was their command. Their lives settled into a rhythm again when little Bobby started sleeping through the night.

～

Hazel looked forward to meeting her friends at the roller rink on Friday nights. She was meeting Grace and Elizabeth tonight. They always had a great time. The skating was fun, and you never knew who you might meet!

Her friends were waiting for her when she arrived. Dressed in her prettiest frock, Hazel quickly put her skates on and glided out on the polished wood floor. The organ was playing a lively tune. Being an excellent skater, she was whirling and twirling in time to the music. Soon, she, Grace, and Elizabeth were playing a game of tag.

She glanced up in the balcony and noticed a young man sitting up there. *Oh! He's looking at me!* Her heart skipped a beat. It was one of the Crane boys! *I think it's Blanchard*, she thought.

His name was Blanchard Crane. He couldn't take his eyes off her. *She sees me too*, he thought. *Every time she circles the floor, she glances my way. I have to find out what her name is.* He moved from the balcony to a bench on the main floor.

When the music stopped for a short intermission, Hazel sat down nearby. Blanchard approached her and asked if he could sit down beside her. She shyly nodded her head, and they exchanged names.

He was struck with her beauty. She had lovely blue eyes with long lashes. An abundance of strawberry blonde hair, styled in the latest fashion, was held in place with a Paris blue taffeta ribbon. She was a tiny little thing, barely five feet tall. She was wearing a white dress with a dropped waistline. *I bet I could put my two hands around her waist*, he thought. *She's so small.*

When the music started, Hazel went back on the floor, her heart pounding. She was so excited. She wanted to know more about this handsome man with the dark blue eyes. Every time the music stopped, she went back to sit down beside him.

Near the end of the evening, he asked if he could walk her home. She was happy to say, "Yes." Hazel said goodbye to Grace and Elizabeth, and she and Blanchard left together.

On that mild September night, the sky strung with a million stars, Blanchard escorted Hazel home. They seemed to be floating on air. They were happy, just being together, holding hands. Hazel was shy, but Blanchard was easy to talk with. When they reached her front porch, he didn't kiss her, but asked if he could walk her home from the rink again the next Friday.

Hazel couldn't wait to tell Edna all about it. She went in Edna's bedroom, and they chatted like the old times before Edna got married. Edna was delighted to see Hazel so happy, and Hazel couldn't wait for next Friday to come.

CHAPTER 6

Hazel hadn't seen Blanchard during the week that passed, and when she, Grace, and Elizabeth met to walk over to the roller rink, all she could think of was, *Will Blanchard be there?* When she saw him standing by the door, his skates in his hand, she greeted him with a warm smile.

They skated every musical number together, holding hands. When the organ played a waltz, it was a perfect excuse for Blanchard to place his hand on her waist, and she put her left hand on his broad shoulders. Gliding smoothly across the floor, Hazel gazed into his dark blue eyes.

Hazel was wearing another pretty dress in lavender with a lace collar and matching cuffs. Blanchard learned that evening that Hazel worked at the Owosso Casket Company.

Hazel knew that Blanchard worked at Owosso Carriage and Sleigh Company but was surprised to learn that he was also a blacksmith. They had so much to learn about each other. That night was just the beginning.

He asked permission to walk her home again. As they walked hand in hand, they couldn't stop talking. Blanchard told Hazel about his family—brothers Grant, Glen, and Seward and his sister, Geneva. Hazel knew he had brothers but wasn't aware that he had a sister. Geneva was four years older than Hazel.

Hazel was eager to share about Edna and her new baby, and that she had appeared on stage with her husband. Blanchard knew about her brother Clarence through his barbershop. Hazel's love for her mom shone through in their conversation, but she didn't mention her father.

They walked to the park and sat in the gazebo, talking for about an hour. Hazel said that she better get home—she didn't want Blanchard to become acquainted with her father's temper. So they slowly walked the rest of the way to her house. Blanchard kissed her that beautiful September night under a star-spangled sky. It was the beginning of a romance that would last a lifetime.

Hazel's head felt like it was spinning. *Is this what swooning is?* she wondered. She couldn't wait to tell Edna.

She quietly crept to Edna's bedroom, so excited to share her news. She stopped in the doorway, hearing a muffled sob. She tiptoed over to Edna's bed, careful not to awaken Bobby. Edna was crying. Hazel put her arms around her, and they hugged each other until Edna was able to talk.

She hadn't had a letter from Al for two weeks—not even a postcard. She had written to him every day telling him how much she missed him, how she longed to be with him, and sharing all the cute baby things that Bobby was doing, sitting up alone and cutting his first tooth. But there was no response for two weeks.

She couldn't understand what was going on. After the baby was born, Al came to see her often, but always said that it was too hard for them to travel with the baby. Something just wasn't right. It seemed he was always too busy now to come to Owosso to see her and Bobby. But never had it gone two weeks without a letter or postcard.

Edna was worried, Katie was worried, and George was furious. He was going to find out what was going on.

George tracked Al down at New Castle, Pennsylvania, where he was appearing in a vaudeville show. He bought a ticket to the evening performance and took a seat near the back of the theater. When Al came onstage for his skit, he was solo—no partner.

George went backstage after the program to find Al's dressing room. Al couldn't believe his eyes when he opened the door and saw his father-in-law standing there. And George was equally surprised to see that Al did indeed have a partner, and she was visibly expecting a baby.

7

Hazel and Blanchard were together every moment possible. Sometimes on Friday nights when the weather was splendid, they would skip the roller rink, take a long walk, and just talk for hours in the gazebo in the park.

They wanted to learn everything about each other and never grew tired of chatting. Blanchard's family called him "Blanch" and Hazel did too. He told her about his ancestors, who had been in this country almost three hundred years.

The Crane family came to America from England in the early 1600s. Jasper Crane was born in 1605. When he was twenty-five, Jasper and his wife, Alice, set sail for a new life in America on the ship Arabella. They traveled in a group of eleven ships that had over a thousand Puritan passengers onboard. They planned to make land-fall in Virginia, but ended up in Massachusetts.

William Seward Crane (Blanch's father) was eight generations removed from Jasper.

Will and Mary Crane lived on a farm near the tiny village of Oakley, Michigan. For being such a small village, Oakley's one-block downtown area had one school, three dry goods stores, two grocers, two pharmacies, and two hardware stores that provided supplies for the 350 people that lived in the village and nearby farms.

The Crane farm was neat and well-kept, their outbuildings whitewashed. Their home was made of white clapboard and had a large front porch with pillars and gingerbread trim. Painted white and trimmed with bright blue shutters, it was very charming.

Mary was thin as a spindle and full of energy. She was always busy and seemed to be wound tight, ready to spring. Mary liked to rock, and if she was upset, that rocking chair would fly! She wore flowered cotton dresses for everyday wear, and her hair was kept neat with a hairnet over it. A half apron always covered her dress, and she often had a cup of tea in her hand. Mary was a "no-nonsense" person and not one to argue with. She would very firmly let you know that she was right!

Mary loved to garden, and their yard was a cascade of various colored blooms—dazzling white daisies with puffy sunshine yellow centers, bright-colored zinnias, black-eyed susans, purple petunias, and lavender gladiolus. Out in the back were the tomatoes, green beans, cucumbers, squash, and other vegetables that added freshness to their meals.

Will wasn't a big man, about five feet and nine inches, with dark blue eyes, long dark lashes, and a thick mustache. He wore work pants held in place by suspenders and blue cotton shirts. When he hitched up the wagon to go into town for supplies, the clothes were the same, just a clean set.

Will had a violin that he enjoyed playing. He was surprisingly good at it, being self-taught, and could sure make that violin sing. He knew both the popular music of the day and also opera pieces. He even had an offer to travel with Barnum and Bailey Circus and play his violin. That was quite the feather in his cap and kept the townspeople busy talking for a while, but he couldn't just leave his family and the farm and travel the country, so had to turn the offer down.

Will and Mary had been married five years before they were blessed with their first child, a baby boy, who they named Grant. Two years later, they had another little boy, Stephen. Tragedy came into their lives when precious baby Stephen was stricken with croup and died when he was only ten months old.

Will and Mary were grief-stricken beyond belief when they lost their sweet baby boy. The heartache was unbearable. They were deeply depressed, but they had Grant—a busy two-and-a-half-year-old that needed constant care. Will had to take care of the animals and keep the farm going. They couldn't just give up. They had to go on.

God gave them a miracle that helped them overcome their grief and depression. Mary was expecting again and soon delivered a beautiful baby girl, Geneva. Will hadn't played his violin since Stephen went to be with the Lord. He opened the case and took the violin out and filled their home with music once again.

In the years to follow, Will and Mary had three more children—all boys. There was Blanchard V, Glen Hiemsel, and finally Seward. Blanchard had no middle name, just the letter "V," but if he had to provide a middle name, he just wrote down "Vet."

Will ran the farm with the boys' help, and Geneva helped her mother with house chores for the family of seven. The children attended the one-room schoolhouse down the road. Mary was a midwife and was called on in times of need to deliver babies.

My Dad's one room school house class. Dad has dark shirt on, second row. His sister, Geneva, top row, far right, dark dress

The Crane boys resembled each other greatly and were considered handsome men. They had blue eyes like their dad, and they all had dark hair except Glen, who had lighter, sandy-colored hair.

There's a story told about the Crane family that's been handed down through generations. It was said around town that Mary only cared for the boys and that she had no love for Geneva. It seems impossible not to love a child you give birth to, but this story has persisted through the years, told by Geneva and her children, so I guess it's true.

When Christmas came one year when Geneva was in her early teens, all the boys had a small gift under the tree, but there was nothing for Geneva. So Will bundled up in his heavy mackinaw, fur-lined hat, and knee-high boots and on that snowy Christmas Eve walked from the farm into town so Geneva could have a gift under the tree too. The Sanders family lived over their general store. Will knocked on their door and asked if he could make a purchase. He bought a bright red ribbon for Geneva to wear in her hair and lovingly placed it under their tree.

My Dad, Blanch, on right with younger brother, Glen

8

By bits and pieces, Hazel learned about Blanch's life growing up on their farm in Oakley. She learned most from Blanch through their endless conversations, some was shared by his younger brothers who loved to hang around and tease, and some from friends. She was falling in love with Blanch more every day.

It was the early 1900s, and America was moving forward in many dramatic ways. Automobile production of the Model T had begun. Wilbur and Orville Wright had made a short flight in the first airplane. These two events alone were starting to revolutionize the world. The effects were felt as far away as Owosso where many new businesses had been started.

Will and Mary considered selling their farm. Farming is a hard life, demanding seven days a week from early morning until after sunset. Some years, you can work your heart out and lose your crops. It was a difficult decision, but Will and Mary sold their farm and moved to Owosso where they felt sure they could get jobs.

They found employment easily. Will was hired at Robbins Table Company as a sander of quality furniture. He was soon joined by Blanch, who worked alongside him at the same job. Grant was a driver for the C. W. Jennings Company while simultaneously being schooled in the ministry.

My Dad, Blanch
when courting

My mother, Hazel
when courting

With the newly acquired jobs, the Crane family began to prosper. The work wasn't as tiring as farming, and the boys liked that. The Crane boys got along well and loved doing things together. They enjoyed playing cards, chess, dominoes, checkers, cribbage, and tossing horseshoes as much as the usual rough and tumble sport of football or getting a gang together for baseball. And the boys watched over Geneva as she attained the age where she was dating. All those who came to court Geneva were aware that the Crane boys were her brothers and her protectors.

After a while, Blanch moved on to a job at the Owosso Carriage and Sleigh Company where the wages were higher. When younger brother Glen was old enough to work, he was hired as a clerk at Roth and Sullivan's. Geneva met a fine young man named Raymond Signs and, with her parents and brothers approval, got married. Seward, the youngest, was still in school.

Grant completed his ministry training and married Pearl, a graduate of Olivet, a Bible college. Although Mary and Will did not attend church, their firstborn was now pastor of a church. God works in mysterious ways.

Blanch and Glen, with little brother Seward tagging along, were out for a walk on a warm September evening and decided to drop in at the roller-skating rink. It was a pleasant fall evening, and it appeared that a lot of people had come out to enjoy the skating. The roller rink was where the younger crowd came on Friday nights to have fun, get a soda, and catch up on what their friends had been doing all week. Outside of church, it was the best place to meet a girl. It was a blessing that Blanch and his brothers stopped in at the rink. As it turned out, that was the night when he met Hazel, his forever sweetheart.

9

Hazel and Blanch made plans to be together every time they could. They took long walks or went skating together every Friday night. They both had bicycles and enjoyed riding along the woodland paths, stopping to steal a kiss. Sometimes on Sunday afternoon, they shared a picnic lunch in the gazebo while the weather was still nice through September and October. Their head-over-heels romance could be called love at first sight. They didn't want to be with anyone else.

The Crane family readily welcomed Hazel into their family circle even though Mary had a difficult time sharing her sons with any other woman. The boys all thought Hazel was a perfect match for Blanch, and she was such a pretty little girl. Geneva too was friendly toward her and often had them over to have dinner with her and Ray.

Hazel's mom thought the world of Blanch and was so happy that Hazel had fallen in love with a man who would be good to her. He was a hard worker and would provide well for her.

Hazel and Blanch were already talking about getting married. Her father groused around, protesting that she was too young to even be thinking about it, but he had no ground to stand on. He had married Katie when she was fifteen.

Her sister, Edna, shared Hazel's excitement and was so happy for her. They shared every secret, every detail. It was especially hard for Edna because of what was taking place in her own marriage, but she put up a good front for Hazel, sharing in her happiness.

When her father had returned from New Castle with the earth-shaking news, Edna filed for divorce from Al. She was so brokenhearted. Her very soul was torn apart. She had suspected Al was being unfaithful, but when actually confronted with the truth, it crushed her heart. She didn't know what she would do.

Little Bobby was barely two years old. She'd have to get a job. So much to think about, her brain felt muddled. Didn't Al love his baby boy at all? Didn't he love her anymore? How could he change so fast? Everything was so hard to understand. They had only been married four years. Much of that four years, they were separated—he traveling to see her and, sometimes, she traveling to be with him. Their reunions were always magnificent. Now this.

When Al was served with the divorce papers, he was remorseful and wished he could undo the travesty he had created. He still loved Edna. Part of her wanted him back too, but in her heart, she knew she could never trust him. He had another woman in his life, another baby on the way, another life to live.

Edna had the support of her family, a home to raise Bobby until she could get her own place, and had acquired a job at the jewelry shop downtown. Still, her heart was grieving when she signed the divorce papers. Bobby would never know his father.

⚬⌒⌐

Hazel and Blanch set their wedding date for June 13, 1914. Her mom would create Hazel's wedding dress and prepare a delicious wedding supper, just as she had for Edna. There were so many details to take care of, but most could wait until it was closer to the date. Hazel prayed that her father would be on his best behavior.

Happiness for Hazel and sadness for Edna filled their home. Hazel was saving everything she could from her job and purchasing lovely things to put in her hope chest. She bought sheets and pillow-cases that she adorned with their monogram and added lace trim or a crocheted edge. There were gorgeous bath towel sets and kitchen linens. A hand-crocheted tablecloth was a special gift from her mother. The chest also held a Battenburg lace tablecloth with eight matching napkins. Her bureau drawers held all new lingerie and a lovely night dress for their wedding night, pale aqua trimmed with cream lace and accented with a pink satin rosebud at the neckline.

Katie was now supplementing their household income working as a furrier at a local business. She created fur coats, capes, jackets, and hat and muff sets. She also enhanced wool coats by adding a fur cape or collar. The wealthy ladies in town coveted her one-of-a-kind creations.

Katie had a trunk full of fur scraps at home that she used to enrich her clothing and also for Edna and Hazel. As the winter chill set in, she made both of the girls matching hat and muff sets. With their sewing skills and being able to create their own clothing, they always looked elegant.

As the plans for Hazel and Blanch's wedding progressed, a distant rumble was being heard overseas—events taking place that would start World War I.

CHAPTER 10

As Hazel's wedding date grew closer, the excitement raised dramatically. Her mother had created a lovely wedding gown for her. It was all finished except for the final fitting. Hazel was overjoyed with it, and it looked gorgeous on her tiny little figure. She weighed eighty-three pounds and was under five feet tall.

Made of ivory satin, the gown had a sweetheart neckline and puffed sleeves. Alencon French lace overlaid the bodice that was further enhanced with scattered pearls. A fitted waistline with tiny tucks accentuated Hazel's slender waist. A small bustle added interest to the back, and the gently flared skirt had satin-covered buttons from the bustle all the way down to the hemline.

A Juliet cap crowned her hair and was adorned with seed pearls, each one individually sewn on by hand just as the pearls on the bodice were. A floor-length veil made of silk tulle completed the look. On her wedding day, Hazel would wear ivory satin sandals with the strap held in place by a single pearl.

It seemed forever for June 13 to arrive! All the final plans were in place. Blanch and Hazel went early that morning to get their marriage license. It was legal to obtain your marriage license and get married the same day back then, but was unusual. They lingered momentarily, not wanting to part, and then, each went to their home to get ready for their wedding.

They were united in marriage at the home of Rev. C. R. Wolford. Edna was Hazel's matron of honor, and Glen, Blanch's younger brother, performed the duties of best man.

Hazel was stunning in her wedding gown. Her eyes were sparkling as she saw her beloved, her smile glorious. Blanch was attired in the latest style. His dark blue suit was the fashionable slim-tailored cut. The jacket had narrow lapels, and the trousers broke at his shoes, which were polished to a high sheen. He wore a French-cuffed white shirt with silver cuff links and a narrow blue tie. They gazed at each other a moment before the ceremony could begin, their eyes misting a bit.

Edna had styled Hazel's hair for her in a becoming style that was complemented by the Juliet cap. Hazel's flawless complexion actually appeared to be glowing. She carried a bouquet of pale pink roses interspersed with baby's breath, satin streamers flowing to the floor.

Hazel's mom and Edna had fulfilled the "something old, something new, something borrowed, something blue" tradition. The "something old" was the pearl necklace her mother had worn on her wedding day; the "something new" was a new coin placed inside of her shoe; "something borrowed" was a lace handkerchief belonging to Edna; and for the "something blue," her mom had sewn a blue ribbon tied into a small bow inside of Hazel's wedding gown.

Immediately following the ceremony, the wedding party went to Hazel's home where her mom had prepared a delicious wedding supper. The fifteen members of the Crane and Yats families were in attendance and a few friends. Katie served beef tenderloin, baked potatoes with shredded cheese, onion crisps and crumbled bacon on top, and roasted vegetables. The triple-layer wedding cake was topped with fresh pale pink roses.

Blanch had reserved the wedding suite at the Washington Hotel for their wedding night. They were happy to finally be alone. Hazel was sweetness personified, and her smile melted his heart. She never thought she could love anyone as much as she loved Blanch. As he tenderly cupped her face with his hands, he had to admit his heart was no longer his own, for he had given it to the sweet lass he married.

11

Reverend Wolford presented Hazel and Blanch with a wedding booklet that every newlywed couple should have. Godly instructions in the book detail how to have a blessed marriage. For the husbands, "Husbands, love your wives, even as Christ also loved the Church and gave himself for it" (Eph. 5:25).

Husband means literally "the band of the house," the support of it, the person who keeps it together, as a band keeps together a sheaf of wheat. He is the head of the home and represents the worthiest elements in an ideal state of society.

The husband in the model home will love his wife.

Paul says, "Husbands, love your wives." Marriage begins in love. It must continue and end there. The husband must see that the early, tender affection never fails—that the gentle tone of life's meaning does not grow harsh. He must love his wife through all the avenues of life, down through the declining age to the sunset years, with a love that makes wrinkles beautiful and infirmities precious.

Tell her how much you love her still. Tell it more and more as the years go on. Never allow the white roses of affection to fade on your lips and your tongue to grow silent. Let little attentions and delicate thoughtfulness for her welfare never cease. Do not lay up food for sad reflection when death comes, and plant the thorns in your pillow against that hour.

The time to love, honor, and help her is when these things are needed. When death has entered and plucked the roses from her cheek, it will be too late then to lighten her lot or speak her praises.

And for the wives, "Wives submit yourselves unto your own husbands, as is fit in the Lord" (Col. 3:18).

Wife means weaver. In the primitive home, one of the principal employments was the making of clothing. The wool was spun into threads by the girls, who were therefore called spinsters; the thread was woven into cloth by their mother who accordingly was called the weaver or wife.

It is the duty of the wife to cultivate the ability of making the home happy, keeping her house bright and attractive, and at the same time being equal in position and influence with her husband. "God did not take her out of the head of man to be over him, nor from his feet to be under him, but out of his side to be equal with him, from under his arm to be sheltered and protected by him, and from near his heart to be loved and live in sympathy and helpfulness by his side." The wife and husband are in a true sense one. Whatever is good for her is good for him. She owes no duty to him that he does not owe to her. The love and honor the wife requires of her husband that let her give to him. It is an even thing.

Let every good wife remember that she is heaven's last best gift to her husband—his angel of mercy; his minister of graces innumerable; his gem of many virtues; his casket of jewels; her voice his sweetest music; her smiles his brightest day; her kiss, the guardian of his innocence; her arms, the pale of his safety, the balm of his health, the balsam of his life; her industry, his surest wealth; her economy, his safest steward; her lips, his faithful counselors; her bosom, his softest pillow in distress; and her prayers, the ablest advocates of heaven's blessings on his head.

The weekend newspaper printed the following details of their wedding:

Crane–Yats

Owosso Young People Quietly
Married by Rev. C. R. Wolford

Miss Hazel Yats was united in marriage
with Blanchard Crane, Saturday evening at 8:30
o'clock at the home of Rev. C. R. Wolford. They

were attended by Mrs. Edna Leybourne, sister of the bride and Glen Crane, brother of the groom. Following the ceremony the wedding party repaired to the home of the bride, 205 Oak Street, where a delicious supper was served to a few friends and relatives.

The bride has been employed for some time at the Owosso Casket Company while the groom is in the employ of the Owosso Carriage and Sleigh Company. Their many friends extend hearty congratulations.

Hazel and Blanch set up housekeeping in a little house they had rented. It was a typical newlywed "starter" home, but completely adequate to fill their needs. A four-square, the house had a living room, kitchen, and two bedrooms all equal in size. Hazel loved putting her personal touch on the décor. Outside too, she planted flowers in the two window boxes that added a "welcome" to their little place.

Hazel wasn't working outside the home anymore. Blanch had willingly accepted responsibility for all the household expenses, quite unlike her father. She was concerned about her mother who not only continued to work for the local furrier but also had started a furrier business from home. All three of their children were grown, but Katie was still the one providing for the household expenses. Edna and Bobby were still living with them, and Edna helped every way that she could—keeping the house tidy and cooking the meals for them.

Hazel and Blanch were a joy to be around. Their love for each other was contagious. They had a lot of friends and enjoyed having other couples over for dinner or an evening of board games. Oftentimes, their conversation would turn to the situation in Europe. Tensions had been brewing throughout Europe for many years. On July 28, 1914, just weeks after Hazel and Blanch got married, World War I broke out in Europe. The president of the United States, Woodrow Wilson, was determined that the United States would not get involved, but everyone was concerned about it.

When Blanch opened his Christmas presents that year, one small package held a tiny blue angora baby bonnet. He looked at Hazel, a bewildered look on his face. She nodded "yes." "Is it a boy?" he exclaimed. Hazel explained that she didn't know if it was a boy or a girl, but with both of them having blue eyes, she was pretty certain the baby would have blue eyes too. She was knitting a pink one too, just in case. They were so happy it seemed as though they were floating on air. Blanch picked Hazel up and twirled her around the living room, both laughing and crying. They could barely contain their joy. Their baby's date of arrival was sometime in July.

12

It was 1915, the same year Hazel was expecting her baby, that the Lusitania, a British passenger ship, was sunk by a German ship. Passenger ships, even during wartime, should be off-limits. Over a thousand people were lost in that attack, and 128 of them were Americans. Outraged American citizens put pressure on the U.S. government to enter the war, but President Woodrow Wilson was still reluctant to involve our country in the dispute overseas. However, that situation was on everyone's mind and about all anyone talked about.

Even with that cloud hanging over them, Hazel and Blanch couldn't help being thrilled, anticipating the arrival of their baby. They were so very happy. Hazel and Grandma Yats were busy crocheting baby bonnets and sweaters in pastel colors, suitable for a boy or a girl. Long gowns were stitched out of the softest flannel for nightwear. For daytime, they created gowns from pure cotton for those warm July days. Edna pieced a quilt for this blessed baby-to-be in pretty pastel colors. Stacks of diapers were cut from yards of flannel. The chest that Hazel and Blanchard had in the nursery was filled to overflowing, the baby's layette complete.

Clarence's wife, Agnes, hosted a baby shower for her, and she received many more things—hairbrush and comb set, more handmade gowns, blankets, sheets, bibs, a soft teddy bear, teething ring, powders, and lotions. It seemed they had everything needed to welcome their little prince or princess. The bassinette was waiting to receive this blessed little bundle.

Their sweet little baby arrived on July 16, 1915. A girl! They named her Lucille Violet. Such a good little baby! Hazel just wanted to hold her all the time, cuddle her, hold her close to her heart, rock her, and sing her a lullaby. She was so happy.

Hazel felt guilty at times when she thought of the unhappy marriage her mother had lived through all these years with her dad. She knew that without strength from God, her mother never could have done it, but Katie had been determined to keep their family together until the children were on their own. She prayed continually that George would change, but that hadn't happened. She was still a victim of his outbursts of temper. It didn't seem to make any difference that Edna and Bobby were there to hear everything that took place.

Clarence and his wife, Agnes, also knew the joy of wedded bliss. He was doing well in the barber trade, managing Hochfield's Barber Shop, and they had recently found out that Agnes was in the family way. Sometime around the first of February, they would be welcoming a little one into their loving home.

~~~

Just recently, Edna had started spending time with a friend that lived nearby, a fine young man named Lester Brown. He was kind and soft spoken—a gentle man. Edna admired that about him. He was very attractive with light sandy hair that was a bit unruly and the softest gray eyes Edna had ever seen. Edna used to take Bobby to the park to play, and it seemed every time they went, Lester would turn up at the same time. That mystery was solved one day when she saw him come out of one of the houses across from the park.

Lester had noticed that even on Sunday afternoons, there was no father for the boy with her. He could just stroll over one day and see if she was wearing a wedding ring, couldn't he? He did and was very happy to see that the ring finger on her left hand did not have a ring. They sat in the gazebo and talked. Edna really enjoyed his company, and before long, it became obvious to both of them that their attraction to each other was more than friendship.

Lester had never been married and liked Bobby so much. He would have no qualms about raising another man's son. Edna wasn't so sure about trying marriage again. She had been betrayed by Al. He had quickly gone on with his life, and Bobby was no part of it. She didn't know if she could ever trust anyone enough to give her heart away again.

Edna and Lester continued to spend time together. He asked Edna to marry him. He would gladly adopt Bobby and raise him as his own son—they would be a family. Edna had grown more than fond of Lester and wondered what her life would be like without him now. When he proposed a second time, she said, "Yes." They set their wedding date six months away—a Christmas wedding. They would be married the weekend after Christmas on December 27, 1916.

Edna was looking forward to her upcoming marriage to Lester. She and Bobby would be moving into his home across the street from the park. She had to admit she'd be glad to finally be away from her father's unkind words and outbursts of temper. She was equally sad to leave her mother under those conditions. She didn't know how her mother had taken it all these years. She knew it was unusual to get a divorce—most women just stayed no matter what the situation was. It was almost considered a scandal to get a divorce, yet she had divorced Al. Some things are just too difficult to bear.

Hazel was so happy for Edna. She and Blanch had invited Edna and Lester to their home many times—had gotten to know him well—and deemed him worthy of Edna. They felt sure that he would love her with all his heart, never hurt her in any way. Edna and Lester asked Hazel and Blanch if they would stand up with them to witness their wedding. Of course, they were honored to do it.

Edna and Lester were planning a small wedding—just their immediate families. It was not to be a formal wedding, but her mom would create a pretty dress for her to wear. Hazel offered to take care of Bobby while they went on a brief honeymoon. Bobby was all for that. He loved coming over to play with their baby.

Katie created an ivory velvet suit for Edna's wedding. The jacket was scalloped around the bottom and had vintage lace peeking out of the wrist-length sleeves. From her trunkful of fur scraps, she found enough autumn haze mink to create a pill box hat and matching muff. It was simply elegant, and Edna would look gorgeous in it. She would wear suede pumps tinted a soft brown. An orchid worn at her shoulder would be the floral offering. How beautiful she will look, Katie mused, as she stitched the ensemble. Only two more weeks until the wedding.

When George came home from work that night, he was drinking and furious about something that had happened at work. As often was the case, he took his fury out on Katie. He picked up a kitchen chair and tried to strike her with it. Katie moved quickly and missed the fullness of the blow. As he tried to strike her again with the chair, Edna rushed from her bedroom and intervened. When that attempt failed, he did the unthinkable. He struck Katie in the face with his fist. He knew he had crossed over the line when he heard a small voice shout, "Grandpa!" When he saw Bobby, tears streaming down his face, George spun on his heels and left the house.

All of Katie's children hurried to her to make certain she was all right and to offer their comfort and support. Katie was stunned, and the children were shocked that their father went to that extreme. All three of them, Clarence, Edna and Hazel, said she could no longer stay with their father. She had put up with verbal abuse for years, but physical violence was too much. It just could not be tolerated. So with Edna's wedding only two weeks away, Katie, against her godly principles, filed for divorce.

Edna and Lester hesitated about their wedding, wondering if they should postpone it for a time, but Katie insisted they go ahead with their plans.

Christmas was a solemn affair that year for everyone except Bobby and baby Lucille, who at six months was loved by everyone and passed from one to another for cuddling or a soft kiss on her rosy cheek. Bobby got the bicycle he had been wishing for, and he couldn't wait for spring to come to ride it.

No one really felt like celebrating Christmas, but they had attended the Christmas Eve candlelight service and the Christmas morning service together to honor and glorify Jesus—everyone except George, that is.

George had gone to see his son, Clarence, the previous week. He was remorseful for what he had done, but Katie wouldn't agree to talk to him. They had been married thirty-one years, and almost from the beginning, she had suffered from his abuse. George told Clarence he was moving to Flint.

On the Saturday after Christmas, Edna and Lester were married at the home of Rev. C. R. Wolford. Hazel and Blanch stood up with them as witnesses. The only guests present were their immediate families.

Edna and her second
husband, Lester Brown

Edna was resplendent in the lovely outfit her mom had created for her—a lovely Christmas bride. The love that she and Lester shared couldn't have shone brighter as they held hands and spoke their vows. A few tears were shed, but they were tears of joy. They left for a brief honeymoon following the ceremony, and Bobby went home with Hazel and Blanch to stay until they returned.

The war in Europe was raging and soon would tear everyone's life in America asunder.

CHAPTER 13

The new year brought many changes. As he had told Clarence, George left Owosso and moved to Flint. Katie's life was more calm and peaceful than she could ever remember, but was also filled with loneliness. All of their children were married now and doing well, which left Katie alone in their big house.

Clarence and Agnes were overjoyed to be having a baby soon—only a couple of months now. Clarence's work at the barbershop was always steady, and Agnes was a healthy girl, responding well to her pregnancy.

Edna and Lester were head over heels in love, enjoying life as a family in his home across from the park. Their home was very welcoming with its wraparound porch. They loved sharing their home with others and invited company over often. It was very pleasant sitting on their front porch sipping a lemonade or iced tea and watching the lively activity at the park. They enjoyed the company of Hazel and Blanch, and the two couples went back and forth for dinner often. Many times, Agnes and Clarence would join both couples for a supper together or perhaps to play board games.

Hazel and Blanch had fixed up a darling nursery for Lucille and were getting her used to sleeping in her crib rather than in the bassinette in their bedroom. Hazel was also busy making plans for the baby shower she was giving for Agnes.

All of Katie's children lived nearby, which was a tremendous blessing. She was able to see Bobby and Lucille anytime, and they always filled her heart with joy. And anytime now, Agnes would be having her baby.

Agnes and Clarence Yats

Agnes' "sometime in early February" baby made his arrival on the seventh. Even though Clarence had secretly wanted a boy, he never said so. But he couldn't contain his happiness when Agnes had a boy. He made the rounds to all his male friends handing out the traditional "It's a boy!" cigars. They named him Charles after Agnes' father.

Agnes, who had a healthy pregnancy and no complications with the delivery except for the long labor of twelve hours, did not seem to be recovering. She was nauseous all the time and had pain in her abdomen that was so severe it hurt just to adjust her position in the bed.

She was unable to get out of bed; the pain was so acute. If her stomach got accidently bumped, she could not help but cry out; the pain was so intense. Being her first childbirth, she and Clarence didn't know if this was normal or not. Clarence asked his mother what they should do. Katie was alarmed and said, "Get the doctor over here right now."

The doctor verified Katie's fears that something was gravely wrong. Agnes should have been up and around by now. Even trying to hold her baby was torture because of the pressure on her abdomen and the necessity of moving. Agnes continued to get worse, and when her temperature rose to 102 degrees, the doctor knew the worst had happened. Agnes had peritonitis. Her intestinal tract had been punctured during childbirth, and infection had set in. There was nothing he could do to save her. The doctor told Clarence to go get the priest to come to the house to give Agnes the last rites. Charles was just two weeks old when Agnes lost her battle with the deadly disease.

There was no consoling Clarence. His beautiful, beloved, sweet girl was gone. It was more than he could believe—it didn't seem real. How could he ever go on without his darling Agnes? He held their baby in his arms and sobbed uncontrollably.

Clarence went to Rev. Fr. P. J. Slane at St. Paul's Catholic Church, and together, they made arrangements for her funeral, which would be held at the church she so dearly loved.

Clarence was simply lost without Agnes. They had been married seven years. She was so young, only twenty-seven years old. She had been so happy about the baby, and now, she was gone.

Katie had Clarence bring baby Charles to her house. He carried him over in his little basket. Katie insisted that Clarence stay for a few days too. She knew he was in shock.

Blanch's mother, Mary Crane, sometimes performed midwife services, and she knew of a wet nurse they could get to nurse Charles.

Agnes had died not knowing that her baby was born with a hydrocele, which is a buildup of fluid around the testicles. Because she was in such severe pain, she could not care for Charles and had never changed his little diaper.

The doctor told Clarence this condition is quite common in male newborns. Even though it looks frightening, it usually is not a problem. This was not the case with Charles. His hydrocele was accompanied with inflammation. His temperature rose to 104 degrees. He was barely responsive, just sleeping. At four o'clock in the morning, just three weeks after his mother had passed away, baby Charles joined her in heaven.

Newspaper articles shared the sad news:

Mrs. Clarence Yats Dies of Peritonitis
Highly-Esteemed Young Woman
Was Born in This County
Funeral Friday

Death came Tuesday night at 8:45 to Mrs. Clarence Yats at her home, 703 East Main Street. Peritonitis was the cause. The funeral will be held Friday morning at 8:30 o'clock from St. Paul's Catholic Church. Rev. Fr. P. J. Slane will officiate and interment will be made in the Catholic cemetery.

Miss Agnes Riley was born in New Haven Township 27 years ago. She was the daughter of Mr. and Mrs. Charles Riley, prominent New

Haven farmers. For a number of years she resided in Caledonia with her grandparents and made Owosso her home for a short time before her marriage. In 1910 she was united in marriage to Clarence Yats and they have since made their home here. The deceased was a member of St. Paul's Catholic Church and was highly regarded by all who knew her.

She leaves besides her husband, a son, Charles Robert, two weeks old. Her father and two brothers, Henry Riley, of New Haven and Joseph Riley, of Flint, also survive. The family have the sympathy of the entire community, in their bereavement.

Requiem high mass was sung at the funeral of Mrs. Clarence Yats, which was held this morning at 8:00 o'clock from St. Paul's Catholic Church. Rev. Fr. P. J. Slane officiated and interment was made in the Catholic cemetery. The church was filled with sorrowing friends and relatives of the young woman. The barbers of the city attended the funeral in a body. The floral offerings were numerous and beautiful.

Clarence Yats again Bereaved
Infant Child Dies

Charles Robert, the five-weeks-old son of Clarence Yats, East Main Street, died at 4 o'clock this morning after an illness of slightly over a week. The infant's mother, Mrs. Agnes Yats, died when the child was two weeks old.

The funeral will be held Wednesday morning at 7:30, Rev. Fr. P. J. Slane officiating, and interment will be made in the Catholic cemetery.

Clarence just could not comprehend all that had taken place—first his wife and now his baby in five weeks' time. Sometimes, he thought he would go insane with grief. He couldn't work, didn't want to be around people, couldn't partake of food even when his mother prepared his favorites, couldn't sleep, but just walked the floors at night and sat in the dark with his head in his hands and sobbed.

Clarence was beside himself with grief. There were rumors that the United States was going to join the Allied nations in fighting Germany. If they did, he had decided to volunteer. Life just didn't seem to make sense to him anymore.

14

Over there, over there,
Send the word, send the word, over there
That the Yanks are coming,
The Yanks are coming,
The drums rum-tumming everywhere;
So prepare, say a prayer,
Send the word, send the word, to beware
We'll be over, we're coming over,
And we won't be back 'til it's over
Over there.

The great war in Europe continued, costing thousands of lives and devastating both cities and countryside. The president of the United States, Woodrow Wilson, wanted to keep America neutral and broker peace. He had done so even after the Germans sank the Lusitania, a passenger ship. Over a hundred Americans were lost, and the pressure to get involved was increasing. An unexpected event changed everything.

In January 1917, the British intercepted a secret telegram from Germany to Mexico and were able to decode it. Germany proposed that Mexico join forces with them against the United States, and in return, Germany promised Mexico the territories of Texas, New Mexico, and Arizona. That telegram was published in the United States press on March 1 and immediately set off a nationwide demand for war against Germany.

The telegram was the final straw. Joining forces with the Allied nations had to be considered. The president went before Congress, shared what had taken place, and asked them to declare war on Germany. The United States officially declared war on Germany April 6th.

Clarence couldn't wait to be on his way. He joined the Army and was soon in France serving in the cavalry.

All males between the ages of twenty-one and thirty were required to register for military service, so Blanch had to register in the draft but was not called to duty because he had a child. Lucille was almost two years old now, such a darling little girl. She was busy as could be, running all about the house, usually clutching her little doll in her arms. She was the joy of their lives.

The Crane family was affected too. Blanch's younger brother Glen, being single, was among the first to go. He was sent to France, serving in the Army.

As all of this was happening, another momentous event took place. Katie and George's divorce was finalized. They had to appear in court. George was charged with extreme cruelty and nonsupport. Katie had to stand before the judge and testify that the charges were true. She testified that George had escalated from verbal abuse to physical violence and that for years, he had not contributed to their support. The divorce was granted, and George was ordered to pay Katie's attorney $50 and court costs of $11. What should have been a blessed union with three wonderful children legally came to an end on June 9, 1917.

With so many of their loved ones serving overseas, it was difficult to keep things normal on the home front. Katie was saddened over her divorce, remembering how happy they were in the beginning and how that joy had eroded. She believed in one man, one woman, one marriage. She was saddened too that her firstborn daughter had suffered the heartache of divorce, but deeply grateful that Edna had found happiness with her recent marriage to Lester.

Katie had handled the sale of Agnes' and Clarence's home, and new people were living there now, but it tugged at her heart every time she passed the house on Main Street where two precious lives had been lost.

Clarence Yats on right

Hazel and Blanch did their best to keep things positive. Hazel invited her mom, Edna, and Bobby over often to play with Lucille. Their conversation always centered on those who were overseas. "What news have you heard?" Clarence was good about keeping in touch with his mother; and Blanch's brother, Glen, had sent a postcard to his parents from France that had his photograph on it, letting them know where he was and that he was safe, for the moment.

Stateside families were able to get mail to their loved ones overseas too. First routed through Britain, a letter would reach the frontlines in two weeks. Millions of letters and cards were sent to keep the "doughboys" spirits up.

Overseas, life in the trenches was overwhelming. There was little heroism or excitement as many had imagined. Men were living outside for days or weeks on end. In the winter, there was cold, wind, rain, and snow to contend with, while in the summer, heat and sun. Landscapes were reduced to rubble and endless mud in many areas. Oftentimes, the soldiers were standing up to their knees in the slime of waterlogged trenches.

The incredible noise of rapid firing artillery, machine-gun fire, and cannon volleys, both enemy and friendly, could wear on your nerves. The troops endured some of the most brutal forms of warfare ever known. For the first time, Germany used poison gas shells that could paralyze. Tanks were new weapons on the battlefield too.

For some, the day-to-day things were most difficult. Dysentery was common, and they were wet all the time as trenches collected rain. Their uniforms and their boots would get soaked, and there was no way to get them dried out. Seeing your best friend get killed and unable to bury them, not getting a letter from home, and never having a decent meal—life in the trenches was grim.

In the fall, as Christmas grew close, memories of the Christmas Truce of 1914 were retold over and over again. If you were among the soldiers present at that time, it was unforgettable. The United States had not entered the war when this took place, but the doughboys couldn't hear enough about what had happened.

It began about a week before Christmas. All would be quiet when suddenly, jovial voices would call out from both friendly and enemy trenches. Then, the men from both trenches would start singing Christmas carols and songs. Next came requests not to fire, and before long soldiers were gathering in no man's land, the area between the trenches, laughing, joking, and sharing gifts.

The meeting of enemies as friends was experienced by hundreds, if not thousands, on Christmas Eve that year. As soon as the sun was up on Christmas morning, it began again. Songs were sung, and rations tossed to one another. Soon no-man's-land became somewhat of a playground. They played football and soccer together. The men exchanged gifts and buttons, every sort of souvenir. Addresses were given and received, and photos of families shown.

In other areas, in the lull of battle, they simply had burial services for their fallen comrades, prisoner swaps, or recovered bodies.

Found recorded in one man's diary was the following:

> The English brought a soccer ball from the trenches, and pretty soon a lively game ensued. How marvelously wonderful, yet how strange it was. Thus Christmas, the celebration of Love, managed to bring mortal enemies together as friends, for a time.

It was the most incredible occurrence, strictly unofficial, orchestrated by the soldiers themselves—enemies extending the hand of goodwill, peace, love and Christmas cheer.

Movies have been made about it, and books have been written about it. Historians have recorded through the ages about the miracle when there was peace on earth for a span of time that Christmas.

Back on the home front, even though the war stretched on, there was some joyous news to share at Christmas! Hazel was expecting again, and next summer, Hazel and Blanch would be welcoming a new baby. The entire family was excited about that news. And Lester had not as yet received his call to serve his country. He and Edna hoped desperately that the war would end before he was called up.

15

The war that everyone thought would be "over in a few weeks" when it started was now into its fourth year. Everyone in America was affected by the war in many ways. Families gathered several times a day around the radio to hear the latest news.

It was an extremely bloody war. Millions of young men were slaughtered, and the loss impacted everyone's life.

Clarence and Glen were remembered in prayer many times a day by their families and thanks given every time a letter from them arrived. They were safe! Then, the thought would begin to burrow into their minds that something could have happened during the time elapsed since the letter was mailed.

The war grinding on was torture for the boys overseas. There were no more truces like the Christmas truce that took place in 1914. Soldiers on both sides fought from the trenches. The only way to overtake the other side's trench was for soldiers to cross "no-man's-land," the area between the trenches, on foot. Out in the open, thousands of soldiers raced across this barren land in hopes of reaching the other side. Usually, most were hewn down by machine-gun fire and artillery before they even got close. But if they did make it, they knew the horror of looking the enemy in the eyes while trying to kill them.

By the time the United States entered the war, the Allies were starting to run low on young men. While the European troops were weary from years of war, the Americans offered new, fresh troops into the battle. Before long, a change would be seen—Germans retreating and Allies advancing.

Back home, every effort was made to help the troops. Women filled jobs traditionally held by men in the factories, on the police force, in the post office, and serving at fire stations—everywhere they could, replacing the vacancies left by men. For the first time, African-American women were hired as elevator operators and waitresses. Millions of women volunteered for the Red Cross.

The Food Administration, a government agency, produced pamphlets to help housewives prepare nutritious meals with less waste using the foods available. One of their pamphlets urged people to "Eat more cornmeal, rye flour, oatmeal and barley. Save the wheat for the fighters." Americans were encouraged to participate in "meatless Mondays" and "wheatless Wednesdays."

Bobby's school was part of a government program where children helped raise money for war bonds and stamps to aid in the war effort.

Hazel had organized a group of ladies including family, friends, and neighbors to meet at her house on Tuesday evenings to roll bandages for the Red Cross. Even the ladies who were now working outside the home were eager to do their part, and they too joined the group. With many of their husbands now in service, they were grateful to come together once a week to share any news.

Katie still did her furrier work from home and had also added sewing to her business line, but on Tuesday evenings, she would join the ladies at Hazel's home. Edna too was able to attend, as thankfully, Lester had not been called up yet. They were so in hopes that his job as a mechanical engineer at one of the plants producing war goods would make him exempt. They were so grateful for every day they were able to spend together. Blanch's mother, Mary, and his sister, Geneva, were also a part of the Red Cross group.

Hazel was seven months along in her pregnancy the spring of 1918. As May flowers were blooming and the trees budding out, she gave thanks for the life within her. She was so grateful too that Blanch had not been called into service yet. He had to register, but with one child already and another on the way, she prayed he wouldn't have to go.

With the advent of spring, everything seemed hopeful. Tulips, daffodils, and hyacinths bordered the front porch at Hazel and Blanch's home; and the backyard was fragrant with the sweet aroma of lilac bushes. Hazel had discovered a robin's nest in the hydrangea bush outside her dining room window, and she and Lucille made a point of spending part of each day checking to see if all was safe in the little nest.

They watched while the mama robin built the nest. The female is primarily responsible for creating the nest, and this mama worked hard for two days making sure the nest was perfect. She formed it using twigs and mud and then lined it with dry grass. Hazel even saw a bit of string mixed in the nest materials and a snippet of aqua ribbon.

Hazel and Lucille were so excited one day to see three light blue eggs in the nest. It would now take more than a month for the baby robins to develop inside the egg. During this time, Papa robin helped. So that Mama could sit on the eggs, Papa would gather worms and fly to the nest and give them to Mama, keeping her well-fed so she wouldn't have to leave the nest.

The robins were always a topic of conversation on Tuesday evenings for the Red Cross ladies. They never failed to ask, "Have the babies hatched yet?" You can imagine the excitement when they arrived one Tuesday to learn that one of the babies had hatched that afternoon. Everyone had to look and see. They gathered at the dining room window, but Mama was sitting on the nest keeping the baby and the other two eggs warm, safe, and dry.

The other two babies hatched the next day, and Lucille was so excited. She kept exclaiming, "Baby!" "Baby!" They discovered that both Mama and Papa robin help care for the newborns.

Mama robin sat on the nestlings for almost two weeks after they hatched. Papa played an important role during this period. He worked furiously bringing worms to Mama who in turn fed the babies.

The babies were born with their eyes shut and first opened their eyes about five days after hatching, so the Red Cross ladies were able to behold this wonder of nature at the meeting the following week. They were so excited about the baby robins they forgot momentarily to ask Hazel how she was doing in her pregnancy. After all, most of them had had a baby! The birth of the baby robins was a novelty for them!

Before long, the babies started trying their wings. They would sit on the nest and flutter and then get back in the nest. They would try again—get on the very edge of the nest and flutter their little wings. It only took a few days for them to gain courage to fly. One by one, they teetered on the edge of the nest, fluttered their wings, and glided off, dipping down slightly before their upward flight.

Hazel was sad to see them go. It was a beautiful experience being a part of one of God's miracles of nature. Blanch told her that sometimes, robins reuse their nests, so they were very careful not to disturb the nest, hoping they would return.

In a few months, sometime in July, they would experience another miracle from God of their own—the birth of their second child.

CHAPTER 16

Hazel and Blanch's little bundle of joy arrived on July 22, 1918. Another girl! She was a little darling and full of energy from the very beginning. They named her Agnes, in memory of Clarence's wife, who had passed away the year before.

Much to everyone's dismay, Lester got called up in the draft that summer to serve his country. Even though he had legally adopted Bobby, he had to go. Edna and Lester were devastated. They had found such happiness in their short time together, but there was no choice. When his departure day arrived, Lester hugged Bobby tightly and told him to take good care of his mom. Then, he held Edna close, tears flowing down their cheeks. He kissed her goodbye unaware that it would be the last time he saw her alive.

Lester was sent to Allentown, Pennsylvania, to train for service in the Army and would soon be sent overseas.

With Lester in the Army, Edna and Bobby moved back home with Katie and rented their lovely home across from the park for added income. Bobby and his friends played war all the time, and he had a little soldier's uniform "just like my dad's" that he wanted to wear every day.

Lester was faithful about writing Edna every day. They were dreading the time when he would be sent overseas. The war had shown evidence of the Germans retreating, so both Edna and Lester held on to the hope that it would end before he had to be shipped out.

By the time fall arrived, peace was on the horizon. Deep within the trenches, the men had fought the most brutal of conditions. You would think it couldn't get worse than what they had been through when something erupted worldwide that seemed as benign as the common cold. The influenza that year proved to be far more than a cold.

It was called the Spanish flu epidemic because Spain was hit hard first, but it quickly spanned the entire globe. Surprisingly, most of the victims were young, healthy adults, most being between the ages of twenty and forty.

In the United States, citizens were ordered to wear masks; and schools, theaters, and other public places were shuttered.

Victims died within hours or days after the symptoms appeared, their skin turning blue and their lungs filling with fluid causing them to suffocate.

It was the most frightening disease you could ever imagine. People were struck with the illness on the street and would be dead within hours. Others told of people on their way to work and suddenly dying within hours. One truth was told about four women playing bridge together late into the night. Overnight, three of the women died.

The toll from the flu was so great it sometimes took entire families and left countless widows and orphans in its wake. Funeral parlors were overwhelmed, and bodies piled up. Some people even had to dig graves for their own family members.

With the war showing signs of coming to an end, Edna was beginning to believe that Lester would not be shipped overseas. She came home from work at the jewelry shop one night and remarked to her mother how exhausted she was. With the flu epidemic taking center stage in the news side by side with the war, Katie immediately felt alarm. She asked a neighbor to go to the doctor's house to see if he could make a house call. The doctor sent word back with the neighbor that he would be at Katie's house early the next morning.

Katie tenderly tucked Edna in bed that night, praying over her for God to protect her and heal her. She helped Bobby with his bath, tucked him in bed, and kept watch over Edna throughout the night.

At eight o'clock the next morning, the doctor was on Katie's doorstep. He commented that he was making calls day and night, with the flu epidemic running rampant. He took Edna's temperature and listened to her heart and lungs. In many victims, the flu virus would invade their lungs and cause pneumonia. He was almost certain that was the case with Edna.

There was no vaccine to combat this deadly strain of flu. He would treat Edna with what medication was available, but he knew it wouldn't help her. He was overwhelmed with helplessness seeing so many of his patients needing help, and he had no help to give.

Edna continued to get worse. Katie and Hazel took turns holding vigil over Edna so she would never be alone, continuously praying over her, pleading with the Lord to heal her.

It was not to be. Edna went home to be with the Lord after a two-week struggle, succumbing to pneumonia caused by the influenza. Katie and Hazel were both with her as she passed. They had their hands on her, praying for her, when she took her last breath. Mother and sister, heartsick over their loss, held Edna in their arms and sobbed.

There is no heartache, no sorrow as great as losing a child. Someone once said, "Grief is the last act of love we can give," when we lose a loved one. Katie's grief over Edna's death was heartbreaking. Still in shock, she had to make arrangements for Edna's funeral.

Katie asked Blanch to contact the Army to let Lester know the sad news. She couldn't even imagine how he would accept that news, but was grateful he was still stateside.

Hazel too was overcome with grief—just lost. She and Edna were so close. From the time they were youngsters, they shared every happiness, every hurt. They were not only sisters but also best friends. They had been beside each other through marriage, childbirth, Edna's divorce, and their mom and dad's divorce. What would she do without her?

The Owosso newspaper reported Edna's death, saying that she died that Friday afternoon, October 25, at her mother's home, and gave the cause of death being pneumonia, which developed from influenza, after an illness of two weeks. The funeral was to take place the following Monday. It told of her husband being in the Army and that he was stationed in Pennsylvania. The survivor's names were listed. Just words on paper. Just facts that cannot begin to tell of the heartache of the loss.

Blanch had notified the Army of Edna's death, and they were to contact Lester. That should not have been difficult because he was in the United States, stationed in Pennsylvania. They knew right where he was; still, the funeral had to be postponed until Tuesday because as of October 27, they still had not informed him.

Lester had sent Hazel a postcard dated the 27th, two days after Edna passed away, and he was still unaware of Edna's death. Incredible! But the Army finally reached Lester with the sad message, and he sent a telegram saying that he would be home for the funeral, which took place on the 29th, five days after her passing.

Still in shock and brokenhearted with grief, Lester stood beside Edna's coffin—his dearly beloved. He closed his eyes, and he could see his beautiful bride, the one person he loved with all his heart. He loved her in life; he loved her still.

Edna's father, George, handled the burial arrangements. She was laid to rest at Oak Hill Cemetery in Owosso where he purchased a four-grave plot. On her tombstone, he had her name engraved as Edna Yats, not even acknowledging her marriage to Lester.

As soon as Lester returned to Pennsylvania, he requested that he be sent overseas. His request was granted.

Katie would raise Bobby and, while trying to cope with the loss of her daughter, would help Bobby to overcome the loss of his mother.

CHAPTER 17

World War I ended on November 11, 1918. Armistice Day took place when Germany and the Allied nations signed an agreement in France. The war was to officially end on the eleventh month on the eleventh day at the eleventh hour, Paris time. And it did. Arms were laid down. The war was over. It marked a victory for the Allies and a complete defeat for Germany, although not a formal surrender.

At the frontlines at the eleventh hour, there was some spontaneous fraternization between the two sides. But in general, the reaction was muted. A British corporal reported, "The Germans came from their trenches, bowed to them, and went away. That was it. No celebration."

As far as the Allies, euphoria and exultation were rare. There was some cheering and applause, but the dominant feeling was silence and emptiness. They were exhausted and just wanted to think of going home, returning to the embrace of loved ones.

In some cities, people were celebrating, dancing in the streets, and drinking champagne. The celebrations were overshadowed by the sadness of the millions of lives lost not only in the war but also by the flu epidemic. There were more lives lost due to the flu than in the war—over half a million in the United States alone. Together, it was a global catastrophe. An unforgettable time of suffering and death.

Back home, everyone was anxiously awaiting the return of their loved ones. Clarence returned home safely and talked very little about the war. His beloved wife, Agnes, gone as a result of childbirth and the baby passing away too, tempered his happiness in coming home.

His house was gone too, sold while he was overseas; there were too many memories for him to live there anymore. He stayed with his mother while he decided what was next in his life. His job as manager of Hochfield's Barber Shop was waiting for him.

Glen, Blanch's brother, returned safely too. Being younger and more boisterous, he was more open about talking of his experience overseas—not much about the war, but about the French girls. Glen was very handsome with his unruly sandy blond hair and blue eyes. The French girls found him to be very attractive. His war stories were about the few times he met the French beauties, not about the horrors of war.

Lester had barely gotten overseas when the Armistice was signed, and he returned home. Still grieving over Edna's death, he returned to Owosso. Bobby, his adopted son, was living with his Grandma Katie. He was six years old now. He had only known Lester as his father for a year. Lester planned to move west to be near his family, and it was agreed by all that it would be best for Bobby to stay with his grandma, to continue growing up with those he had known in his young life—Grandma Katie, Uncle Clarence, Aunt Hazel and Uncle Blanch, and his little cousins Lucille and Agnes. Yes, it would be cruel to tear him away from all those familiar to him who loved him so much. That was the final decision.

Glen, as a returning veteran, quickly found work driving a truck and delivering soda pop to businesses. His heart's desire was to go back to farming, the way he was raised, but driving the truck would do for now. It seemed so good to be back home with his family that he just wanted to relax for a bit.

Postwar America was changing too. During the war, the United States was booming economically due to production of war goods. With the machinery of war no longer needed, factories were changing back to prewar production goods.

With all the veterans coming home and returning to their former jobs, unemployment would soon become a problem.

The suffragette movement was stirring worldwide and was won by the ladies in America in 1920. They gained the right to vote on the platform that during the war, they had to fill in for what was known as "men's jobs" and should have equal rights to vote. The nation agreed.

As the women were gaining the right to vote, Hazel was quite content to be a stay-at-home mom, and she and Blanch had a sweet announcement to make in the spring of 1921 just as the flowers were in full bloom. They would be having an addition to their little brood sometime around Christmas.

18

The roaring twenties changed America with a deafening roar! The twenties ushered in the birth of a new, modern lifestyle, as war-weary Americans wanted to enjoy themselves and began to value convenience and leisure over hard work and self-denial.

The twenties brought advances in technology and prosperity with new labor-saving inventions that led to the use of automobiles, telephones, the radio, motion pictures, and electricity. These devices gave people more time for leisure. Young people wanted to forget the horrors of war and enjoy life again. Movies and "speakeasies" took up much of their leisure time. You had to know the code word to gain access to speakeasies where you could get illegal liquor, but the code word was easy to come by.

America was beginning to prosper. Automobiles were sold by the millions, and Americans roared around in their new vehicles. Gone were the former means of travel—horse and buggies and bicycles. Automobiles began to fill city streets.

Many Americans believed the morals of the nation to be in sharp decline. Prior to the 1920s, women didn't wear makeup. It was not really accepted in American society, but now, women began wearing makeup copied from the movie stars they saw at the local cinema. People smoked cigarettes, drank prohibition liquor, and enjoyed wild dancing. Some women dressed in clothing considered by many to be too revealing.

Traditional values were challenged, and the new morality glorified personal freedom and youth by the lifestyles of the "flappers" who danced the Charleston to the new music of the Jazz Age.

Women could now vote, attend college, and acquire a career. They were clamoring to learn how to drive. The confining nature of the old-style clothing with long skirts and corsets was thrown aside for new fashions worn by the "flappers" and movie stars.

Changes took place in small town Owosso too, but not nearly to the extent of the big cities. The smoking, drinking, vivid makeup, and scanty clothing didn't reach most people in small towns. They liked the old ways. Let the big cities have the new, wild ways. They wanted no part of it.

Hazel and Blanch's little brood increased on December 9, 1921, when Hazel gave birth to a baby boy. They named him Donald Reed. He was healthy and plump, perfect in every way. Blanch was overjoyed to have a boy. Lucille was five now, and Agnes was three. Their little baby boy was a perfect addition to their family. They were filled with joy and probably thought their family was complete.

～

George had moved to Flint and opened up a restaurant. Flint was in high production mode of automobiles. There were several plants producing automobiles on assembly lines and other plants producing parts. One of those was Chevrolet Manufacturing at the foot of a hill on Chevrolet Avenue, named after the inventor of the Chevrolet automobile, Louis Chevrolet, who made his home in Flint. It was known as the plant "in the hole" because of its location at the bottom of the hill. George was the proud owner of one of their products, a new Chevrolet automobile.

Prohibition was still in effect, and the manufacture and sale of alcohol was still banned. George decided that since he couldn't sell liquor, he would sell food. He purchased a building "in the hole," just a few steps away from the Chevrolet plant. It was immensely popular with the workers there because of its location. The workers could easily make it to George's restaurant, get a quick lunch, and be back to work on time.

There was another auto plant on South Saginaw Street in Flint. George encouraged Clarence to open a restaurant across the street from that factory, and Clarence agreed that it would be a good thing, and that's what he did. He moved from his mom's where he had been staying since the war and opened his restaurant. In a very short time, he was successful in his business, location being a huge factor. He never cut a head of hair again.

Blanch found himself in a predicament—one that he hadn't thought would develop so rapidly. With all the automobiles being built postwar, no one was buying carriages or sleighs anymore. The Owosso Carriage and Sleigh Company where he worked, their only source of income, was going to be closed down. There was no need for his blacksmithing trade either. It was rare that he was called on for that service anymore. And three little ones in their family now—it was a worry.

After a few weeks, Blanch heard there were jobs in Saginaw at Malleable Iron Works. So the move was made from Owosso to Saginaw, a city famous for the lumber industry that was about forty miles from Owosso.

Hazel was sad about moving away from her mom, but they had to go where the work was. She was sad too to say goodbye to all of her friends—all the memories she had in Owosso. Leaving their dear little home where Lucille, Agnes, and Don had been born was going to be difficult. The move to Saginaw was made in 1922.

Hazel and Blanch were able to rent a lovely home with the sizeable increase in the pay scale at the Iron Works. It was a large two-story, pale green in color with white trim. There was a large bay window in the parlor. There were four bedrooms, a grand upscale from their little two bedroom in Owosso. Hazel would enjoy decorating this beautiful home.

Hazel was beside herself with joy when she found out that Ferris Brothers Furrier had a store in Saginaw, and they would be pleased to hire her mom. After all, Katie had years of experience in the fur business, and there weren't many people with her skill in that field. Would her mom make the move to Saginaw? She would! Bobby was twelve years old now, and he was happy to once again be living near his aunt and uncle and three little cousins. God had worked out a miraculous plan for their lives.

Wonder of wonders, soon after Katie's move, Mary and Will Crane followed the trek to Saginaw because of the work available. Glen was still living at home, not really having settled down after the war. Blanch's youngest brother, Seward, was fifteen now and still in school.

Blanch's eldest brother, Grant, and his wife, Pearl, who were pastors, accepted a call from Christ to become evangelists and travel the country to preach the gospel. Their home base would be Saginaw.

Another miracle from God had brought both families together again.

CHAPTER 19

The 1920s was a time of hope, prosperity, and change. For the first time, more Americans lived in cities than on farms. There was great economic growth, and Americans were being swept into an affluent, but unfamiliar "consumer society." They had extra money to spend, and they spent it on ready-to-wear clothes and home appliances like refrigerators, washing machines, and vacuum cleaners. Above all, they bought radios.

The first radio station hit the airwaves in 1920, and within three years, there were more than five hundred stations across the nation.

Because of nationwide radio programs, people from coast to coast listened to the same music, did the same dances, and even used the same slang words.

Many, in fact probably most, people in the United States were not ready to accept these changes and still clung to old-fashioned family values. However, for a small handful of young people in the nation's big cities, the twenties was indeed roaring.

There was also a delightful change in Hazel and Blanch Crane's family. Their little brood increased by one when Hazel gave birth to a darling baby girl. Edna Louise was born on June 23, 1923, soon after they had moved to Saginaw. Edna was delivered by her grandmother, Mary Crane, who lived a few doors down the street from Hazel and Blanch. The new little baby was named Edna in memory of Hazel's beloved sister who had passed away in the flu epidemic five years before.

When Hazel was fully recovered from the new baby's birth, she set about decorating their home. It was a big change from the four-square they had in Owosso. It was twice the size. Where that home had four rooms, this one had eight. The first floor had a parlor that was on the front of the house overlooking the street and featured a handsome bay window. This room wasn't used by the family, but was closed off by pocket doors, always in readiness for company. If a friend or neighbor unexpectedly dropped by, the parlor was always neat and tidy, no toys strewn about.

The parlor proudly held a phonograph and several records. Being a recent invention, Blanch and Hazel were among the first of family and friends to own one. It was great entertainment when they had company over. The parlor had hardwood floors and an area rug that could be rolled up if the evening called for dancing. Popular dances of the day were the Hesitation waltz and the One Step. There was also a game table with four matching chairs in a quiet corner where they played board games and cards or perhaps served guests afternoon tea or coffee and dessert.

The living room was behind the parlor, adjacent to the kitchen, and that's where the family gathered. The radio was in there, and after dinner in the evening, Hazel and Blanch turned on the radio to listen to the world news. You could also listen to weather reports, musical entertainment, sporting events, stories, lectures, and stock market updates. And always, there was an abundance of advertising. Comedy shows became a great favorite of the nation's listeners, especially the *Amos and Andy Show*.

The phonograph and the radio were luxuries to Hazel and Blanch, but before they were added to their household, Blanch had bought Hazel a washing machine. A new invention, Hazel loved it more than any of their possessions. Before that, she had done washing for their family of five (now six with the new baby) on a washboard and two metal tubs. Backbreaking work!

First, she had to heat the water. Then, she scrubbed the clothes in one tub that was filled to the brim with sudsy water, rinsed in the other tub of clear water, wrung the clothes out by hand as dry as possible, dropped them in a wicker clothes basket, and then carried them down four steps to hang them outside on the clothesline.

This procedure was the same, summer or winter. There was a small area of their back porch that was closed off for doing laundry. There was no heat there for the winter months, but it did have a window that allowed a breeze to stir the air in the summer. The clothes still had to be hung outside in the winter. Hazel's hands would get so cold. She heated the clothespins in the oven to help a bit. The clothes would freeze stiff as a board on the clothesline, and she had to bend them to get them in the basket to carry inside. She warmed the clothes in the basket by the stove before hanging up or folding them to put away. No wonder Hazel loved her new washing machine and felt as though it was a gift from the Lord.

Most of the clothing required ironing, another long, time-consuming task. The flat iron had to be heated on the stove before use, but did a passable job of removing wrinkles from their clothes.

Hazel had a ritual she seldom varied from—Sunday was devoted to church, washing on Monday, ironing on Tuesday, and thoroughly clean the house on Friday. With Saturday being a "free" day and Blanch home to watch over the children, Hazel joined a ladies group called the Good Luck Club. There were twenty-five members, and they gathered once a month. The second year that Hazel was a member, she was elected president of the club.

The local newspaper put an article on their society page each month detailing what the activities included at their meetings. The article for July's meeting read,

> Mrs. M. L. White was hostess to about 25 members of the Good Luck club at her home on Genesee Street Saturday afternoon. Mrs. Blanchard Crane, President, called the meeting to order and various business topics were discussed. The Secretary, Mrs. William Borial, read the minutes of the last meeting and the annual dues and fees were paid to the Treasurer, Mrs. Lyle Coy. A musical program followed by a social hour was enjoyed by all present, after which the guests were served to a pot-luck supper in the dining room. The tea tables were centered with bouquets of garden flowers and greenery, with four guests seated at each table.

My mother, Hazel, a young married

Three new members were admitted to the club, Mesdames L. Wickware, Alice Hayes and Irene Scharer. On August 18, Mrs. Lyle Coy and Mrs. Ernest Lytle will entertain the club at a porch party at the home of the former at 213 Goodhue Street.

This was a big affair for the ladies, and they looked forward to the third Saturday of each month. It gave them a chance to dress in their finery and enjoy a pleasant afternoon.

Most of the ladies wore their hair in the fashionable bobbed style. Their dresses were a bit shorter, and many had dropped waistlines. Since the corsets had been replaced by camisoles or chemises, this style dress was becoming on just about any figure. Accessories might be long strands of pearls, a chiffon scarf, a feather boa, or headband. Cloche hats were very much in vogue. But the latest fashion trend was rolled down stockings. Shocking! They were rolled below the knee and held in place by elastic garters. One by one, the club ladies gave in and joined this new trend. What a pleasant breath of freedom from the corsets with garters!

I wonder if they rolled their stockings above the knee for church the next day.

~⁀〜

Another pastime Hazel and Blanch enjoyed was going to the movies. Occasionally, Grandma Katie or Grandma Mary would come over and watch the children so they could have a night out. Going to the local cinema was a very special treat. Strolling home from the movies one night, Blanch brought up the idea of buying an automobile.

Hazel was taken by surprise. Many of their friends owned automobiles, but she had been content without one. She thought Blanch was too. Everything was within walking distance—their extended family, their church, Blanch's work, and the grocery store. She just never saw the need for the expense and didn't know that Blanch cared that much about it.

Blanch confessed that he yearned for one. It seemed as though all the men he worked with had autos, and the topic of conversation at work often centered on their automobiles. Blanch was a good provider, and their radio, phonograph, and washing machine were all paid for. She agreed they should start saving for one.

It took them a whole year to save enough money for the down payment for their auto. The cost of their new car was $260. They paid half down and got the other half on credit. Blanch was so proud to drive his 1926 Ford Model T Touring car home that beautiful spring morning. It had nickel=plated headlamp rims and balloon tires. It also had a large compartment under the rear deck that would easily hold their picnic basket.

They had a splendid time taking the children for rides in the car. They would pack a picnic lunch and find a pretty place to spread out a blanket and enjoy eating outside. The children loved it. It was the most summer fun they had ever had as a family.

They had made one payment on the car when Hazel became aware that she was expecting again. That was quite an unexpected surprise—definitely one they had not planned on with the payment they now had on their new Ford. They would have to be extra careful with their money now.

Hazel adjusted their budget by foregoing the movies and using that money for gas so they could continue their summer outings. The children so enjoyed their picnics out in the country. Their summer was the best ever. The "baby on the way" was due around Christmas.

It was in November when Blanch and Hazel, with all the kids piled in the car, decided to drive over to Bay City for a little outing. They would see what the town was like and stop somewhere and let the kids choose a penny candy. The children were chattering with great anticipation about what they would choose with their penny.

Lucille thought she might choose a taffy sucker or candy corn, but was also considering lemon drops because they would last longer. Agnes was toying with the idea of a chocolate-covered cherry or a Clark bar, but they would be gone too quick. She decided on chocolate caramel creams. Don didn't have to think too long about his choice—it would be a jawbreaker, for long-lasting goodness. Mom would help Edna make a choice, maybe a bit of chocolate.

They were just nicely getting started on their trip when a light mist began to fall. Before long, the road began to ice over. Suddenly, the auto slid to the right, and with Blanch desperately trying to stop it, the Ford tipped over in the ditch. Hazel was thrown from the auto and pinned under it.

Passersby gathered to help, and several men were able to lift the auto to free Hazel, who was taken to the hospital. Blanch had the children taken to Grandma Katie's house and then made arrangements to have the car towed to a garage before heading to the hospital.

Hazel stayed overnight in the hospital, and the doctors determined that she had suffered no lasting injuries, and the baby was not harmed. Another miracle from God. Although Hazel had no broken bones, major organs injured, and no internal bleeding, they let her go home but insisted on one stipulation—she must stay in bed throughout the remainder of her pregnancy. Grandma Katie came over every day to care for Hazel and the two little ones who weren't in school yet.

Blanch was so remorseful and felt totally responsible for what had happened. There was no way Hazel could convince him that it was an accident, no way he could have known the road would turn icy, no way to prevent it. Still, he couldn't forgive himself. He felt he was to blame and knew he could have caused great harm to his entire family. He vowed never to drive again and sold his Ford Touring car that he had wanted so badly.

To add to their grief, Grandpa Crane, Mary's beloved Will, passed away quietly in his sleep just before Christmas. That, coupled with the accident, was almost too much to bear.

Christmas was a quiet affair at the Crane household that year. Hazel had obeyed doctor's orders and stayed in bed so no harm would come to the baby she carried. She and Blanch had made the decision to have a doctor present to deliver this baby because of the circumstances.

Christmas came and went, but still no baby. On New Year's Eve, Hazel's water broke, and Blanch went to get the doctor. Hazel had a long labor, and the only help the doctor had to alleviate the pain was a cone of chloroform. Into the valley of the shadow of death. At noon on New Year's Day, the baby arrived. A baby girl! The doctor hefted the baby in his right hand and announced that she was beautiful, perfect in every way, and weighed about ten pounds. They had a name chosen for the baby. If it was a girl, her name would be Arlene Marie.

I am born.

CHAPTER

20

There were so many spectacular happenings that occurred in 1927:

- The first transatlantic telephone call was made from New York City to London.
- Charles Lindbergh gained international fame as the first pilot to fly solo and nonstop across the Atlantic Ocean in "the Spirit of St. Louis." The aircraft industry was just emerging and produced over 4,000 planes.
- Baseball became a popular spectator sport, and Yankee Stadium was built.
- Ford had sold 15 million Model T automobiles, and that alone revolutionized the American way of life. In 1927, Ford Motor Company introduced the Model A as its new automobile.
- The advent of talking pictures emerged when "the Jazz Singer" debuted in New York City.
- The first live demonstration of television was viewed at the Bell Telephone Company in New York.
- The Holland Tunnel opened to traffic as the first Hudson River vehicular tunnel linking New Jersey to New York City.
- On the first day of the first month of the new year at high noon on Saturday, January 1, 1927, Arlene Marie Crane was born.

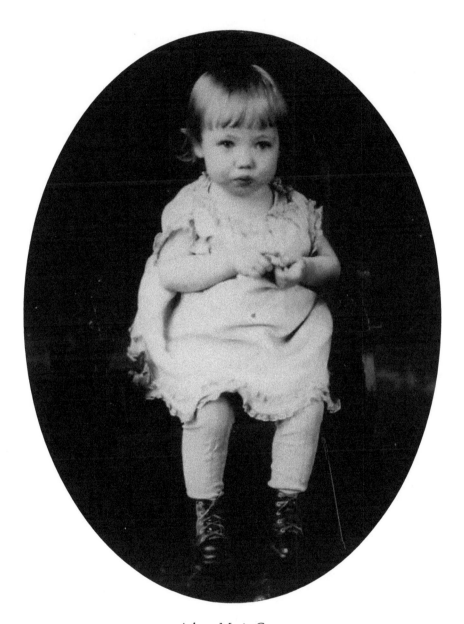

Arlene Marie Crane

I was born into a loving family. My mom and dad, Hazel and Blanch, were happy in their marriage, and that reflected in their home. They loved each other with that "forever" kind of love that you commit to in your marriage vows. They loved their children with their entire being and were so proud of them.

When I was born, Lucille was twelve, Agnes was nine, Don was six, and Edna was three. They all doted on their baby sister. Lucille wouldn't go to school in the morning 'til she rocked me to sleep, and I've been told that it's a wonder I ever learned to walk because they all wanted to carry me around.

My dad was a hard worker, a good provider for his family. He was still working at Saginaw Malleable Iron Works when I was born. It was hard physical labor, so hard that when he sat down to eat lunch, his hands trembled. He never regretted giving up his car. He never could have forgiven himself if any harm had come to Hazel or any of us kids when the car turned over.

Mom has told me many times how they almost lost me again that first year. That winter, I came down with pneumonia. The doctor came to the house every day to check on me, but my condition continued to get worse. On the fourth day, the doctor told my mother that I probably wouldn't make it through the night. Mama had to have been exhausted beyond belief, but she never left my side that night. About three o'clock in the morning, my fever broke, and I was able to take nourishment.

～つ

My mother was love personified. She was totally content being a stay-at-home mom and also very happy to have her mother living nearby. Katie was still working at Ferris Brothers Furs, and from her home, she was creating the one-of-a-kind original ensembles so coveted by the wealthy. My mom used to do handwork in the evening to help her mother. It was relaxing for her, and she, like her mother, enjoyed creating. They would add collar and cuff sets of lace or satin, crochet lovely lace edges, and add smocking or pleating on rich satin, silk, velvet, linen and organza outfits. In the fall and winter, they designed fur collars, capes, muffs, and millinery. Their lovely work was in great demand.

Keeping house kept Mom very busy throughout the day. She cooked on a wood stove, so the fire wood had to be laid and started before any cooking could be done. There was no refrigerator either, just an icebox where you had to remember to empty the tray at the bottom or you would have water leaking all over the kitchen floor.

She was ever thankful for the new washing machine Blanch had bought for her, but it was still long, tedious work; so after the children were in bed, she enjoyed very much sitting in a comfortable chair, listening to the radio, and doing her handwork.

America was prospering. With all the new inventions coming on the market, there were plenty of things to spend their money on.

Hazel and Blanch listened to their radio along with twelve million other households. Movies were an inexpensive form of entertainment, and by the late 1920s, Lucille, Agnes, and Don went to the movies every week where they laughed over the antics of Mickey Mouse just like most other Americans.

Some people thought morals were in a tailspin, declining rapidly. Birth control devices became available, and that introduced the element of sexual freedom. And many claimed that autos gave young people too much freedom—that they were able to go where they pleased and do what they wanted to do, earning the nickname "bedrooms on wheels" for their automobiles.

Life was good at the Crane household. Blanch had a job earning good money, so they were doing well economically. They didn't have a car payment, so they had extra money. That meant a movie for the three older kids and an ice cream cone on the way home every Saturday afternoon. They looked forward to that treat; all the other neighborhood kids got to go too, and it was a fun time.

It was a happy, peaceful time, and Hazel was giving thanks because she wasn't expecting!

21

Hazel and Blanch enjoyed living in Saginaw. It was a prosperous city. Logging was a big business, in part because of access to the Saginaw Bay. There were a lot of mansions built in Saginaw by the wealthy lumber barons.

Hazel and her mother, Katie, could easily spend an afternoon strolling down the streets with the huge, beautiful homes. While the older children were in school, they often took a walk down the tree-shaded streets with Edna and Arlene, gazing at those handsome homes. The two little ones liked riding in their red wagon with its big rubber tires.

Hazel and Blanch were an attractive couple and very popular with the young married set. Even after having five children, Hazel's figure remained trim. She still retained her delicate heart-shaped face and porcelain-smooth complexion. Blanch too remained trim in stature with broad shoulders and still narrow waist.

They enjoyed having company over to play board games in their parlor, dance to the music played on their phonograph, or play Charades. They belonged to one group that met once a month for a potluck dinner, with each couple taking their turn at hosting the group. And the Saturday Good Luck Club was still high on Hazel's list of social gatherings.

The kids missed their rides in the car and the picnics in the country, but there were so many other things to do. There were a lot of playmates in their neighborhood—no shortage of friends.

Don loved playing Cowboys and Indians with his young friends. They could hoot and holler around the neighborhood to their heart's content. They were just as noisy when they played Soldiers and War. They let their imaginations run wild and take flight.

In his quiet time at home, Don played with his little metal cars and his train that ran on an oval track. But his favorite times were when his Dad and Uncle Seward helped him get his kite to soar in the sky or if they would get up a game of baseball with all his neighborhood buddies. That was the best of times—the most fun for him.

Lucille and Agnes had different "likes" altogether and wanted nothing to do with the boys. Of course, they had their dolls and loved to dress up and play house. The cool shade of the maple trees in the backyard was a perfect place to set up their "house." They had a small table with two little chairs where they could "eat" their mud pies and sip their "tea." They had child-size rocking chairs where they could rock their "babies" to sleep. They loved to get Edna and Arlene out there where they could "mother" them.

Another favorite pastime was making flapper headbands to play movie star or play ballet. Hazel had gathered tulle on a grosgrain ribbon waistband that they could tie around their waists. Many a sunny summer afternoon was spent pretending to be a prima ballerina.

On a quiet afternoon, they might play paper dolls or sort through Grandma's button box. They liked to play Jacks, Old Maid, and hopscotch with their neighborhood friends.

There was no doubt though that their favorite thing to do was go over to Grandma's house and get in her trunk that was full of scraps. She had all kinds of fur, fabric, lace, and millinery flowers tucked inside. Next came the box of high-heeled shoes and the hats that Grandma was famous for. They dressed themselves up to the nines and played "rich ladies."

Edna was easily entertained with the wooden hobby horse that her Dad had made for her, and the soft Raggedy Ann doll Mom had created. She had wood puzzles and alphabet blocks to play with when she wasn't being "little sister" in Lucille and Agnes' playhouse.

My Mom always said I was a good baby. It's no wonder. I had three sisters who fawned over me, did anything they could to make me happy. I was the perfect "baby" for their playhouse where they could pretend feeding me. They could stroll me up and down the sidewalk in my wicker buggy. Lucille was old enough to change my diaper. They had lots of fun playing the mother role. I'm sure I loved all the attention, too.

Sundays were reserved for church. We were always in Sunday school.

Life was calm and serene in the Crane household. It was the American dream. Such a wonderful time to be raising a family. Innocent times. A golden era.

Hazel and Blanch were young and in love and enjoying life to the fullest with their little family. Little would they have dreamed that their world of happiness would soon change. The prosperity that America had known since the end of World War I was about to end. The worst depression in our nation's history was right around the corner.

22

The roaring twenties had been an exciting period in America with new inventions, technical advances, and changing lifestyles. Jobs were plentiful because manufacturing companies were changing over from wartime to peacetime goods.

Many Americans had adopted the new phenomenon of "Live now, pay later" and bought expensive products like automobiles. Credit terms were enticing, and it was easy to become overextended in debt.

Blanch had given up his car, so they weren't in debt, but Blanch was worried about his job. The Saginaw Malleable Iron Works had been laying off workers, and by seniority rights, Blanch's name would be coming up soon.

Mom and Dad tried to keep their worries from us kids, but we could hear their whispers after we were in bed. There were heat registers in the living room ceiling, and their quiet voices filtered right up to our bedrooms. I didn't have any idea what was going on. I was too young to understand. Nor did my sister Edna, who was five. We just knew something was really wrong and making Mom and Dad sad. But the older kids got the gist of it.

That dreaded day came in the fall of 1929 when Dad came home from work and said that he'd been laid off. They had a little savings in the bank, but not much—not enough to live on, pay rent and feed five kids. Dad was heartsick. He would find "daywork." He was willing to do any kind of work. It didn't matter what kind of work it was or hard it was; he would do it for his family.

It wasn't long before their savings was used up. The rent was due with no money left in the bank to pay it. They didn't know what to do. Dad was feeling like a failure because he couldn't provide for his family. It didn't matter that Dad was a hard worker; there just weren't any jobs out there. It wasn't just Dad. Everyone was finding that there was no longer any work available. Dad's brother, Glen, had lost his job too. It seemed so hopeless. Grandma Katie moved in with us to share what she had.

When they thought things couldn't get any worse, on October 29, 1929, the stock market crashed. That was the onset of the greatest depression this country has ever known.

The Great Depression began in the United States and quickly spread throughout the world causing unbelievable hardship. There were beggars on the streets in downtown Saginaw. Men were seen wearing signs around their necks "Wanted—a job. War Veteran with family." Children too were out on the streets with signs reading "Please give my dad a job."

There was a man and two ladies standing on a street corner in front of a bank. They were well dressed—the gentleman in a suit, white shirt, and tie. The ladies were both dressed in lovely coats with fur collars. Obviously, they were wealthy people before the stock market crashed. They were selling apples from a crate for five cents each. That's how desperate people were. They were trying anything to make a few pennies.

God created a miracle for our family. Unbeknownst to my mom and dad, Grandma Katie wrote a letter to Clarence, who was barely getting by with his restaurant in Flint. She told him of the drastic situation that Hazel and Blanch had—no income, savings gone. Clarence, in turn, told his father. That's how it came about that we moved to Flint. Grandpa hired a man with a truck to come to Saginaw to rescue our family. There was also a promise of a job for my dad at Grandpa's restaurant at "the bottom of the hill" on Chevrolet Avenue.

Thank you, Lord. That was a miracle indeed because the depression only kept getting worse. But for the grace of God and Grandpa's help, we would have been on the street.

On the way to Flint, we passed a family of five trudging down the road. Their dad was leading the way with a single suitcase for all five family members. Another family of five joined them. They had a little red wagon that their dad was pulling. It held all their worldly possessions. Their youngest child was perched on top of their belongings.

I was only three when we moved to Flint, so some of this has been told over the years. But the depression was to linger on for years, and I have many vivid memories of my own. But on that day, with Mom and Grandma Katie riding up front in the truck with me on Mama's lap, and Dad and the other four kids in the truck bed with our household goods, we felt very blessed.

CHAPTER 23

Before Flint became famous for the auto industry, the city was a major lumbering area on the historical Saginaw Trail. From there, Flint became the leading manufacturer of carriages, earning it the nickname of "Vehicle City." Over the years, Flint grew into an automobile manufacturing powerhouse.

In the early days of the auto industry, there was a group of men in Flint unlike any other in our country, probably in all the world. The major players in the birth of the automotive industry in Flint were Billy Durant, Louis Chevrolet, David Buick, Albert Champion, Walter P. Chrysler, James H. Whiting, Charles W. Nash, William S. Ballenger, Dallas Dort, and A. B. C. Hardy—all familiar names to Flintites. But the one best known to Flint residents would without a doubt be Charles Stewart Mott, not only for his part in the automotive industry, but also because of his love for the people of Flint and the city itself.

Charles Stewart Mott's personal life was marred by sadness for a time. He married his first wife, Ethel, in 1900. Together, they had three children. It was during this marriage that Applewood, the Mott estate, was built. Applewood was a self-sustaining farm located on what was then the outskirts of Flint. The residence and grounds encompassed many acres, the orchard alone having twenty-nine varieties of heritage apples.

The entire community mourned with Mr. Mott when Ethel died in 1924 after falling from a window of her second-story bedroom at Applewood.

Mr. Mott remarried three years later; and his wife, Mitties, died most unexpectedly the next year from tonsillitis. The following year, Mr. Mott married Dee, a socialite from New York. She filed for divorce later the same year. Some said that she didn't like rural life.

Charles Mott married the fourth time to Ruth, with whom he had three more children, and he shared the rest of his life with her.

The Mott's were very wealthy and could have lived a much more opulent lifestyle, but they chose to share their wealth with others. Both were committed philanthropists, and over the years, the Charles Stewart Mott Foundation has disbursed over a billion dollars, much of it geared to education and providing students with nutritional support, sports, adult education, and community assistance. It would be impossible to fully express how generous the Mott's have been to the city of Flint or how many lives they have touched.

❧

It was 1930 when we rolled into Flint in the truck. America was deep in the throes of the Great Depression. If Grandpa Yats hadn't helped us, there's no telling what would have happened to us. There was no social security or unemployment benefits to help people at that time.

Mom and Dad found a house to rent on Matthewson Street between Third Avenue and Bluff Street. It was a small house, not like the one we had left behind in Saginaw. There were four rooms downstairs—a living room, kitchen, and two bedrooms. Another bedroom was upstairs that had been fashioned from an attic. The rent was reasonable; everything was down in price because of rampant unemployment. It was just a few blocks from Grandpa's restaurant, and Dad could easily walk to work.

Grandma Katie went to live in a house that Clarence owned, a rental property that he had on Corunna Road. He was so happy to be able to provide a home for his mother.

The truth is always stranger than fiction. You just can't make things up like this. The rental property was two doors away from Grandpa Yats, who also lived on Corunna Road. Yes, Katie and

George, who had been divorced thirteen years previously, spent the last years of their lives separated by a single house.

~

Have you ever tried to recall your very first memory? I have, many times. I always go back to the same place.

I am three or four years old, sitting on the steps leading to the cellar of that house on Matthewson Street, eating Argo starch. I can pinpoint my age because we lived in that house from 1930 to 1931.

The cellar in that house was called a Michigan basement. It had dirt walls and a dirt floor. It was really just a hole dug in the ground with the house built over it on a concrete block foundation. A single light bulb dangled from the ceiling. I was watching my mama wash clothes in her beloved Maytag washer. That's my earliest memory of being alive on this earth. I was to learn many years later that if you crave starch, it's caused by a lack of iron in your system, and our family did not have much red meat during those depression years.

Grandpa made good on his promise to give Dad a job at his restaurant. His duties were to help with the cooking and serving, clerk, keep the place clean, and make himself available to play cards at the tables if someone wanted a game. My dad was an excellent card player.

I can still envision Grandpa's restaurant. Up front by the cash register were two big glass cases that held an assortment of candy bars and gum. Behind the cash register against the mirrored wall was an array of cigarettes, cigars, and chewing tobacco in tins.

Beyond the cash register, a counter with stools extended to the rear of the building. Six round tables with four chairs encircling each filled the rest of the space.

Prohibition was still in place, so Grandpa couldn't sell liquor. The food he sold was simple fare. The men still fortunate enough to be working at the Chevrolet plant kitty-corner across the street used to run over for lunch. Because it had to be quick, he served hamburgers, hot dogs, and fried potatoes off the grill. There was always a big pot of chili or bean soup going on the burners. The coffee was always piping hot. Behind the counter was a big red "Coca-Cola" cooler with a variety of soda pop drinks.

The menu board for the day might read,

> Hamburg 3¢ Chicken Noodle Soup 2¢
> Hot Dog 3¢ Stewed Prunes 1¢
> Fried potatoes 2¢ Cereal 1¢
> Vegetable Soup 2¢ Cold Milk 2¢
> Bean Soup 2¢ Coffee 1¢

There was a stairway that led to two bedrooms and a bathroom over the restaurant. Those two rooms were rented out to a couple of single gents that worked at the Chevrolet plant just a few steps away.

My mom cleaned those two rooms and bathroom every Friday, taking the bedding home to launder. She was paid $2.00 a week.

I had to go with her when she cleaned the rooms because the other kids were in school. I looked forward to cleaning day. The two roomers, Joe and Robert, knew that I came with my mother, so they started leaving a penny on their bedside table for me to find every week. Two penny candies! What a treat!

And that huge candy case—it looked as high as a mountain to me. Grandpa would ask me if I wanted a candy bar. I was so shy that I would just twist and turn and keep my head down, shrugging my shoulders. I would have been thrilled to have any of them! He said that when I could tell him what kind I wanted, I could have one, and he turned and walked away. Lesson learned. When he asked me the next time, I quickly answered, "Milky Way."

⌒

If you went up the little hill on Matthewson Street, you would practically run into Third Avenue Baptist Church, and that's where we went to church. It was a beautiful red brick building that stood on a corner. There was a huge leaded glass window behind the pulpit depicting Jesus with a lamb in His arms.

All of us kids were in Sunday school every week. I still remember my "Sunday" dress. My mom made it for me, and I loved it. It was made of white dimity with tiny pink roses printed on it. Ruffles over the shoulders formed sleeves. We wore the same outfit every Sunday.

My mom cut down an old suit of Grandpa's to make a suit for Don. It had knickerbocker pants, and he wore knee-high argyle socks with it.

Lucille and Agnes sang duets in church. They looked so grown up to me standing in front of that elegant stained glass window of Jesus. I was so proud of them and thinking how scared I'd be to get up in front of all those people and sing.

We lived in a happy home. This does not in any way mean that we escaped the effects of the depression.

Mom planted a garden and canned everything she could to supplement our food supply. She utilized foods that you could stretch for a family of seven—soups, beans, noodles, rice, and cheaper cuts of meat. It was said that some even cooked horse meat during the depression, but not at our house.

When Mom cooked a chicken, she cooked every usable part. For seven of us, there were two legs, two wings, two thighs, two breasts, liver, gizzard, heart, neck, back, and the "part that went over the fence last." The breasts were cut in half to deliver more white meat. Dad always ate the tail, the back, the liver, and the gizzard. All of us kids wanted the heart, so Mom made us take turns. I clearly remember standing by the stove while Mom fried the chicken when it was my turn to make sure I got it.

I can also remember Mom taking a tinned can of roast beef just slightly larger than a can of tuna and pairing it with homemade noodles to stretch far enough for seven. And it was delicious. Mom was such a good cook.

With four girls in the family, outgrown clothes were handed down. My older sisters traded clothes with their girlfriends just to have something different to wear.

When the soles of our shoes wore through, Dad would cut cardboard to fit inside so we could get more wear out of them.

Dad used to walk along the railroad tracks and pick up pieces of coal that had dropped off the boxcars to heat our house.

We were blessed more than most. Dad worked hard, and the hours were long at the restaurant, but he retained his dignity. We were poor, but I didn't know it. Over the years, I've heard my siblings say the same. Our home and our family life was like a cocoon immersed in love.

Across town, also growing up in Flint, was a youngster of five years old. He was growing up in very different circumstances than I was. He was an only child. Adopted. Little did I know that he would become the love of my life—the man I would marry someday. His name was Jack Curns.

24

When the United States entered World War I in 1917, Manley Leo Curns enlisted in the Army. He served honorably and faithfully, and according to his discharge papers, "No AWOL." He was discharged on December 20, 1918, and was "paid in full $13.53." He was happy to return to his hometown of Flint, Michigan, and just in time to celebrate Christmas with family.

Jack's Dad Manley Leo Curns

Manley was twenty-three years old, weary from the war, and just wanted to get on with his life. After the new year began, he secured a position as a conductor on the interurban that ran between Flint and Saginaw.

He dated several young ladies, but the one who won his heart was a young lady from church, Lois May Goodrich. She was beautiful, and he enjoyed very much being with her. He could envision spending the rest of his life with her. He asked for her hand in marriage, and they were married just a year after he got home from service.

Lois was a milliner, and with their two salaries combined, they were able to purchase a home. They chose one on Beach Street, downtown Flint. It was a two-story home—yellow with brown trim. There was a wide porch extending across the front of the house that was almost completely enclosed with ivy.

They had a happy marriage and enjoyed a busy social life. They were blessed with many friends and were active at the First Baptist Church.

Before long, Manley made a decision to change professions. He wanted something local instead of "riding the rails." He went to Barber College, and upon graduation, he secured a position at the barbershop located in the Dresden Hotel, downtown Flint.

They were both fulfilled with their work, but something was missing. Only one thing marred their happiness. They were unable to have children. Six years had passed, and they had not been blessed with a baby. They both wanted a child badly. They decided to try for adoption.

In the city of Ann Arbor at the University Hospital on January 14, 1925, a child was born. A beautiful baby boy weighing six pounds and two ounces. Two weeks after he was born, the birth mother signed a release of her parental rights, and this precious baby boy was put up for adoption.

Adoption is not easy, but Manley and Lois met all the qualifications required. It took a few months, but near the end of May, that baby boy was placed in Lois' arms, and they brought him home.

There was a lot of cooing and butterfly kisses, and soon, he wrapped his tiny fist around one of Manley's fingers, closed his blue eyes, nestled close to Lois' heart, and went to sleep. He was home. They named him Jack.

Manley and Lois couldn't wait to show him off to all their friends. He was a churchgoer from the very beginning, being baptized right away and a new member of the nursery. He received his Cradle Roll Certificate before he was a year old.

The adoption agency made regular checkups to see how Jack was doing. Their report stated he had "a very good disposition and had been very well. Jack was a bright, attractive little fellow with a winsome smile."

By the time he was a year old, he had cut four teeth, and others were breaking through. He was walking by holding onto furniture.

The adoption agency's last entry in his portfolio was when he was one and a half years old. They reported, "Jack was developing splendidly, had all of his teeth, walked alone, and was in very good physical condition. He is a very attractive child with light brown hair, hazel eyes, and rosy cheeks."

The notation about "hazel eyes" was definitely an error. No one had eyes more blue than Jack. His blue eyes fairly sparkled.

Jack was a sweet little boy, doted on by his mom and dad. They were so proud of him.

Jack had a bout with pneumonia and overcame it quickly—just a healthy little boy. He had a sandbox in the backyard and a little tricycle to ride up and down the sidewalk. He was promoted from the Cradle Roll Class to the Beginner's Class at First Baptist Church.

Life was good for the Curns, and they were doing well. Manley had established a good following in the barber trade, and Lois was now a stay-at-home mom. They were the proud owners of a new car.

Manley opened his own barbershop on Dayton Street near Dupont Street. LeMieux's Drug Store was on the corner, and Manley's barbershop was joined to that. His customers followed him to his new shop, and everything was falling into place nicely for them.

Jack M. Curns

It was the summer before the stock market crashed that Manley and Lois took the giant step to build a house. They bought the northwest corner lot at Dupont and Dartmouth Streets and set about to build their dream home. It was just a few blocks from Manley's barbershop.

It was a big home—two stories. On the first floor, there was a living room, dining room, kitchen, breakfast nook, two bedrooms, and a bath. All were large rooms. The best of materials was used. The kitchen and bathroom had ceramic tile counters and floors.

The upstairs was divided into two apartments, each having a living room, kitchen, bedroom, and bath. The kitchens and baths upstairs also had ceramic tile. A two-car garage that housed their new car completed the property.

Manley had correctly planned that the income from the two apartments would pay for the mortgage on the house. The cost of the home was $12,500—a large sum of money in that day.

Things couldn't have been any better for Manley and Lois. They built a little cottage at Houghton Lake. Manley worked six days a week, but a couple of times a month on a Saturday evening, they would drive up to the lake and enjoy Sunday at their little lakefront cottage.

One of the games Jack played while passing time on those drives up to Houghton Lake was playing "cars." When he was four years old, he could recognize every car on the road by the headlights coming toward them. There wasn't the variety then that there is now, but that was still quite an accomplishment for such a little guy.

<hr />

When our family was making the move from Saginaw to Flint, Jack was just beginning school. That fall, he would attend kindergarten at Civic Park School.

One of Jack's earliest memories was from that time period. On his walk to school, he passed a house that had a dog chained inside of their fence. It was a white Spitz Eskimo dog. Somehow, Jack got inside of the fence. Before the lady that lived there could get out of the house, the dog came at Jack. He was off his chain! The dog lunged at Jack, and being surprised, Jack hit him on the end of his nose.

Jack driving the travelling goat cart

The lady found out Jack's name and contacted Lois to tell her what happened. After that, Jack always stopped in to play with the dog, and they became great friends. The people ended up giving the dog to Jack. He named him "Snowball" because he loved to sleep in snowbanks.

~⁓~

So this is how two different families were living at the beginning of the Great Depression. Our family with five children in a rented home and no car. Across town, the Curns have a large home, their own business, a small lakefront cottage, a new car, and income from their two apartments.

If it sounds like I'm complaining about our circumstances, I'm not. We were blessed beyond belief compared to most others. We never lived on the street, and I don't ever remember being hungry. I'm happy for anyone who was able to escape the hardship of the depression. I'm simply trying to express how two families, whose lives were destined to cross, survived the depression.

This was just the beginning. The depression would linger on for many years.

25

We moved from Matthewson Street to Third Avenue, just a few blocks from Dad's job and a few short blocks to Durant School where I started kindergarten. The only photograph I have of my dad and me taken together is a snapshot taken on the front porch steps of that house.

I attended Durant School for kindergarten, first and second grades from three different houses, the one on Third Avenue and two separate addresses on Joliet Street. Apparently when you have five kids and rent houses, you move a lot. I was too young to know the reason why we moved. It was the height of the depression, and perhaps, the owners needed the houses for themselves or a family member. Or maybe we got behind on the rent. I don't know, but we moved four times in four years.

One thing I do remember is our moving day lunch. The gas or electric for the stove at the new place was never turned on by noon, and the lunch was simple and always the same—Dad would get a ring of Koegel's pickled bologna, a brick of cheese, and a box of crackers. No stove required.

The Great Depression peaked in 1933. The average family salary, if you were fortunate enough to have a job, was $1500 a year. Think of it—$125 a month for a family to live on. Banks closed at an alarming rate. In all, 11,000 banks failed, 4,000 in 1933 alone. Millions lost their savings. Those who had been reluctant to buy on credit and put their money in the bank for safekeeping lost their life savings anyway when the banks collapsed.

Two million people were homeless and living in tent cities and shanty towns. Others were living in cardboard boxes. My sister, Lucille, had a friend who was living in a chicken coop with her mom, dad, and two sisters.

There were bread lines and soup kitchens—signs for free soup, coffee, and doughnuts for the unemployed.

All over the country, farmers were forced to let crops rot in the fields because they couldn't afford to harvest, while millions went hungry.

Women coped by being as frugal as they knew how, and still, it wasn't enough. Clothing was sewed, patched, handed down, or traded with other families. When flour companies learned that women were making dresses out of their sacks, they started printing them in flowered patterns.

Many women took in boarders or did laundry to earn money or exchanged their services for food. Extra rooms went to cousins or in-laws who had lost their homes. In many cases, two or more families crowded together in a single family home or an apartment.

Bread was selling for 9¢ for a one pound loaf, butter 56¢ a pound, coffee 56¢ a pound, and five pounds of sugar for 35¢; but most didn't have the money to buy it.

But the saddest thing ever was a photograph in a newspaper of a mother sitting on her porch steps, her head buried in her hands, surrounded by four adorable children—no way to take care of them and depressed beyond belief. A sign stuck in the dirt beside them read, "4 children for sale."

If it had not been for Grandpa's gift of a job for Dad, that could have been our family. Only by the grace of God.

But kids will be kids, and I have many fond memories from that time period. My sister, Agnes, asked for a Brownie camera and a quart of chocolate milk for her birthday when we lived on Third Avenue. She received both, and the camera started a new phenomenon in our family as she snapped photos. Thank you, Ag, for taking that photo of Dad with me—the only one I have, a treasure that I cherish.

Ag took the quart of chocolate milk in her bedroom and locked the door. That's all right. It was her special day.

On my special day, my birthday, Mom made my favorite dinner. Homemade noodles and lemon pie. I chose the pie instead of birthday cake every year; it's still my favorite.

Ag and Don were the rascals among the five of us kids. Lucille was a gorgeous seventeen-year-old by that time and couldn't be bothered with some of the things Ag and Don came up with.

One day, Mom went downtown to her favorite meat market—Bazley's. She was a steady customer there and stopped in every Friday. Most Fridays, Mr. Bazley would have a soup bone saved for Mom that he would give her free of charge that turned into a delicious pot of vegetable soup or broth for Mom's wonderful homemade noodles.

Before she left to do her shopping, mom gave us 25c to get bread and lunch meat for sandwiches for our noonday meal. Ag and Don went across the street to the drug store and bought five frozen Milky Way bars instead. That was our lunch. Delicious!

They were the two who put the mattress out the window onto the front lawn and were jumping off the porch roof when Mom got home too. What those two didn't think of.

Ag got caught smoking with some neighbor boys in their dog house. They would have gotten away with it too, but someone saw smoke coming out of the dog house door, and they got busted.

One night, a bunch of us kids went sledding on the hill at Mott Park Golf Course. There was a pileup on the sleds, and Ag got cut near the eyebrow with a sled runner. The doctor came to our house, laid her on our dining room table, and stitched her up right in front of family and friends. I'll never forget that!

On a Saturday morning, Don and I went grocery shopping for Mom. She gave us money and a list and off we went to A&P. Don would go in and buy one article; then, I would go in and buy one article. We figured by buying one article at a time, we'd save a few pennies in tax money and treat ourselves to some candy. We were stockpiling the groceries in a banana box at the back of the store. It didn't take the store owner long to figure out what was going on, and he told us to bring in our list, and he'd fill our order and give us the tax money. So we got our treat after all.

The Crane Kids
Front row: Don, Arlene, Edna,
Back row: Lucille, Agnes

One year for Christmas, I got a baby doll from my Grandpa Yats. My mom and dad gave me a green wicker doll buggy to go with it. The wicker sunshade that went over the top had round side windows where I could peek in and make sure my "baby" was doing fine. It also sported spoked wheels with rubber tires. I loved playing "mother." It's a wonder I didn't wear those tires out.

Edna and I had our favorite thing to play that kept us entertained for hours—office! We had two little chairs that we would sit back to back about six feet apart. A string was looped around the chairs that we could draw back and forth pulley fashion. We had a little purse that we snapped shut over the string. *Oh, the messages we sent back and forth in that little purse.* Ag's camera recorded that too.

And her camera captured forever photos of the Crane kids in their Sunday best, ready for church. She was in them too, so Mom must have taken those.

From those early years at Durant School, I remember having milk period. The milk came in little half-pint glass bottles with cardboard caps. It cost 2¢ a week for white milk and 3¢ a week for chocolate. Mom used to tie my money in the corner of a handkerchief so I wouldn't lose it.

I didn't get to walk to school with the older kids, because my kindergarten class was in the afternoon. There was a dog on the corner by our house that used to bark at everybody. I was so scared of him because he always jumped up on me. It was his way of playing, but I didn't understand that, and I was afraid of him. My dear mom would walk me past that house, past the dog that seemed so ferocious to me, and then, I would continue on alone. After school, all the kids were walking by and the dog was inside, but I still hurried past that house.

Dad wanted to pull my tooth. It was just one of my baby teeth, hanging by a thread, but I was scared it would hurt. His plan was to tie a string around my tooth, tie the other end of the string around the door knob, and then shut the door. "It won't hurt a bit," he promised. My plan was to run out the door before Dad could catch me. I ran around and around our house, and Dad finally just decided to let it go. That night at supper, my tooth fell out, right onto my dinner plate. I guess Dad's plan would have been painless after all.

When prohibition was voted in, middle-class Americans had hoped to turn the clock back to an earlier, more comfortable time, but that didn't happen. It only drove those who wanted alcohol underground to the speakeasies.

Prohibition was repealed in 1933 because it simply did not work. It not only failed to prevent people from drinking but also led to crime and violence.

So Grandpa could sell liquor now. His restaurant was turned into a saloon like he had started out in business way back in Owosso.

∽

Across town, Jack was growing into a fine young boy. There were a lot of kids in his neighborhood, and some that he was friends with remained friends throughout his life.

His memories of the depression were that they had a beautiful car setting in the garage, but oftentimes had no money to buy gas to drive it. It was a maroon Auburn with a black leather top and black fenders. The interior boasted plush wine-colored mohair upholstery.

He also remembered hearing his dad say that he didn't have 50¢ to put in the cash register to open his barbershop for business that day and hoped that his first customer had the right change.

26

Moving again. New school. Make new friends. Pickled bologna, a wedge of cheese, and a box of crackers. It must have been so hard for Mom and Dad to be moving all the time like that.

This time, it was Williams Street, in the second block from Saginaw Street, the main artery through Flint. Our house was on the south side of the street, so if you turned right from our house and walked two blocks, you would see Doyle School (where I attended school). On the corner of Williams Street and Saginaw Street, there was a branch of Citizens Bank, Kennedy's Grocery Store, and the Ritz Theater. What a wonder living that close to a theater!

There were several theaters scattered along Saginaw Street, and they only cost 11¢, a dime for the theater, a penny luxury tax for the government. We loved our Saturday afternoons at the theater. It was cheap entertainment and took people's minds off the depression that was still going on. America was having a difficult time getting stabilized.

By the time we moved to Williams Street, Lucille had married a local boy, Sam McMonagle, and they were living in an apartment. Sam always called Lucille "Peg," and everyone picked up on it, so she was Peg from then on.

Peg used to come over on Monday nights to go to the Ritz with Mom. On Monday nights, they gave away a piece of china with gold trim on the edge—an incentive to get people out on a slow night—and the ladies packed the theater to collect that china.

Ag and Don were still filled with mischievousness, and I remember them chasing each other around our oak dining room table. It was never over anything that really mattered. They just enjoyed antagonizing each other like siblings sometimes do.

Ag had another habit different from the rest of us kids. Mom was a wonderful cook, but Ag never wanted to eat what was on the table. She would beg for a bologna sandwich, and quite often, she got it. There was a little neighborhood grocery, not Kennedy's, but a little mom-and-pop grocery just a few houses away. It was mixed right in the residential area with the houses. So Mom would give Ag a nickel; then, she'd run to the store and get two slices of bologna. She'd make a sandwich and sprinkle pepper on that bologna 'til it was covered.

Our house on Williams Street was a two-story. There was only one problem—it didn't have a bathtub. We used to take a bath in a large round laundry tub in the middle of the kitchen floor. Mom heated water on the stove to fill the tub; then, the four of us kids took turns bathing. Thank goodness it did have the other necessary facility!

The Curry family lived next door to us. They had a lot of kids too, all about the same age as us. One summer day, both of our families got a puppy, a brother and sister, from the same litter. That was a first for us, having a puppy. We got the female and named her Ginger; they named their male Pepper. There was a wire fence between our two houses with openings about three or four inches square. Ginger and Pepper used to squeeze through those tiny openings to play together. They were so cute!

My best friend was Jean Horton, who lived right around the corner on Chippewa Street. We were in the same grade at school. There wasn't a father present at Jean's house, and her mom worked. We used to go to her house after school, pierce a slice of bread with a fork, and toast it over the gas flame of their cooking stove until it was burned black and then slather it with peanut butter. Scrumptious! We probably would have had our after-school snack cut off if either of our mom's knew what we were doing. We could have easily caught our clothes on fire, but we didn't think about that—eight years old and playing with fire.

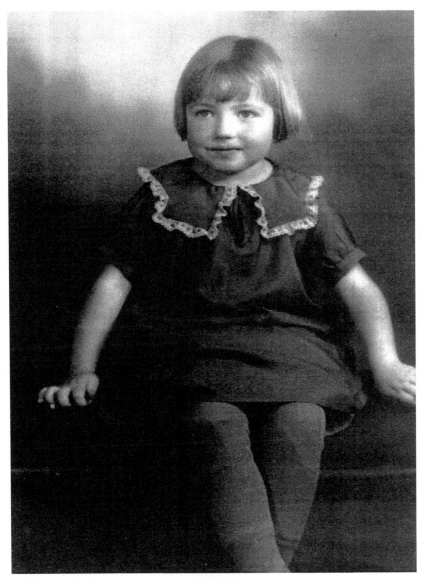

Arlene
Handmade silk dress
and long underwear

I was never fond of eating breakfast when I was a youngster, so Mom bought me a special cereal bowl to encourage me to eat. It was bright red celluloid and had a picture of Mickey Mouse on the bottom inside of the bowl. On the first day, I downed my cereal in a flash to see Mickey. The next day, I was dawdling, and Mom said, "Don't you want to see Mickey Mouse?" "No," I replied. "I saw him yesterday."

Edna and I still enjoyed playing "office" and "school." We played hopscotch, jump rope, jacks, hide-and-seek, tag, and all the other childhood games with the neighbor kids. I had a tricycle that I was allowed to ride to the corner and back. The Maxwell's lived on the corner. Their son, Frank, and my brother, Don, were best friends from the time we moved there until the day they were separated by death. Frank's life would intertwine with our family forever as a result of that move to Williams Street. God sure works in mysterious ways.

The Ringling Brothers and Barnum and Bailey Circus was coming to town, and I could barely contain my excitement! Dad and I got up very early that morning, and he took me down to watch them unload all the animals from the railroad boxcars. Moving the circus from city to city is quite a show in itself. I saw lions, tigers, and elephants—everything. I thought it was the real thing and didn't find out for quite a long time that I hadn't really been to the circus. I had a wonderful time and a great memory of time shared with my dad.

We didn't have around the clock news back in the 1930s. We depended on the daily newspaper and the evening news broadcast on the radio to keep up on the news. When something spectacular happened, the newspaper would put out an extra edition. News carriers would go up and down every street, even in the middle of the night, shouting "Extra! Extra!" doing their best to wake people up.

I remember such an "Extra" while we were living on Williams Street. It was the night the Dionne quintuplets were born. The night Mrs. Dionne gave birth to five baby girls—an event that people all over the world had been waiting for.

We had a continual procession of transients at our door on Williams Street. It was so close to downtown. Hoboes would knock on our door asking if we could spare a meal. They were never turned away. Whatever we had, Mom and Dad were kind and generous about sharing. Dad always thought our house was marked in some way so others would know they could get a meal at our door.

~~⌒

Grandma and Grandpa Yats were still living almost side by side on Corunna Road. Grandpa had a live-in housekeeper now, Mrs. Carr, who prepared his meals and did all the housework. Our family was invited over for dinner occasionally, and Mrs. Carr would fix a nice meal for us. Grandpa and Mrs. Carr spent the winters in a little cabin in Tampa, Florida. I thought Grandpa must be very rich.

Grandpa had a player piano and a cabinet full of piano rolls. The rolls were pierced with holes, and when they were inserted in the opening in the front of the piano, you pressed your feet up and down on the pedals and beautiful music poured out. I thought that was the most fantastic thing I had ever heard and wanted so much to pump those pedals. Grandpa didn't really want us to play it. Sometimes, he'd let us play a little bit, but not much.

Grandma's health was declining; she had developed sugar diabetes. Mom used to go over once a week and clean house for her. Years ago, Grandma taught my mom to make homemade noodles. Now, that she was older and not in the best of health, Mom would make the noodles and bring a container to Grandma to enjoy.

In the summer, when I wasn't in school, I went with her. We'd take the bus downtown, transfer, and go out to Corunna Road. It was a little adventure for me, because our family still didn't have a car.

Grandma had a metal glider on her front porch. The cushions were made of fabric with faded roses. The glider squeaked when you rocked back and forth in it. When the cleaning was finished, Grandma, Mom, and I used to sit out there on the glider and have a cool iced tea or lemonade and watch the traffic go by until our bus arrived at the corner to take us home.

~~⌒

Across town, Jack attended Civic Park School all through elementary—no changing schools like me. But Jack was not a spoiled child. His parents made him toe the mark; in fact, they were very strict, and if he disobeyed, he got the razor strap from his dad—quite severely at times.

His mom and dad were still attending First Baptist Church, downtown Flint. When Jack was ten years old, he started attending Sunday school with his neighborhood pals at Flint Gospel Assembly. It was on the corner of Dupont and Dayton streets, near his dad's barbershop, and close enough to home that he could walk there. They had Vacation Bible School in a big tent, like a circus tent. Jack liked it so much he started going there all the time. He remembered the Sunday schoolteacher using "felt graphs" to explain the gospel—pieces of felt in cutout shapes that stuck in place where you put them. He invited Jesus into his heart as his personal Lord and Savior at the tender age of ten right there in the big tent and held fast to his faith in Jesus all his life.

27

No one could possibly understand the joy in my heart when I was ten years old, and we moved to Crosby Street. If I was that overjoyed, imagine how thrilled my mom and dad must have been. We were not renting this time, but buying. Oh! To own and not rent! No more leaving friends behind and having to make new ones. No more changing schools. I was ecstatic!

Dad had secured a job at AC Spark Plug, a division of General Motors. He was hired as a maintenance man on the third shift. We had Grandpa to thank for getting us over the rough spots on the way to a permanent job, making it possible for Mom and Dad to buy their first home.

I absolutely loved our home on Crosby Street. It was large and comfortable—a tranquil place of peace and joy.

There was a porch that extended across the entire front of the house. Dad hung a wooden swing at one end of the porch. We also had a pair of metal armchairs that had a little "give" in them, and you could bounce a bit in them. Mom had a wicker planter that she filled with ferns. It was a fitting welcome to everyone who came to visit.

Hydrangea bushes bloomed in profusion on either side of the porch steps. Beside the one-car garage out in the back, hollyhocks and rhubarb flourished in a yard shaded by magnificent red maple trees.

A spacious living room extended the width of the first floor, with a stairway to the second floor at the right. A large dining room opened off the living room, and the kitchen was to the left of the dining room. Upstairs were three large bedrooms and a bathroom complete with a tub! No more bathing in the middle of the kitchen floor.

When we first moved to Crosby Street, we didn't have a refrigerator. We had an old-fashioned icebox. The ice was delivered by a man driving a horse and wagon. Mom would put a card in the window that displayed how many pounds of ice we needed, 25, 50, 75, or 100. The delivery man would chip off the appropriate number of pounds with his ice pick, grasp the block of ice with his big clamp, and carry it on his shoulder to the side door leading into the kitchen and place it in the top of our icebox. While he was doing that, every kid in the neighborhood gathered at his wagon and ate the loose ice chips that were broken off.

My beloved childhood home Crosby Street, Flint, Michigan

We didn't have a car either, since my dad had vowed never to drive again after the accident in Saginaw where our car slid off the road and turned over. My mom and dad (sometimes with me along) walked all the way to Hamady's Market on North Saginaw Street to get groceries and draw them home in my little red Radio Flyer wagon—about a two-mile round trip.

The church that we attended from that home was a little basement church located on Mary Street, about four blocks from our house. It was mixed right in with the neighborhood houses and for some reason never got completed. The only thing aboveground was a door with a stairway leading down to the basement level.

It was called First Methodist Protestant Church and was pastored by Reverend A. G. Frost. I recall with great fondness my Sunday schoolteacher Jeanette Wolf and her husband Dale. Mrs. Wolf was a faithful servant of the Lord, as was her husband. They owned Dale's Health Foods. One Saturday, Mrs. Wolf had the class over to her home for lunch and an afternoon of games. I got to wear my Sunday dress. I thought that was such a nice thing for Mrs. Wolf to do. I felt like royalty being invited to her home because I respected her so much. After all of these years, I still remember her kindness.

There were lots of kids in the neighborhood, and they were quick to include me in their circle, which added to my joy.

My two closest friends were Rita Stachowiak, who lived across the street, and Barbara McDowell, one house down from me, but there were at least a dozen girls my age in a two-block radius, and all of them were friendly. We used to have the best times together.

In the summer, we were outside all day. We played all the games every kid played—kick the can, hide-and-seek, jacks, jump rope, tag, hopscotch, Annie-I-Over, Ring around the Rosie, and drop the handkerchief. We had roller skates that clamped on the soles of our shoes, and we skated on the sidewalks and the street too, because there wasn't much traffic on Crosby Street. There was a vacant lot at the corner, and we played baseball there. Sometimes, we could get a few boys to play with us, making bigger teams.

The girls still played "dolls" and "house." Our neighbors on the corner, the Awreys, had a mulberry tree in their side yard. The branches cascaded to the ground, leaving an open space in the center just perfect for our little "playhouse." Mr. and Mrs. Awrey were older and didn't have any children living at home, and they let us play in the center of their tree any time we wanted to. Rita, Barbara, and I spent many afternoons playing "house" under the branches of their tree, shaded from the sun. Being kids, we probably snitched some of their mulberries too.

Eileen, who lived around the corner next door to the Awreys, was an only child. Her mother set a game table up on the front porch, and we often gathered there for Monopoly, Old Maid, or Go Fish. Sometimes, we'd leave the Monopoly board set up for days and continue playing whenever.

I used to make "hollyhock dolls" fashioning a lovely ball gown from an upside-down bloom and creating a head from a bud. Childish imagination can dream anything. Paper dolls and coloring pictures with Crayolas were favorite ways to pass time too.

There were two favorite places for my quiet time—the swing on the front porch was one. But my "secret place" was a built-in window seat in the bedroom that Edna and I shared. It had a storage chest with a lid that lifted up to hold blankets and pillows. The window and the seat were in a little recess, creating a perfect niche to read, which has always been a favorite pastime of mine. There's a whole world to be discovered within the covers of a book. Some of my childhood favorites were *Anne of Green Gables, Little House on the Prairie,* and *Nancy Drew Mysteries.* I loved to sit and read in that little "secret" nook.

When the streetlights came on, we had to report home. Sometimes, play would continue, but we had to let our folks know where we were. Rita, Barbara, and I liked to spread out a blanket in our backyard and gaze at the velvet blue sky studded with stars. We could pinpoint the evening star, the North Star, the Milky Way, and the Big and Little Dipper; and once in a while, we would catch sight of a shooting star. If there was a full moon, we were certain something weird was going to happen.

There were four movie theaters within walking distance of our house—the Regent, Ritz, Star, and Della. That didn't include any of the ones downtown, and there were several in that area too. I loved the movies, and Edna and I went every Saturday. A special favorite, for me at least, were the Shirley Temple movies. My mom could put my hair in long curls just like Shirley's. That was so much fun. Shirley Temple and I were the same age.

Then, there were all the musicals with Ginger Rogers and Fred Astaire. The comedy films with Laurel and Hardy and the Three Stooges and who can forget the *Our Gang* comedies. I guess the movies were a love affair with most Americans to forget their troubles for a while.

My brother's best friend Frank Maxwell who lived by us on Williams Street was now working at the Genesee Dairy on Saginaw Street across from Doyle School. Edna and I would stop in after the movie to get an ice cream cone. Frank is the only person I know that could pile a quart of ice cream on one of those little cones. And they were only 5¢. It took me a while to figure out why our cones were so big. Don wasn't the only one in our family that Frank was interested in. He was falling in love with Edna.

~~~

We had a telephone for the very first time when we lived on Crosby Street. It was a party line shared with three other families and when a call came through, the phones at all four houses would ring. The sound and number of rings were different for each home, so we would know when to pick up. Every call came through a switchboard, so an operator had to be on duty day and night in case a call came through. Having a phone was very exciting for us kids. We had strict orders never to listen in on anyone else's call.

The Crosby Street Gang
I'm top row, center

Before we were blessed with our own phone, if we had to make a phone call, we had to locate a pay phone. You rarely see a phone booth any more where you can pay to make a call. They used to be scattered in downtown areas, gas stations, even drug stores. The cost for a local call was a quarter and there was a coin box where you could drop the coins for your call. There was a local phone book chained to a small shelf, although they were usually missing. Pay phones have virtually disappeared from the landscape with the advent of land lines and cell phones.

Don taught me a new trick, and I did it once or twice at Barbara's house because there wasn't anyone home there in the daytime. Her mom had passed away, and her dad and sister were working. We would dial a store and ask, "Do you have Prince Albert [tobacco] in the can"? If they said, "Yes," we would say, "Well, let him out. He can't breathe." We thought we were so clever—ten-year-old humor. The storekeeper probably wanted to wring our little necks.

Don got a two-wheel bicycle for Christmas one year, but he didn't have it very long when it was stolen right off our front porch. None of us four girls ever got one. I wanted one so bad and almost got one once. A boy who lived one block away from us had a little bike he wanted to sell. When I say it was little, it was very small. The wheels may have been 12" across. It was old and rusty, and he wanted $2.00 for it. He rode it in circles in front of our house for two days, tantalizing me. He even let me "try it out." Mom and Dad considered it but in the end decided against it because they wondered if it might have been stolen, because it was newly acquired by the boy. So my hopes were crushed—no bike!

Crosby Street was just a nice friendly neighborhood. Everyone knew everyone else and what was going on in each other's lives. Everyone had front porches, and the folks would sit outside in the evening while the kids played.

We never had a vacation as a family. One week during the summer, Don, Edna and I were invited to spend a week at Aunt Geneva and Uncle Ray's house. They had matching kids to pair up with each one of us. Our visit coincided with the Shiawassee County Fair, where my cousin, Faye, played the guitar and sang in the country music show. I was pretty impressed with Faye being up on stage. Because she was "part of the show," we got to ride on a float in the parade through town with Faye playing and singing. All the rest of us kids had to do was set on a bale of hay. It was great fun.

I liked every part of that week except the cold beans. We were always pressed for time to get to the fair, and Aunt Geneva served pork and beans right out of the can. I never did develop a taste for that.

~

Peg and Sam had been living in an apartment, but when a house kitty-corner across the street from our house came up for sale, they bought it! Peg was pregnant and would be having a baby soon. Ten years old, and I was about to become Aunt Arlene.

Ag married a local boy, Estel (Ed) Escue, and Dad built an apartment for them added onto the back of our house. Dad could do anything. It was a nice apartment with a living room, kitchen, and an open stairway leading to a bedroom and bathroom upstairs. I loved having my family so close.

Ed worked at Freeman's Dairy. He used to bring cream home for us. We'd pour it in a mason jar, and with the top securely on, we would shake it until it turned into butter. Another thing we did as a family was shell popcorn. In the fall, Dad would purchase a bushel of popcorn on the cob. Yes, popcorn grows on ears of corn just like corn on the cob. The kernels were so hard and sharp. You would take two ears of the popcorn and rub them together to get the kernels to fall off. That wasn't fun to do, and it really tore your hands up, but it was so good when it was popped, and we were nibbling on it. The kernels were stored in mason jars.

One day, Ag came running into our house calling for Dad. "Come quick!" she screamed. "There's a mouse in my wastebasket!" Dad went into the apartment and, sure enough, heard a mouse rustling around in the bottom of the wastebasket. He filled the plastic basket with water and put a cardboard cover over it. Dad and Ag sat down to wait for the mouse to drown. After a time had passed, Dad went to the kitchen and carefully lifted the cover off. There, sitting on top of a cereal box, was Mr. Mouse. Dad said, "Little buddy, if you want to live that bad, I'm going to let you!" He carried the basket outside and set the mouse free.

In the fall, all the neighbor kids put away their roller skates and exchanged them for ice skates. As soon as the ponds froze over, we were out there every night. Our favorite places to skate were at Dort School where you could skate for free, and sometimes, we walked to the Ballenger Park Ice Rink.

Ballenger Park had a heated building where you could put your skates on, the rink was lighted, and they played music. I kind of remember that it cost a dime to skate there, so most every night was at Dort School.

My curfew to be home was 10:00 p.m., and there was always a group of us walking together. Dad had to be at work at 11:00 p.m. to start the third shift, so I was just getting home when he was getting ready to leave for the night. I would come in half frozen, chunks of snow stuck to the legs of my snow pants, and my hands so cold I could barely move them. Dad would have me sit down in front of the floor register in the living room, help me get my snow pants off, and rub my feet. Oh, that felt so wonderful. Did I ever tell you, Dad, how much I appreciated that? I love you, Dad.

◦⌒◦

When September arrived, I was enrolled in the Fifth grade at Dort Elementary on North Saginaw Street.

I was thrilled that one of my best friends, Barbara, went there too; and we could walk back and forth together. We were the only two; all the other girls went to the Catholic school.

Overall, I enjoyed attending Dort School, but it was there, in the sixth grade, that I had a humiliating experience that I remember to this day.

When I was young, I was painfully shy. Even family members could sometimes embarrass me and cause my face to flame. A sudden question asked where all attention was turned on me was torture. Someone verbally teasing me caused embarrassment.

It was worse at school. One day, our teacher announced that each student had to get onstage—alone—and do a "talent" act. I was terrified even to the point of losing sleep over it. In a group, I was fine, but to get up there alone, I just couldn't do it. We had until the end of the school year to do it.

The teacher would have a few students each day do their "act." Some were eager to do it, so she took volunteers at first. When that base was depleted, she started calling students by name. When my name was called, I said that I didn't have anything ready.

This continued to the very last day of class when she announced that anyone failing to take part would not pass. So I did it. Shaking like a leaf, face red as a beet, I squeaked out a popular song of that day entitled "Rosalie." It was a horrible rendition by any standard, and in my entire life, I don't believe I've ever been so humiliated. To this day, I remember the words to that song.

I don't believe forcing someone to do that accomplishes the purpose, but that teacher had a mission, and it was her way or no way if you wanted to pass. It took me until adulthood to overcome the fear of speaking before an audience, and I believe I conquered that fear by myself, not by a well-meaning teacher who coerced me into it.

The infamous sit-down strike against General Motors took place the same year we moved to Crosby Street and put Flint, Michigan, on the map. The auto workers went on strike to stop GM from sending work to nonunion plants and to establish a fair wage.

The strike actually started on December 30, 1936, when early that morning, a small group of men simply sat down at Fisher Body Plant 2, the plant on Chevrolet Avenue "down in the hole." Soon, Fisher 1 joined and Chevrolet Factory 4.

The entire city of Flint was emotionally torn apart. Sympathizers on the outside and wives of those on the inside took part in the strike by picketing and supplying food to those inside. It went on for forty-four days through bitter cold winter weather, and before an agreement was reached between the United Auto Workers and General Motors, the Michigan National Guard was called in.

For one night, the evening of January 11, 1937, gunshots were heard, and blood was spilled at what came to be known as "the Battle of the Running Bulls."

It began quietly enough with pickets pacing in front of Fisher Body Plant 2 "down in the hole." Earlier in the day, heat in the plant had been shut off by GM, and ladders to the second-floor windows were removed, cutting the food supply to the sit-downers.

As word spread, a crowd gathered. Sit-downers used ropes to haul food and coffee to the second floor.

Before long, police officers advanced down the hill, firing gas shells. Soon, there was the sound of glass smashing. The strikers fired back with water hoses, bricks, bottles, door handles, and hinges—anything they could lay their hands on.

A second and third charge took place. Before it was over, the Emergency Room and surgical floor at Hurley Hospital were filled with those injured. Fourteen strikers were wounded and a dozen police officers.

The United Auto Workers won control of the huge Chevrolet Engine Plant. An agreement was signed between the UAW and GM granting some of the worker's demands. Among other things, they received a 5% pay increase and permission to speak in the lunch room!

⁓

On the west side of Flint, the boy who would become the love of my life someday was quite the entrepreneur. Jack was twelve years old when the strike against General Motors took place. He sold ice cream bars from a basket attached to his bike. He went down to the plant on Chevrolet Avenue that was "down in the hole" and sold ice cream bars right through the windows to the strikers. Sometimes, the men who were there with the National Guard let him wheel right up to the gate, and the strikers would send someone out to buy several bars. It was very cold, December and January. He went there three times a day on weekends. The bars cost 10¢ each, and he made 2.5¢ profit on each one sold.

Jack sold ice cream bars at the fire station in the north end of Flint too. One day, the firemen invited him in, let him wear one of their big hats, slide down the pole, sit in the fire truck, and clang the bell. Big day.

When Jack was thirteen years old, he dug graves at Gracelawn Cemetery after school hours. The pay was 35¢ an hour, and it was hard work. There were two workers assigned to a grave, and the only tools were a pickax and shovel.

Another "big day" in Jack's life was when he attended the auto shows with his mom and dad when the new model for the year was introduced. Back then, it was kept under wraps, literally, until they brought out the new models. They were shipped on railcars or the big trucks that haul cars. They were covered with canvas tarps until "show day," when they were revealed to the public. The unveiling was a big affair.

It was at this age that Jack began to ask questions about his birth parents. He was told by his adoptive parents that his birth parents were getting a divorce, that there were five other children in the family, and that his mother was expecting another baby. She couldn't afford to keep another child, so when he was born, she gave him up for adoption.

The story that Jack was told was a big lie—not a shred of truth in it. It was a total fabrication that could break a teenage boy's heart and spirit. He lived all his life believing that his mother kept the other five children, but gave him up. It couldn't have been further from the truth, and why the truth was never told to him will always remain a mystery. Such a tragedy. Someday the truth, which was so foreign to the story Jack was told, would be discovered.

28

With the advent of World War II, which started in Europe when Germany invaded Poland, America was able to claw its way out of the economic slump that had hung over our country for ten years. All kinds of war goods were needed for export overseas. Manufacturing flourished, and unemployment was no longer a problem in the United States. America was booming.

On the west side of Flint, Jack was entering his teens, just two years ahead of me. His neighborhood was blessed with lots of kids too. His teen chums were Frank Watson, Dale Green, Bob McGraw, Don Fetkenheir, and Bob and Bill Bennecasse. Frank Watson was his best buddy, and they remained close friends throughout their lifetimes.

These neighborhood chums practically lived outside, just like the kids in our neighborhood. Their favorite activities were sidewalk roller-skating, cowboys, cars, tree camps, baseball, football, kick the can, hide-and-seek, shooting marbles, trying to master the art of spinning a yo-yo, and swimming at Haskell pool. In the winter, they switched to sledding on the Jackson Street hills, hockey, building snow forts, and having snowball fights.

Their neighborhood gang used to play pranks too, but being boys, their pranks were more than a phone call asking someone to let Prince Albert out of the can.

Flint had electric trolley buses back then, and there was one that came down Chevrolet Avenue, turned left on Dayton Street, and went to Civic Park School to make a turnaround at the end of the line. In the summertime, the gang would throw chains over the trolley and pull the cables down, cutting off their electric power so they couldn't go. The driver would have to get out and hook the trolley back up. Sometimes, the kids would have them down again before he could get going. In the winter, the trolley buses had to stop at Chevrolet Avenue and Dayton Street. When it was icy, the kids would slide the bus over to the curb and hold it there so it couldn't get traction to go.

Jack and his friend, Warren Harrison (who would later stand with him as best man at our wedding), got in some trouble one day. They carried water-filled balloons up the outside stairs leading to the roof of his Dad's barber shop. They dropped the balloons on unsuspecting passersby. They thought it was hilarious until Jack's Dad caught them. They both got the razor strap for that.

Jack and his best friend, Frank Watson, weren't involved in this prank, but they retold the story over the years. Some of the older boys in their neighborhood tied ropes around an old car and hoisted it to the roof of Civic Park School. I think they always wished they were part of it - but the older boys wouldn't let them.

Then, there was the Halloween prank they did one year that was really bad. They went a little north of Pasadena; there was nothing out that way back then except a scattered house or two. They thought it would be fun to tip over an outhouse. They didn't know that the outhouse was occupied. They had pushed it over with the door down, and the only way out was through one of the portholes. The man slipped and fell in the hole. If that man could have gotten ahold of those kids that night, I dread to think what he would have done to them.

～

A big part of Jack's life centered on Houghton Lake. His dad had built a cottage on the lake shortly after they adopted Jack during the Great Depression. It was a little two-bedroom cottage with an outhouse. Jack loved going to the lake to swim, fish, and hunt. He went hunting with his dad before he was legally of age to carry a gun.

Jack's Grandma and several aunts and uncles on his dad's side lived at or nearby Houghton Lake. He liked to visit his Aunt Gertie and Uncle Frank's farm. They had cows, horses, and a big goose named "Pete" that was mean. He would fly right into you, beat you with his wings, and bite you. It was a square-off match that Pete usually won unless you could outrun him. And if you got ahead of him, he'd chase you, trying his best to bite your butt.

⌇

Jack was lying on his bed one night, doing homework, when he heard his mom crying in the other bedroom. He knocked on her door, and she told him he could come in. When he asked, "What's wrong, Mom?" he was stunned to learn that his mother and father were getting a divorce. He didn't know what to say or think except to say "Why?" His mom said that he should ask his dad.

The next few weeks were the hardest in his young life. His dad was leaving for another woman. His mom was crying day and night, willing to forgive him. "Just please don't go," she pleaded. None of the begging or crying was enough; the thrill of lust was too great— his dad was leaving.

It was a crushing blow, not only to his mom but also to Jack. He was at an age where he needed a strong guiding hand. He had always looked up to his dad, and now, that was all shattered, their home broken. He pleaded with his dad too, but nothing or nobody was changing his mind.

Lois asked their pastor to talk with Manley. He wouldn't go to the pastor's office, so the pastor went to his barbershop. The pastor waited until two customers were taken care of to talk privately, but to no avail. The divorce was going forward.

Lois struggled for a time to keep their big home, with the income from the two apartments, but it was impossible, and after a time, she sold the home they had built together and loved so much. She and Jack moved to a smaller, older home on Wood Street. It was very hard for them, but with the help of the Lord, they would make it.

⌇

One day, Jack was riding his bike on Dort Highway when he saw Graff's Tractor Sales towing a car into their dealership. It had hay and chicken poop and feathers on the top and on the upholstery. The tires were rotten, and it had no battery and no starter. It didn't make any difference to Jack; it was love at first sight.

It was a 1931 Model A Ford Roadster. It had come out of a barn in Lapeer and was being traded in for a new tractor. Jack rushed into the dealership, so excited, talked with Mr. Graff, and told him he wanted to buy that car. Mr. Graff told him it was $12.00. Jack asked his dad to take a look at it. His dad gave his permission, and Jack was the proud owner of a car at fourteen. Back then, it was the law that you could get a driver's license when you were fourteen, so Jack got his license right away.

They had the car towed to Otto P. Graff's automobile dealership on South Saginaw Street across from the court house. Being the owner of a car, Jack got a job at the Standard Gas Station next to Lippincott Oldsmobile on North Saginaw Street. He got paid $9.00 a week and a tank of gas once in a while

His boss Charlie helped him in the restoration of his new vehicle. There were two tires in the fender wells, but they had some dry rot. They put new tubes in the tires, and Charlie rubbed the tires with oil to make them shiny and to prevent further dry rot. They put on new canvas wheel covers. Charlie let Jack buy four new tires and tubes at $10 each and a new battery for $8.00. A total of $48.00; Charlie took $2.00 out of each check, so it took almost six months to pay it off. Charlie didn't know it, but he was also helping to mend a young man's heart.

Jack got a starter for his car from a wrecked Model A that belonged to one of his cousins—Bill or Paul Bingley. He had it rebuilt for $1.00 and paid 25¢ for a bushing—$1.25 in total.

Mr. Schultz lived on North Saginaw Street, and he did upholstery work. The seats had been plugged with rags and taped. The roof leaked too. Mr. Schultz did all the upholstery work in a garage behind his house. He put in a new front seat, a new rumble seat, and a new top with side curtains all for $40. Then, it was in perfect condition. The paint was excellent, having been stored in a barn. It was black with red wheels and a red pinstripe and the new top was black.

Now, it was ready to roll! A dollar's worth of gas would last a week. Jack wasn't allowed to drive his car to school.

Jack's lifelong romance with cars had just begun.

CHAPTER 29

When I received my diploma from Dort Elementary School saying I had graduated to junior high, I was elated. I had successfully escaped the clutches of the "evil" teacher who had tried so hard to build up my confidence. I felt free as a bird on wing and ready to enjoy the summer.

Don, Edna, and I were the only three kids living at home now. Peg and Sam were living across the street from us. Ag and Ed were living across the street too! The house next door to Peg and Sam came on the market, and Ag and Ed bought it! Now, our family owned three houses on Crosby Street.

That was so much fun! Peg and Sam had two baby girls, Phyllis and Marilyn, born on the same day exactly one year apart.

Ag and Ed had a baby girl, Margie, just halfway between Phyllis and Marilyn—three babies for me to play with and babysit for right across the street!

I still enjoyed very much reading on the porch swing. It was that summer too that Mom taught me how to crochet. You could buy handkerchiefs at Kresge's in their needlework department for 10¢. They had little holes perforated around the edges ready to accept the crochet stitches. I crocheted a handkerchief for every female in our family that summer to give as Christmas gifts. When I ran out of hanky recipients, Mom taught me how to embroider.

Don, Edna, and I used to sleep on the front porch sometimes or on the living room floor to catch any cool breeze that might come our way. No air conditioning, just open doors and windows. No one locked their doors back in those days.

On the hottest summer days, I hooked up our sprinkler, put on my bathing suit, and invited the neighbor kids over to play. The sprinkler was a small metal circle, only about ten inches across, but it put out a pretty good spray, and we had a lot of fun running through it.

My friends and I had put away our dolls, but found a new love that summer. Our clamp-on skates were replaced with white shoe skates. Rita, Barbara, and I all got them the same summer and started roller-skating at the Rollerdrome on Louisa Street. Oh! How I loved that. It was in my blood, after all! My mom and dad met at a roller rink.

It was that same summer that I begged to take piano lessons. There was a sweet lady at our church, Mrs. Will Brewer, who taught piano, and she only lived a few blocks from our house. For $2 a week, Mrs. Brewer patiently taught me the scales and easy classical pieces. As simple as it was in the beginning, I loved it. Where most kids had to be threatened to get them to practice, they had to beg me to stop. I loved it so much I didn't care if it was only scales, and I played them over and over.

Mrs. Brewer held a recital each year at our little basement church for all of her students. I had no problem playing my numbers in front of the audience because I loved what I was doing and had confidence that I was doing it well, not like the traumatic experience I had suffered in the sixth grade at Dort School.

After three years under the teaching of Mrs. Brewer, I changed over to Jack LaRose. He taught at Wurlitzer, a music store downtown. He taught me to improvise using chords. With that system, I could play every piece of sheet music placed in front of me—all the new modern songs that everyone was singing or listening to on the radio. When our family got together, it always ended up with everyone gathered around the piano singing. Often, Don and Frank would join in with their coronets; we had so many good times.

And we listened to the radio! It's difficult to envision a world without television, but of course, when I was young, there wasn't any. We had radio, and the whole family would gather round and listen to our favorite programs. There was *Major Bowes Amateur Hour, Fibber McGee and Molly, Amos 'n' Andy, Burns and Allen, the Jack Benny Show, Little Theater off Times Square*, and so many more. There were soap operas every day too. We just couldn't see them—only got to hear them—but you could picture it in your mind, and they were very exciting.

I loved going downtown shopping with Mom. Mom had tiny feet, size 4. They were so small most stores didn't carry shoes in that size. She wore the salesmen's sample shoes, so when the stores had a pair to sell, they would call Mom. If it was in the budget, and the need was there, we would go shopping.

Downtown Flint was a magical place. Flint was a prosperous town because of all the auto manufacturing right here in my hometown. The array of stores downtown was tremendous. Ladies shops, men's clothing stores, department stores, shoe stores, jewelry shops, restaurants, several movie theaters, hardware store, furniture stores, candy stores, drug stores, and banks—just about any kind of business, Flint had it all.

On the way downtown, we passed the smallest skyscraper in the world. It was actually written about in "Ripley's Believe It or Not" newspaper column. This skyscraper was six stories high, in the shape of a triangle, with each side being six feet wide. It was owned by Winegarden Furniture Company, and they used to display pieces of furniture in it. It was always a mystery to me how they got an overstuffed couch in that tiny space on the sixth level, but later learned it had a series of trap doors to get the furniture up there.

Next door to the tiny skyscraper was Schiappacasse's Candy Kitchen. They sold handmade chocolates inside the store, but their biggest attraction was outside the store. They sold "hot jumbo peanuts," and the big roasting machine right outside their door drew everyone to their doorstep. The aroma of those roasting peanuts would make your mouth start to water before you even got close. That tantalizing aroma floated through the air of downtown Flint.

When we got to the river, I always had to look over the bridge before we continued on. There was a man who used to do amazing sand sculptures on the banks of the river, and if he was there that day,

I wanted to see his excellent work. He had a circle rounded out in the sand for people to toss coins into. Most people missed the circle, and there would be coins spread all around the target area. If he was there, Mom would give me a nickel to toss.

We would continue on, purchasing Mom's shoes first and then go to Kresge's Five and Ten Cent Store. I loved that place. The candy counter was right inside the front door. We always got a pound of chocolate drops, 10¢ a pound, and then went in search of another hanky to crochet or a needlework piece for me to embroider. I was as happy as a cat with a mouse and couldn't wait to get home and get started on my newest project.

Our neighborhood was saddened that summer by the loss of Mr. Awrey, owner of the house with the mulberry tree where we used to play "dolls." He was lying in state at a funeral home just west of Detroit Street. Mom was making her usual Friday trip to Bazley's Meat Market and walked over to the funeral home to pay her respects to Mr. Awrey. It was around noontime, and no one was in the viewing room, no family member present, or other visitors. After signing the guest book, Mom went up to the coffin to pray. She noticed a fly on Mr. Awrey's lapel, and quick as a flash, that fly flew right up Mr. Awrey's nose. Mom hastily told the funeral director what had happened and left as quick as she could get out of there so he could take care of that matter. She did her praying for Mr. Awrey as she continued on to the meat market.

August was canning month, and since Mom did a lot of it, mason jars took up most of our kitchen counter space that month. The kitchen table was moved from in front of the double windows and into the middle of the floor. The jars were dipped in boiling water to sterilize them. The peaches and tomatoes were submerged in washtubs of hot water to make the peeling easier, and the great kettles were on the stove ready for cooking. Steam filled the kitchen, and soon, the bounty was ready to be dipped into the mason jars. When the rubber rings and the lids were in place, Mom's canned goods looked as beautiful as any pictures in a cookbook. And they were so delicious, lasting until it was time to do it all over again.

Dad always put up a huge crock of pickles that was stored in our cellar next to the shelves holding the canned goods. Mom didn't can meat, but I heard that one of my aunts canned headcheese, so I made a mental note never to eat any of that if we were at their house when it was served. I don't even know what it is, just couldn't get anything with that name past my lips.

Mom made doughnuts too when fall arrived. I'd stand by the stove, but not too close, as she lowered those perfect circles of dough into the sputtering, boiling oil. Just a few minutes, and they would be turned over until the other side was golden. I got to shake the powdered sugar over them while they were still hot. So good!

Dad favored molasses cake with no icing. I can still picture Mom breaking a straw from the broom to test the cake for doneness. Plunge the straw in the center of the cake—if it came up clean, the cake was done.

The summer passed way too quickly, and before I knew it, September had arrived, and junior high school was on the horizon.

CHAPTER

30

Crosby Street was the borderline between Longfellow Junior High School and Whittier Junior High School. I chose Longfellow. By choosing Longfellow, I would be going to school with the kids from Flint's westside who lived in bigger homes and came from more affluent families.

I wanted so much to "belong", and I begged my mom to let me get a permanent wave on my hair. To get a permanent curl, you had to be hooked up to an electric machine that resembled medieval torture, but I wanted curls so bad, my mom finally relented.

The machine itself was on wheels and the apparatus with the curlers hung over my head. The beautician rolled my hair up on rods, and a metal clamp dangling from an electric cord was fastened over every rod. Then the whole thing was plugged into an electric wall socket, creating heat that would curl your hair. It was really barbaric, but if you wanted curls and didn't have natural curls, this was the process you went through. I loved my "new look", and with curls bouncing, was ready to meet the rich kids.

It was such a long walk to Longfellow. Being the borderline street, it was the farthest area away from the school. I had to walk from Crosby Street to Welch Boulevard, go west the whole length of Welch where it crossed Chevrolet Avenue, and then turn south on Chevrolet until I came to the school. It was at least two miles. Rain, shine, sleet, or snow, I made that round trip every school day for three years. My folks didn't have a car, so there were no rides. There were no school buses either—just foot power. Some days when it was snowing, the wind blowing, it was pretty bad. I had snow pants to wear that helped keep my legs warm and fur-lined boots.

It was too far to come home for lunch, but Longfellow had a cafeteria—my first experience with that. A friend of mine, Beverly Thompson, and I used to walk to a nearby dairy bar for lunch on some of the pretty days.

Where I had loved physical education during elementary school, I did not like it in junior high. We were required to wear those ugly tan gym suits with the elastic around the legs that made them look like bloomers. And you had to take a shower after class. The girls who had gym first hour were always unhappy because the shower messed up their hair. Some of the girls tried just turning on the water and then trying to slip out. No! There was a matron at the door to make sure you took a shower by rubbing the back of your robe to see if it was damp. We soon figured out we could get by her by sprinkling a little water on the back of our robes.

Another hallmark in junior high was when they introduced us to the social graces—dancing with boys in gym class. Oh, how we all hated that. They lined the girls and the boys up and paired us off. The only good thing was we didn't have to wear the ugly gym suits on that day.

My school wardrobe that year consisted of two skirts, two blouses, one dress, and a green and brown plaid jumper with two blouses—one green and one brown to coordinate with the jumper. I wore the same clothes every week, but they were always fresh and clean. I was somewhat self-conscious of this. West-side kids. Bigger homes. Nicer clothes. But they were nice. I don't remember any disparaging comments about my clothes.

On my fourteenth birthday, I reached puberty and didn't know what it was. Things of a private nature like that were not discussed in any way, shape, or form. My mom didn't prepare me, my three older sisters didn't share it, it was not taught in school, nor was it ever mentioned by any of my friends; so apparently, my friends didn't know any more about it than I did. So when it occurred on that January day, I was completely in the dark until I went to my mom.

We didn't have sanitary pads back then; at our house, we had squares of flannel that were folded into rectangles and secured in our underpants with two safety pins. These were washed in the washing machine and used again the next month. What a blessing when I discovered a machine in the Phys Ed class locker room where you could drop a nickel in the slot, twist the handle, and a packaged sanitary pad dropped out. Before long, boxes holding a dozen pads were a staple in our house. Thank you, Jesus.

⌒

The Christmases that I remember most from my childhood were the ones on Crosby Street, and oh, how I treasure the memory of them. With my two married sisters living across the street, our family was all nearby to celebrate. Our Christmas wasn't about presents; it was to honor our Savior's birth, who loved us so much that He gave His life on the cross for us. Our nativity scene was displayed on the lowboy china chest in our dining room.

Our Christmas tree was always very special. Mom had to have every tinsel icicle smoothed before it could go on the tree, and believe me, when it was completed, it was a showpiece.

At Christmas, there were always family get-togethers. There was always lots of hustle and bustle, lots of people in and out of our house, a huge dinner around the oak table in our dining room, good times, and sweet memories.

After dinner, I would play the piano, Don and Frank would join in with their coronets, and we would sing carols. Christmas was a lot of fun. Oh yes, and I gave all the ladies their handkerchiefs with the hand-crocheted lace edges, enjoying the "oohs" and "aahs" as they unwrapped them from the red and green tissue.

Just a month later, Grandpa Yats passed away quietly in his sleep. He laid in state in the living room of his home, and the funeral was held there too. I remember coming down the stairway, being able to look directly into the casket, and seeing grandpa lying there. He is buried at Oak Hill Cemetery in Owosso right next to his daughter, Edna. Their names are engraved on the same stone.

The next summer, my brother, Don, got married. He fell in love with Betty Kuss, and after a courtship where they mostly double-dated with Edna and Frank, they tied the knot. Don turned Catholic to marry Betty, but that wasn't an issue in our family. They had a lovely wedding at the Catholic church with a reception following at the Dresden Hotel, downtown Flint. And guess what! They bought a house on Crosby Street! Across the street from us and three houses to the right! Sometimes, life just can't get any better!

My sister Edna and her childhood sweetheart, Frank Maxwell, got married two months later. They didn't buy a house on Crosby Street, but just three blocks away on Root Street. Still close to family.

CHAPTER 31

World War II began in Europe in 1939 when Germany invaded Poland. Great Britain and France declared war on Germany two days later. America supported Great Britain and France by manufacturing their much-needed war goods, but when Japan bombed Pearl Harbor on December 7, 1941, America joined the deadliest war in history. World War II was the most widespread war ever and directly involved more than a hundred million people from over thirty countries.

Jack was in the Navy before we entered the war. His life was totally turned upside down when his mom and dad got a divorce. He was very angry at his dad for breaking up their family and so broken up hearing his mom crying night after night behind her closed bedroom door. There wasn't anything he could do about any of it. He wasn't handling things very well.

A lot of Jack's friends were going in the service. Jack confronted his parents about the possibility of him joining the Navy. He would be dropping out of school, not graduating with his high school class. He was only sixteen years old, but both parents gave their permission, and Jack joined the Navy on June 14, 1941, six months before America entered the war.

He went to boot camp at U.S. Naval Training Center at Great Lakes, Illinois. The new recruits had to train for three months with no liberty passes to come home. Jack hadn't spent much time, if any, away from home, so he was plenty homesick. The last thirty days, they gave the boys passes to come home. I call them boys. When they got finished with boot camp, they were men.

Jack had fun touching base with his friends while he was home and so proud to be serving his country. Even though he was homesick at first, he loved being in the Navy.

At Great Lakes Naval Training Center, Jack was assigned to Gunner's Mate School, a six-week course. He had completed four weeks of the training when an incident occurred that changed the course of his life. He had an afternoon off and, being hungry, went to the galley to get something to eat. There was a sign over the door that read,

Jack joins the Navy—Boot Camp at Great Lakes Naval Training Center

All Unauthorized Personnel Keep Out
And that means you, Sailor

A third-class ship's cook kicked him out. Jack decided then and there that he wanted to be a cook. He would be everyone's friend and let them have something to eat when they were hungry. So he switched to galley and went to Baker's School.

Beans were served every day in the Navy. Evidently, that's where the name "navy beans" originated. I can't really imagine eating them for breakfast, and there was lots of other food available so the men didn't have to eat them, but they were on the bill of fare every day.

Following boot camp, Jack was stationed at Norfolk Naval Operations in Virginia aboard the USS *Augusta*, heavy cruiser. Everyone had specific battle station assignments, and Jack was gun captain on Twin 40s, starboard side. He was also a cook in the galley. When the siren sounded, you stopped whatever you were doing and assumed your battle station.

At that time, before America was in the war, the *Augusta* was escorting convoys to Britain—maybe ten to twenty in a convoy of American and British ships. The British ships would fly American flags and assume American names until they were 75–100 miles from the British shore. Then, the British Navy would take over with Germans attacking with a fury. It's a terrible thing to see a ship go down with the whole crew onboard. The tankers were the worst. Ships on fire. Jack saw men with skin burned right off their bodies. Pretty heavy-duty stuff for a sixteen-year-old.

The USS *Augusta* was also the presidential flagship. Pres. Franklin Roosevelt was the secretary of the U.S. Navy. When the president was aboard a naval vessel, it was the USS *Augusta*. Alterations had been made to the ship—an elevator was installed and bulkhead doors were modified to accommodate his physical condition. He had a stateroom onboard with a brass bed that was bolted to the floor. This stateroom was always in readiness for a presidential visit.

While they were in port at Norfolk, Jack had an incredibly memorable experience. He and his buddies were ashore and came back to the ship pretty late. They were hungry, so they went to the galley. Jack fixed steak, eggs, and hash browned potatoes for the gang. They were setting on wood milk crates eating when they heard a strange noise, a shuffling sound. Suddenly, the hatch flew open, and a Marine shouted "Attention!" They jumped to their feet so fast they almost knocked over the crates they were setting on. Then, the president was helped through the door!

President Roosevelt said that he had smelled the aroma of the food drifting into his bedroom through the ventilation system, and it made him hungry. He wanted to join them, so Jack had the honor of preparing steak, eggs, and hash browned potatoes for the president of the United States. The president kidded around with the guys, telling them not to tell Eleanor, because she wouldn't want him to eat like that at such a late hour.

Some of the guys were seeing President Roosevelt for the first time and were shocked by the sight of his physical impairments. The president was stricken with polio in 1921, and his legs were paralyzed. He was unable to walk without help. It was skillfully hidden by the press because it was believed it would weaken his position as the most powerful man in the world.

President Roosevelt loved kibitzing with the guys, and for Jack, it was a unique experience that was unforgettable.

～

When Japan attacked Pearl Harbor, I was just twenty-five days shy of my fifteenth birthday. Traumatic events make an indelible impression that you never forget. I remember exactly where I was when I heard the news that our country was at war. I was at my friend Barbara's house, two doors down on Crosby Street. We were in her bedroom when her sister came in and told us what happened. I rushed home to find my mom weeping and my dad visibly upset. They knew our family would be greatly affected.

And we were. Everyone's life was dramatically changed. Our entire family was hit like a whirlwind.

Peg's husband, Sam, was inducted into the Army, leaving her alone with their two little girls, Phyllis and Marilyn.

Ag's husband, Ed, was also inducted into the Army, leaving her alone with their little girl, Margie.

My brother, Don, was inducted into the Army even though he was legally blind in one eye.

Edna's husband, Frank, enlisted in the U.S. Air Corps and learned to fly B24s.

I didn't know it yet, but my future husband was serving in the Navy. Every male in our family took part in the war. Even my dad had to register, but because of his age was not called upon to serve. The whole thing was earthshaking.

Just a little after the war started, I enrolled at Northern High School. Back then, they had two graduating classes—one in February and one in June—with the graduation ceremony for both being held in June. I was in the class beginning in February.

I met my forever friend Nelda Bailey in the tenth grade at Northern. We were best friends right from the beginning of the school year. We did everything together, even had some classes together. On weekends, we would have sleepovers. She would be at my house, or I would be at hers. Just inseparable.

Nelda got a job as an usherette at the Palace Theater, downtown Flint, and she encouraged me to apply for a job. I got my working permit, which was required by the state for a minor to work. I was so thrilled when the manager hired me. My first job! The pay was 35¢ an hour. We had to furnish our own uniforms out of that—white blouses and navy blue slacks.

Back in that day, there were no multiple theater complexes. They were all single movie houses, and some of them were really quite splendid. You couldn't just walk in and sit down; you had to wait until the show changed. That's where the usherette job came in. There was about a 15-minute intermission between the 7:00 p.m. and 9:00 p.m. showing with a special 11:00 p.m. showing on Saturday nights.

The lobby would be jammed with people waiting to get in. They had to wait behind velvet ropes guarded by the ticket taker. It was always so full we had to help people find seats. When the lights were lowered, we had flashlights to show people to their seats. Remember that there was no such thing as television then, and the movies were very popular.

Our dressing room was downstairs. Sometimes, that was a scary trip. We had to walk through the darkened theater, across the stage behind the screen (you could see the movie images through the screen), and then downstairs to the dressing room where we changed into our uniforms. It had big mirrors and Hollywood lights. When they had stage plays, the stars used these rooms. There was a second room for the male stars that the ushers used.

They used to make all of the popcorn downstairs too in another room. After they popped it, they would shake it over a big box with a screen on top to remove all the kernels. Then, it was carried upstairs to the concession stand and boxed.

The following article was printed in *The Flint Journal*:

What Flint theater once had animal cages in its basement?

It was the old Palace Theater, located at Harrison and E. Kearsley streets downtown. The Palace was built in 1917 and featured live stage shows and vaudeville acts, as well as silent films and talkies. And those vaudeville acts frequently called for performing animals as well as actors.

(By the way, there were a lot of big-time folks who played at the Palace in the early days. Among the illustrious included Boris Karloff, Ethel Barrymore, Helen Hayes, Kay Francis, and ZaSu Pitts.)

I had a grand time working at the Palace. I loved all the movies. We got to watch them after everyone was seated, but of course, we had to stand up at the back.

I was hooked! Not only on the movies, but also I discovered I loved earning money. When I received my first check, I put a black cashmere Chesterfield coat with a velvet collar in layaway. It cost $40, but I got it paid for with my 35¢ an hour job. I felt like a princess every time I wore that coat.

CHAPTER 32

When America declared war in 1941, Jack was already involved in the battle for the control of the Atlantic Ocean with our country running convoys to Great Britain.

For the most part in the early years of the war, that battle took place in the northern region of the Atlantic Ocean. Once America entered the war, it spread all the way to our coast and as far down as the Caribbean Sea.

The early battles heavily favored the Germans due to the use of their submarines. Travelling in convoys was successful for America and her Allies for a while, but the Germans had so many subs that it was overwhelming.

It was estimated that at least twenty supply ships had to arrive every day in Great Britain for them to continue to fight the war. In 1942 alone, the Allies lost 1,664 supply ships, and over 30,000 sailors were killed on each side. Oh! The insanity of war.

The battle for control of the Atlantic Ocean reached its peak in 1943 when the Allies broke the German secret codes. With that knowledge and the new technology of radar and underwater bombs, it changed the way we fought, and the battle turned in favor of the Allies.

Control of the Atlantic Ocean had a major impact on the outcome of the war. Keeping Britain supplied helped keep Germany from taking over all of western Europe. The United States was able to more safely ship supplies to Britain, including the large number of soldiers and weapons needed for the Normandy invasion, which was already being planned.

Jack was there through all of this. He was destined to be at Normandy too.

Even with all of this going on, the sailors aboard the Augusta sometimes got a leave. Their port when they were in England was Liverpool. It's my understanding that there were a lot of beautiful girls in England, and with their men gone off to war, they loved to see the Yanks come. Overall, the people there were very friendly and grateful to the Americans for joining the war effort.

There was a candy shop in Liverpool named the Sweet Shoppe. Jack went there and told the girl behind the counter that he would have one of these and one of those, as he pointed to his favorite chocolates. She said, "Sorry, Yank. You've got to have coupons to buy sweets. Everything is rationed." Jack asked her who owned the shop. The owner was her father. Jack went back to the ship and brought back five pounds of sugar, a five-pound tin of tea, some Pet Milk, and some butter. When he brought that back to the candy shop and set it on the counter, the owner was so thrilled that he told him he could have all the candy he wanted.

For a time, Jack was stationed in Scotland. His ship was tied up on the Clyde River, near Glasgow, at the British naval base. Most of the fleet anchored there because it was out of range of the German bombers.

He went to a dance at the LeCarnal Ballroom one night and met a nice young lady. She invited him to dinner on Sunday to meet her family. Besides her parents, she had a younger brother, perhaps seven or eight years old. For dinner, they had a little piece of beef, some vegetables, and some dark bread and preserves. Jack helped himself to a nice serving of preserves and then realized he shouldn't have, because they had so very little of everything.

The family was so gracious to him, and the next weekend, he was invited to sleep overnight. For breakfast, they served a cream of wheat type of cereal, toast, and one tiny pullet egg—their only one, which they served to Jack. He had a really difficult time choking that egg down in front of the whole family, but knew they would be offended if he refused their hospitality. For lunch, they had a cookie and tea, no sugar, as everything was rationed.

Jack went back to his ship that afternoon and brought an orange crate loaded with food back to them. A five-pound tin of tea (the Navy didn't use much of that), five pounds of butter, four cans of Pet Milk, two dozen eggs, ham, oranges, white flour, and sugar. The little boy had never seen an orange.

A month later when he was in port, Jack brought the family a lot of meat, ham and Spam—which the father particularly liked in his lunch—roast beef, bacon, three chickens, and more tea.

It's such a shame that wartime friendships weren't maintained. I'm sure they wondered many times what happened to their friend, just as Jack wondered many times about the Scottish family that was so nice to him when he was so far away from home.

～

On the home front, everyone was united and determined to do everything possible to help in the war effort. My hometown of Flint, Michigan, was playing a major role. Our factories were quickly converted over to manufacture war goods.

- Buick Motor Division built M18 destroyers.
- Chevrolet Flint Manufacturing built 1 ½-ton trucks and airplane instruments.
- Fisher Body built tanks.
- AC Spark Plug Division built machine guns.

With husbands, fathers, brothers, and sons off serving our beloved country, one of the biggest changes that took place was the number of women who joined the workforce. Industry of all kinds needed workers, and they filled its ranks with women. They did everything from working in the shipyards to running farms, from clerical work to lawyers, from steel mills to taxi drivers, and everything in between.

We were issued ration books for meat, sugar, fat, butter, fruit, vegetables, gas, tires, fuel oil, clothing, and probably other things I don't recall. Everything went to the war effort. My folks still didn't have a car, but they saved their gas coupons for Don, Sam, Ed, and Frank to use when they came home on leave.

All the silk and nylon went for parachutes, so the only hose available were thick and coarse. When the ladies heard a shipment of stockings was coming in, they would stand in line for hours to get a pair. Most of the younger girls like me went with bare legs and applied leg makeup to make it look like we were wearing hose.

One way folks at home could help was by collecting materials needed in the war effort—rubber, metal, and paper, to name a few. Scrap drives were held. Even little kids helped with these drives by collecting pots and pans, even bottle caps, all to be recycled.

Newspapers were collected too, with kids going door to door. I remember our newspapers being tied up in bundles for collection.

The government encouraged everyone to plant a victory garden and can the goods so that the food in tin cans could go to the troops. We were asked to substitute fruit juice and corn syrup for sugar and to replace butter with oleomargarine. Many a time, I saw my mom knead the oleo. It came in a white brick shape similar to butter. There was a capsule of dye that came with it. By kneading the colored dye into the oleo, it took on the look of butter, but it didn't taste as good as butter.

Some of those who were too old to go in the military helped in other ways. They patrolled our streets at night or became plane watchers as part of civil defense. They scanned the skies with binoculars for enemy planes and learned to listen for planes as well as look for them. We had air raid drills too, and when the siren went off, we immediately turned off our lights and lowered our blackout shades.

The government sold war bonds to raise money. Famous movie stars toured the country giving speeches to raise the needed funds. The kids helped by buying war stamps at school. For 10¢, you got a stamp to paste in a book. A filled book was worth $18.75, and if you kept it for ten years, it could be turned in to the government and you would receive $25 for it. I bet all World War II kids remember those stamp books.

There was no such thing as TV, but we kept our ears glued to the radio constantly for news from the front. For live pictures, we could see the Pathe newsreel at the movies. Other than that, we depended on newspapers for articles and pictures. War news was, of course, always on the front page.

Then, there were the flags hung in windows. If you had a family member in the service, a flag was placed in your window. They were white, bordered in red, and had a blue star in the center for each member serving. If the person died in action, the blue star was replaced with gold.

Fifteen million Americans served; 300,000 would never come home. Everyone at home dreaded getting a knock on the door and receiving a telegram that began with, "We regret to inform you..."

And Americans prayed. Judging by our family, I would say that millions of Americans were praying to our caring and merciful God to watch over their loved ones, protect them, and bring them safely home.

School took place, as usual, even though there was a war going on. I was in the eleventh grade at Northern, and it was there that I learned all of my secretarial skills that would serve me so well later on. I was fascinated with shorthand and typing and really looked forward to those classes. Fifteen pages of shorthand practice every night for homework was a breeze.

I loved school and considered learning a privilege. Attending Northern was my favorite. In place of physical education, I was selected to work in the Dean of Girls' office and decided that was the kind of career I wanted to pursue.

Another change took place when I put in an application for a job at Kresge's $1.00 Store and was hired at 50¢ an hour. Oh boy! Big money! This was a separate store from Kresge's Five and Ten Cent Store. The dime store was much larger. Kresge's $1.00 Store was a smaller store, in the same block downtown, and the two were just a few stores apart. It was located on Saginaw Street between Kearsley Avenue and First Street. The two Kresge's stores were separated by

Lerner's, a ladies clothing store, and Smith-Bridgman's, the largest department store in downtown Flint, and another store or two.

I got out of school at two o'clock in the afternoon and took the bus downtown to work. For 50¢, you could purchase a string of ten bus tickets, so it cost me a nickel to get to work. I walked home from downtown Flint to our home on Crosby Street alone, even at night, safe as could be, never a care in the world about any problems. I so much enjoyed those gentle, innocent days.

My job at Kresge's $1.00 Store was salesgirl in the cosmetics department. My counters were in the very front of the store, center and right side. It was great fun. Nothing was complicated then. There was Pond's cold cream, Vaseline petroleum jelly, Tangee Lipstick, Cutex Nail Polish, bath powders, rouges, and, oh yes, Maybelline mascara. Everything was very inexpensive. I also sold eyeglasses. They were $1.00 a pair, and I sold hundreds, mostly to elderly folks. Together, we would try pair after pair until we found the perfect one for them. Those were the good old days.

Nelda and I weren't working together anymore; but we would meet after work on Friday nights, grab a bite to eat, and then head over to the YWCA to dance. The teen boys were really shy and mostly just lined up around the wall and watched the girls dance.

On Saturday nights, we'd go to the IMA Auditorium to dance. During the war years, they always had big named bands appearing there—Harry James, Glen Miller, Tommy Dorsey, and even Frank Sinatra. The crowds were tremendous and there were always a lot of service men who were home on leave there.

The movies were still a favorite, and Nelda, who was still working at the Palace, got free passes for both of us. We had so many wonderful memorable times together. Sometimes, we'd meet at Paris Candy Kitchen. They had booths in there with tall wooden backs. It was like being in your own private space, and we would share all of our secrets while devouring a hot fudge sundae. Nelda was my forever friend.

And I wrote letters! Letters to everyone in our family that was overseas. Letters to friends who had enlisted and even some who I didn't know because someone said they didn't get many letters. I wrote letters every day and kept a steady stream going overseas. They were harmless letters. I didn't have a boyfriend, so there weren't any love letters, just letters from home. The guys were grateful for any tidbit of news from home. I had a lot of letters coming my way too and was often teased about having my own victory garden of service men.

Getting letters to the boys overseas wasn't easy. It took four to six weeks to travel by ship. The U.S. government came up with V-mail, a unique means of getting the military their mail sooner. It was a real morale builder. You could buy a form for V-mail at Kresge's Five and Ten Cent Store; it was much like a postcard. You would fill in your name, address, and message in the allotted space and send it off. It would be photographed and sent overseas via airplane. Once overseas, it would be reprinted and sent on its way, usually arriving to your loved one in two weeks. I didn't use V-mail. I just wrote often, so there was a steady stream of letters on the way.

Grandma Katie went home to be with the Lord on Mother's Day of 1943. My heart ached for my own mother. She had bought her mom an everyday dress for her Mother's Day gift. She returned it to the store and got her a dress to be buried in. So sad. Mother's Day would never be the same for my mom. Grandma was laid to rest at Gracelawn Cemetery on North Saginaw Street.

33

The Normandy invasion took place on June 6, 1944. Before entering into that battle, all service men received a letter from General Eisenhower, the supreme commander. It started out with, "You are about to embark upon the Great Crusade, toward which we have striven these many months. The eyes of the world are upon you. The hopes and prayers of liberty-loving people everywhere march with you."

Jack was still stationed on the presidential flagship USS *Augusta*. Gen. Omar Bradley, Eisenhower's right-hand man, was stationed on the *Augusta* for that battle. The ship's captain was Captain McCandlish. Jack said that he was a good man and held in high esteem by his crew.

The Normandy invasion began with overnight parachute and glider landings, air attacks, and naval bombardments. As dawn broke, amphibious landings took place on five different beaches simultaneously.

Nearly five thousand ships of all kinds took part in that battle—transports, cargo ships, tankers, and battle wagons. The *Augusta* was at Omaha Beach, and it is recorded that Omaha faced the most resistance.

The landing crafts were hampered by high seas, and many were swamped. Some transport ships let the men out where the water was too deep, and their heavy equipment took them under. Others waded ashore neck-deep in water with the Germans mowing them down before they could get ashore. The ships were giving them cover, and Jack was gun captain on the Twin 40s. The noise was so loud there was virtually no vocal communication.

There were cliffs at Omaha Beach that were one hundred feet high, and the Americans had to scale those cliffs to get to the German army. It was an almost impossible task. The German soldiers were in bunkers above the cliffs firing down on the Americans, and they were just slaughtering them.

Chaos was the rule at Omaha early in the day, but then, order began to take place. By nightfall, 34,000 men were ashore. They were all heroes at Normandy that day. Over 2,000 lives were lost that June day at Omaha Beach alone.

In the evening, the men on the *Augusta* were given permission to go ashore. Jack and some of his buddies went to look for souvenirs. What they saw was carnage that would never be blotted from their memory.

Jack and his friends headed up a path that led to a German bunker. Lying in the entrance to the bunker were two soldiers and others inside, all dead. They stepped over the entrance and collected German helmets, gas masks, coins, a German luger, Iron Cross, belt, and a silver buckle with a swastika emblem. They could have been killed so easily. They never thought that it could have been booby-trapped.

~⁓

While Jack was at Normandy, I was preparing to enter my senior year at Northern. School came easy to me. I loved school and had no problem getting straight As. I continued to serve in the Dean of Girls' office. Working and earning money, I was able to dress well, and that helped tremendously in building my self-confidence.

I filled out an application for a job at Citizens Bank. My sister, Edna, had worked there, and she was such a great employee she paved the way for me. I was hired right away and worked there throughout my senior year.

My job was on the third floor of the main branch on South Saginaw Street, downtown Flint, where the famous weather ball is on top of the building. There were three girls who worked on Check Sort-o-graph machines. We sat at desks similar to a school desk. To our left was the check sorter. It was about six feet long and ten inches wide and slid back and forth on a track. It was fitted with index tabs, one for every customer with a checking account. It was our job to sort the checks by placing them behind the tab bearing the customer's name. The checks were then taken to clerks who wrote by hand every transaction into the individual's checking account record. No one ever foresaw the coming of computers and the way they would revolutionize the world.

While I was working at Citizens Bank, I learned where babies came from! Seventeen years old, and I did not know. It was the same as when I reached puberty—total ignorance. It's hard to believe now; but back then, sex, or anything even remotely connected to it, simply was not discussed. That topic just was not touched upon in the home or in school. Strictly taboo. The biggest scandal I heard about in high school was when one of the girls in my class answered the door in her slip when two boys came to call. How times have changed.

The girl who sat next to me on the Sort-o-graph machine was named Wanda White, and we became good friends. Wanda was getting married that summer and confided in me that she was so afraid she'd get pregnant. I thought the prospect of having a baby was wonderful. My two older sisters had children, and I was looking forward to it someday too. I thought you just went to the hospital and had an operation, and the baby was removed from your stomach.

When Wanda told me how babies came out, I was in total shock. I asked her how they got in there. When she answered, "The same way they get out," I thought I was going to pass out. I remember very clearly the difficulty I had sitting down the rest of that day and for the next several days. Upon learning that, I was sure I was never going to get married!

Before long, fall had arrived, and the Thanksgiving football game between Northern High School and Central High School was right around the corner. With two high schools in Flint, they were fierce rivals over that game. It was kind of a dilemma at our house since Peg, Ag, and Edna went to Central and Don and I went to

Northern. The girls would hang their colors—red and black crepe paper streamers—all around the front porch. Don and I would tear them down and drape our scarlet and gray. There was a lot of good-natured kidding as we would tear down the girl's streamers and Don and I would hoist ours. After a few rounds of that, we would all sit down to an enormous Thanksgiving dinner.

I had my first date when I was seventeen, the summer before I graduated. A young man who went to school with me invited me to go to the movies. It was an afternoon date. He walked to my house and picked me up and met both of my parents. We walked to Saginaw Street and had lunch at a restaurant called the Pink Elephant. Being alone with a boy for the first time, I was pretty shy, and we sort of ate in silence. He was pretty shy too. Maybe it was his first date too. I don't know. After lunch, we boarded a bus and went downtown to the Michigan Theater on South Saginaw Street. When the movie was over, another bus ride dropped us off near my house, and he walked me the rest of the way home. It all took place on a sunny Saturday afternoon, so not even a parting goodbye kiss when we got back to my house. When he graduated, he was scouted by the Detroit Tigers and received a contract. So as it turned out, our first date was also our last.

February seemed to arrive in the blink of an eye, and my public education was completed. Jobs were easy to come by with so many off serving our country. My sister Agnes was working at AC Spark Plug, so I decided to put in an application there.

I was hired right away, and strangely enough, they placed me on a job that my sister, Edna, had vacated. Edna was living down south now, where her husband, Frank, was stationed, serving in the Air Force. Edna had been secretary to the personnel director, Mark Pailthorpe. She hadn't been replaced, so they put me in that position—a prestigious job right out of high school.

162

Arlene
High School graduation 1945

Shortly after I graduated, Mom and Dad sold the Crosby Street house where I had grown up and had so many wonderful memories. I felt really sad about that, but life goes on. There was a general store for sale in the tiny town of Henderson where my dad grew up, and he wanted to buy it, so they did. I wanted my dad to fulfill his dream, but I missed living with Mom and Dad in my childhood home. My sister Ag was now divorced from her husband, Ed; so she and her little girl, Margie, and I moved to an apartment on Jackson Street.

Mr. Bates lived right across the street from us on Jackson Street. He worked at AC too, and he gave Ag and me a ride to and from work every day.

Mom and Dad wanted me to move with them, but about the only place where you could work in that tiny town was at a place that stored beans—I guess it's a beanery; it was kind of like a silo. They said that they would hire me, but I loved my job at AC and didn't want to give it up.

When my graduation ceremony finally arrived in June, I was well indoctrinated in my job at AC and earning good money. I really didn't want to attend the graduation, because I knew no one in my family was able to attend. But my best friend, Nelda, pleaded with me, and I promised her I'd go.

Graduation was held at Atwood Stadium. They seated us alphabetically, so I didn't get to sit with Nelda. The girl sitting next to me asked me who was up in the stands to see me. I told her that none of my family was able to come. She said, "I wondered because all the rest of us are standing up, searching the stands, trying to find our family, and you're just sitting there." Well, Mom and Dad were living in Henderson. Dad wasn't the best driver in the world and couldn't see all that well to drive at night, so they couldn't risk coming. My oldest sister, Peg, had two little girls and no babysitter. Her husband was in the Army. My brother, Don, was overseas serving in the Philippines in the Army. Edna was down south where her husband was serving in the Air Corps and my sister, Ag, had a date. So there was no one for me.

Nelda and I had made arrangements to meet at a designated spot when the ceremony was over. She was immediately surrounded by family—I mean not only her mom and dad and her sister but also aunts and uncles. They had brought cards and gifts and were taking her out to dinner to celebrate. I was just standing there like a dummy, feeling very awkward and out of place. The tears started rolling down my face. I didn't want them to see the tears, so I turned and started walking away. They called to me to stay; they wanted to take me to dinner too, they said.

But I couldn't. At that moment, I felt totally abandoned by my entire family. I had graduated a member of the Sigma Chi Lambda National Honor Society, worked hard for twelve years for that honor, and not one person in my entire family even cared. Oh, I was feeling sorry for myself, having a real pity party even though I knew it wasn't their fault. Nothing could have changed. And nothing could make it better. It must have been at least two miles from Atwood Stadium to my apartment on Jackson Street, but I walked every step of the way in my white high heels, sobbing all the way.

In a calmer moment, I remembered how very much each one of them loved me and that they were proud of my accomplishment. They would have all been there if they could. But the war had changed everything.

CHAPTER

CHAPTER 34

After Normandy, the *Augusta* was sent to the Pacific theater where the Japanese proved to be a formidable foe.

While serving in the Pacific, the homeport for the *Augusta* was Oakland, California. When Jack and his buddies got weekend passes, they would hitchhike to Los Angeles. Everyone was very generous about picking up servicemen during the war and giving them a lift.

The boys used to go to Santa Monica Ocean Park to dance. There were two ballrooms—the Trianon and the Aragon. Tommy Dorsey owned the Trianon. They used to have what they called Swing Shift dances that lasted from eight o'clock in the evening until five o'clock in the morning. There would always be two big bands appearing—Tommy Dorsey, Kay Kyser, Harry James, Benny Goodman, Ted Lewis, Lawrence Welk, and many others. There was a revolving stage. When one band finished playing a set, the stage would revolve, and the second band would commence playing. Jack and his buddies never missed a dance.

The fun times while ashore on leave took the boys' minds off the horror of war for a time, but then, it was back to sea and manning their battle stations. It was while serving in the Pacific that Jack suffered a grievous injury. He was immediately transferred to the Mare Island Naval Hospital at Vallejo, California. He had to have his left leg amputated midway between the knee and hip. He spent several months in the hospital and the rehabilitation center at Mare Island. Neither his mom nor his dad came to visit him.

Jack

The Navy rehab was fantastic. They taught the guys how to adapt to a new kind of life with a disability, even as far-reaching as learning how to roller skate and dance.

Some things they couldn't prepare them for. All of the men there were Navy, of course, and all struggling to learn a new way of life. They became as close as brothers.

One of Jack's friends had been a concert pianist before joining the Navy. In a horrific accident, both of his hands were blown off. The guys nicknamed him "Mittens." One day, Mittens' wife came to visit. She was a tall, shapely blonde, very beautiful. She took one look at her husband, turned around, and walked out. All of Mittens' buddies cried with him that day.

Being all Navy guys, they tried to keep each other's morale up and often played tricks on each other. Many times, a sailor would wake up in the Operating Room where his buddies had wheeled him after he dropped off to sleep the night before.

They had another favorite. The hospital was on a hill. When the guys were able, they would make a train and ride their wheelchairs to the bottom of the hill where there was a Navy facility to get a soda, ice cream, or other treat. When they were ready to go back up the hill, anyone who was able-bodied was required to push them up the hill. They all delighted in catching an officer going up and having him do the pushing, especially if he was with a girl.

Clayton Tragimbal worked at the Rodman Canteen on the naval base. He had lost a leg in the Navy in World War I. Clayton took Jack home to meet his family; he had five children, one a son Jack's age. The whole family took Jack into their hearts and home, treating him like a member of the family.

The guys found another favorite place to hang out that was near the hospital—the Casa de Vallejo Ballroom. They loved going there to listen to the music. They had excellent musicians there, who worked at the naval yard. They could have played with any of the big bands, but didn't want to leave their families to travel.

Jack had a really memorable experience when he was at the Mare Island Naval Hospital. When the guys were able to get around, they were allowed to go into town and were even encouraged to do so. Jack and one of his friends were on the highway hitchhiking on their crutches, when this beautiful convertible with the top down stopped to pick them up. Much to their surprise, their benefactors were Harry James and Betty Grable. Harry James had a big dance band and was in many movies. Betty Grable was a gorgeous movie actress/singer/dancer. She was voted by the Armed Forces to be their pinup girl. Her legs were so shapely they were insured by Lloyds of London for a million dollars—a huge sum of money back then.

They invited Jack and his friend to spend the weekend at their home in Hollywood. Their home was huge—a light colored brick ranch style. It was nicely decorated and had a big fireplace in the living room. In the backyard there was an Olympic-sized swimming pool.

Jerry Colonna, a comedian in the movies, lived next door. He came over to meet the boys and was wearing a wooden barrel over his swimsuit. He jumped in the pool with it on, getting lots of laughs from everyone.

Quite an overwhelming experience for a twenty-one-year-old from Flint, Michigan. Jack said that all of them, for being such famous people, were very nice and down-to-earth people, doing what they could to cheer up a couple of boys, far away from home, who had been injured in the war.

⤳

When my mom and dad moved away from Flint, a new era of my life was opening up. I had a great job at AC and loved working.

Agnes, Margie, and I lived in the apartment that was on Jackson Street, about two blocks off Detroit Street. It was upstairs in a nice two-story home. There was a living room, bedroom, small kitchen, bath, and a big walk-in closet with a window where Margie's crib was kept. It worked out very well for us.

I usually worked overtime on Saturdays. I could get on the bus right across the street from the AC and transfer downtown on the corner by the Vogue, my favorite ladies store. Every payday, I'd buy a new dress and a pair of shoes. Because of the war, the shoes had composition soles, no leather available. I appreciated so much being able to dress well—a carryover from the depression, I guess, when there was so little and I didn't have many clothes for school.

About once a month, I'd take the Greyhound bus to Henderson and help Mom and Dad in the general store. I missed them so much and really enjoyed those times together.

Their store was really quaint, just like the ones you see in the old Westerns —bolts of fabric, notions, jars of penny candy, all the bakery products, canned goods, and fresh meats in the case. None of the meats were packaged. You had to cut it, weigh it on a pair of old-fashioned scales, and then wrap it in butcher paper. The cheese came in rounds and blocks. You had to try to accurately judge the amount the customer wanted and cut off a wedge. An old metal cash register rang up the sales. There was no computer to tell you how much change the customer should receive back.

As common with most general stores of that era, their living quarters were over the store—living room, dining room, kitchen, and two bedrooms. There was no bathroom, but an outhouse in back that I was not thrilled to use, but it was worth it to see Mom and Dad.

~⁀

Ag and I worked hard all week, and when we went out, we had a good time together. Sometimes, we'd double date, but most times, we didn't. One week, I dated five different guys, and all of their names started with "J"— Jay, Jim, Joe, Johnny, and Jerry. I was dating a lot of guys, but nothing serious.

On weekends, though, we never dated; we danced. Friday nights, we went to the Flint Athletic Club and Saturdays to Knickerbocker's. Oh, the fun we had. We always had five or six dances lined up ahead every night. We treated all the guys with respect, and they gave us the same respect. I was underage (the age limit was twenty-one) and was using a friend's identification, but Ag and I never drank anything with alcohol, so no one gave us any trouble. We always ordered a coke cocktail—a Coca-Cola with fruit juice added. We only went there to enjoy the dancing, and we had a wonderful time.

I was spreading my wings—loved working, enjoyed dancing and shopping, and of course still writing letters to every young man I knew who was in the service.

⌇

Germany surrendered on May 7, 1945, ending World War II in Europe. Gen. Dwight Eisenhower had temporary headquarters in a small schoolhouse in Reims, France, and the surrender document was signed there. There was little or no celebration. After the Germans left, those who remained in the room shared some champagne that they drank from mess tins. It was a solemn affair and should have been—so many lives lost.

Japan was determined to continue on, but their navy and air military was pretty much destroyed. The war finally ended when the atomic bomb was dropped on Hiroshima. The Japanese surrendered on September 2, 1945, and the documents were signed aboard the USS *Missouri* in Tokyo Bay, Japan.

When the USS *Missouri* returned home to the United States, it was a wondrous thing to behold. The "Mighty Mo," as she was nick-named, pulled into the harbor at New York, and the reception was unbelievable. Her arrival had been anticipated all day; and when she finally arrived, every horn, every whistle, and every bell on every ship in the harbor went off to greet the "Mo." All the fireboats shot up huge plumes of water. Every inch of the "Mo" was lined with sailors in their whites. I would have loved to see it in person, but was thrilled to witness it on Pathe movie news reel, tears streaming down my face.

The young men started to come home. Two fellows who I went to school with brought engagement rings home for me. I liked both of them very much. They were both handsome, very nice, both Navy, but not for me because God had a different plan for my life. I wasn't to meet my future husband until the next year.

CHAPTER 35

When World War II ended, Jack was still at the naval hospital at Mare Island receiving rehabilitation. The government was exceptionally thorough in preparing those with disabilities to get back to a normal life.

Jack received an honorable discharge from the Navy. His discharge papers listed his history while serving in the Navy.

His ratings throughout his service years were as follows :

- Apprentice Seaman
- Second-Class Seaman
- First-Class Seaman
- Third-Class Petty Officer
- Second-Class Petty Officer

He received the following decorations:

- The European-African ribbon with two stars
- The Asiatic-Pacific ribbon with two stars
- The American Theatre ribbon
- Good Conduct medal
- World War II Victory medal

At a later date, he was presented with a Certificate of Thanks from France.

Jack was given a leave to come home for a visit. All he had to do to complete his discharge was to return to California and formalize the discharge papers. They would be completed and finalized on April 29, 1946. He would be receiving a pension in the amount of $89 each month for the loss of his leg while serving in the Navy.

Jack's mom, Lois, had remarried while he was away in service. She met a nice gentleman named William (Bill) King. Bill worked at the Chevrolet plant down in the hole, and they lived on a small farm on Linden Road, just outside of Flint.

His dad had married the woman who played a part in the breakup of his marriage to Lois, and they were living in Flint. Jack stayed with them because he wanted to be in Flint where all of his buddies were.

One of Jack's first stops was at the Flint Original Coney Island, downtown Flint, to get a couple of Coneys, a huge favorite of his that he had been missing. The owner still remembered Jack's favorite, two with mustard and onions, ordered them up, and brought them to the counter where Jack was sitting on a stool, his crutches leaning against the counter. He shook Jack's hand and said, "Welcome home! Thank you for your service to our country. These are on the house."

Ford Motor Company gave Jack a car. A beautiful new blue car with all the features dedicated to aiding a person with an amputated leg. There was no clutch; somehow, it was fitted with a lever to the steering column.

I don't know much about cars, but it was brand new, and it was a gift from Ford. The auto manufacturers were just nicely getting back into postwar production. I also don't know if a car was given to every amputee by Ford; I only know Jack received one.

Jack sure loved cars. His first car, the much-loved Ford Model A that he purchased for $12.00, was sold by his mother, with his permission, while he was in service. His mom had put the money from that sale in the bank along with the money that Jack had been able to send back home the four and a half years that he was in the Navy. He had a bit of a nest egg and plans in place for what he was going to do with it.

As soon as Jack got settled into his new life, he ordered a bright red Chevrolet convertible and received the very first one delivered to the Flint area. Not many people had a new car right after the war, and here's Jack with two brand new ones.

He was a man about town—home from the Navy, two brand new cars, and $89 a month, which was pretty good money back then. He was living at his dad's, so his pension was gas and fun money. He had no need to work, so he didn't.

He was unwinding from the war years, his injury, and rehab. He was trying to find his place in the world again and wondering what he would be able to do for a job, sometimes worrying he might end up selling apples in front of Michigan National Bank. Would anyone ever take a chance on hiring him? Would anyone ever want to marry him?

Jack, who had always had a great deal of confidence, was at a loss.

There was a Veteran's club on Garland Street. Jack met up with a friend of his, Richie Bush, and they spent some time with other men home from the war, telling war stories, trying to adjust to being home again.

He began dating too.

~⁓

My life was going through a very turbulent period. I missed not living on Crosby Street with Mom and Dad. I was still living with my sister, Ag; sharing the apartment on Jackson Street; and continuing to work in the Personnel Office at AC Spark Plug Division.

Ag worked in the order department at the same plant. There were about forty men and women clerks in that office. When the secretary's position in that department became available, Ag encouraged me to ask for a transfer there so we could work together in the same office. Even though I loved the job I had, I transferred to that job. I knew many of the girls who worked in that department. We socialized outside of work too, and I knew it would be a fun job.

The clerk's desks were set up in rows, and the supervisor and I had desks at the front where he could oversee everything—much like a classroom.

One night, we had an office party. I don't remember what the occasion was, but it was a gala affair. Everyone was dressed in their best, and all were in a festive mood. Midway through the evening, my supervisor asked if he could take me home. He was married and probably twenty-five years older than me. I said, "No, thank you. I already have plans." My plans were to go home with the same group of girls I came with.

The next day, my supervisor told me I was being transferred to the night shift because of seniority. I knew it had nothing to do with seniority. If seniority had been a factor, I wouldn't have been given the job to begin with. Nowadays, a situation such as this would be sexual harassment.

I stewed about it all afternoon and talked with my sister. She couldn't believe what happened. Being on nights would mean taking the bus downtown Flint, transferring buses, and walking home from Detroit Street at two o'clock in the morning. Before I left the office that night, I typed out my own release, left it on his desk, and walked out. The next day, I was hired in at Chevrolet National Parts Division on Bluff Street, in the stenographer's pool. I was no longer a private secretary and no fault of mine.

It was the spring of 1946 that I changed jobs. Soon, I would meet the man I would marry and spend the rest of my life with.

CHAPTER 36

The general store wasn't working out for Dad. In that tiny hamlet of Henderson that had no downtown area, there were two general stores on the two-lane country road going through town, and they were right across the street from each other. There just weren't enough families living in the area to support two stores. When the owner of the store across the street told the bread man he was going to quit buying from him if he didn't stop delivering to the store across the street, Dad knew he was defeated. Of course, the bread man stayed with the established store. Knowing that more of the same from other distributors would follow, Dad sacrificed his dream and closed his store.

Looking back, it was a foolish move to begin with, but Dad had tried to fulfill a dream of "going back home." Sometimes, it just doesn't work out. So Mom and Dad moved back to Flint's east side on Hamilton Avenue—a cute little bungalow. Mom was glad to be back by family and to have a home with an inside bathroom again.

❧

It was a lovely sunny Saturday afternoon. Ag and I were downtown and stopped in the Flint Athletic Club to have lunch, the same club where we danced every Friday night. The restaurant was on the street level, and the dance club on the lower level.

Ag saw a young man that she knew sitting in a booth by himself. When we finished eating, she stopped to say "hi" to him and introduced me. His name was Jack Curns. He was wearing a Navy uniform. We chatted for a few minutes, and when departing, Ag said, "Save a dance for me next Friday night, Jack." He said, "Okay."

I was horrified! When we got outside, I said, "Didn't you see his crutches? He had an empty pant leg." She hadn't noticed and didn't know that he had lost a leg. He wasn't at the dance the next Friday night, but he did come a few weeks later after he had been discharged from the Navy.

We danced together several times that night, and he asked to take me home. Throughout the evening, he was teasing me, saying he was going to take me home in his Model A. Believe it or not, when we came out of the club, there was a Model A parked right at the curb. I assumed it was his. He said, "Oh, I guess I won't take this one. Let's go in this one." He took my hand and led me over to the brand new blue Ford.

I refused to get in even though he had the keys to the car. I didn't believe it was his. Ag and her date, Richie Bush, were in on the joke. All three of them were laughing hysterically. They finally convinced me that it really was Jack's car. We never did find out who the Model A belonged to.

The four of us went out for a bite to eat, and it seemed like we talked for hours. Jack had been back to California where he was formally discharged. He was so nice and lots of fun to be with. I thought he was very handsome too. He had blond hair heightened with streaks of gold, nice facial features, sparkling blue eyes, and a beautiful smile. His upper body was muscular—probably from having carried his weight on crutches—and he had a narrow waist. I was impressed. We had such a good time just being together, laughing and talking. I was hoping he'd ask me out again.

Jack went home, woke his dad up, and excitedly exclaimed, "Dad! I just met the girl I'm going to marry!"

He called the next day and asked me to go out.

Our first official date was on July 4, 1946. We went out to Lake Fenton to swim with Ag, Richie, and Margie. I had the cutest new bathing suit. It was a royal blue two-piece, trimmed with ruffles. Of course, I never planned on getting it wet. But Jack didn't realize that I didn't know how to swim. When we got far enough out in the water, he picked me up and threw me over his head! I came up like a drowned rat, sputtering water, choking, trying to catch my breath. It's a wonder I ever went out with him again. He apologized, saying, "I'm sorry. I thought everyone knew how to swim."

From that first date, we were inseparable. Both of us stopped dating others and were together every moment possible.

We went dancing, but now, we went together. We enjoyed going to the beach together. We went up to his dad's cottage with Ag and Richie, and horror of horrors, it had an outhouse! Sometime in my youth, I heard someone tell about going into an outhouse and there was a snake coiled around the seat. I never forgot the story and was always afraid when I had to go in an outhouse.

We went out to eat a lot. Ag and I invited Jack and Richie over to the apartment for dinner one night. We fixed tuna sandwiches and chicken noodle soup. Guess they didn't think much of our "cooking"; consequently, we dined out quite a bit.

We chose a song to be "our song." It was a romantic song that was very popular then entitled "To Each His Own."

To each his own, I've found my own, one and only you.

And we went riding in his cars—yes, two of them—the blue Ford and the bright red Chevrolet convertible. Jack only brought the convertible out on sunny days.

My friends who I worked with at Chevrolet National Parts Division just couldn't believe that Jack had two new cars. There were hardly any new cars out since the war, and I was claiming that my boyfriend had two. They especially couldn't believe he had a convertible. I insisted, "Yes, you'll see. He'll pick me up in it." At closing time, everyone, and I mean everyone, lined up across the windows in that huge office to see this awesome car, even the plant manager. Jack came in the blue Ford. My face must have been as red as the convertible. I took a lot of teasing over that. The next day was a repeat performance with everyone lined up to see the convertible again, but Jack said that it "looked like rain." I was mortified. When I got in the car, I said, "If you don't come in the convertible tomorrow, don't come. I don't care if it's pouring!" The next day was a beautiful day, and my sweetheart was waiting for me right by the front door with the convertible top-down. You should have seen my coworkers clamoring to get a look. They surrounded that car, taking in every detail—even the plant manager. I was sitting in the front seat, soaking it up, happy as a clam. Jack was forgiven, and I was vindicated.

⌇

Ag moved down to Vero Beach, Florida, to be with a boyfriend. I couldn't afford the apartment without sharing expenses, so I moved back home with Mom and Dad in their little bungalow on Hamilton Avenue.

Jack gave me an engagement ring and asked me to marry him, and I joyfully accepted. I don't remember when we first expressed our love for each other or murmured our first "I love you," but don't think it was very far into our relationship. Jack was comfortable to be with, had an irresistible smile, and had a great sense of humor. We had so much fun together that I wanted to be with him forever. I couldn't have loved anyone more.

Our courtship wasn't without controversy and some bumps in the road. Jack's mother didn't want him to marry me. She wanted him to marry Peggy, a nurse he had been dating, because she thought Peggy would be able to take care of him if he ever needed help with his disability.

My mom and dad didn't want me to marry Jack either. They didn't think that with his disability he would be able to provide for a family. The fact that he wasn't working was a valid point, and I knew it was a source of irritation to them. Mom and Dad didn't like it because Jack would keep me out late at night, and I'd have to get up early in the morning to be at my desk by eight o'clock, while he was able to stay in bed as long as he wanted to. And they had hoped that I would marry Harold, one of the other boys who brought me an engagement ring, and were disappointed because I didn't choose him. He was a nice young man, and I'm sure he would have made a fine husband, but my feelings for him weren't the same as for Jack.

I loved my mom and dad with all my heart and didn't want to do anything to hurt them. I may not have mentioned it before, but I never left the house without kissing my mom and dad goodbye and saying, "I love you." I never went to bed at night without doing the same. I wanted very much to please them because I loved them so very much.

I was under quite a bit of pressure to date Harold. The Bible said to honor your mother and father. I had a measure of guilt because I didn't want to disappoint them in any way. After all, I was their baby girl. I wrestled with it in my heart and mind. Was it possible that Mom and Dad were right and I was making a mistake that I would regret for my whole life? With a heavy heart, I returned Jack's ring.

CHAPTER 37

You never saw a more miserable person. I was heartbroken. Jack didn't call, didn't pick me up at work, or didn't try to contact me at all. And I was crying at the drop of the hat. He was going through the same thing at his end, but was trying to honor my decision. We were a miserable pair.

About two weeks later, Mom, Dad, and I were in the living room listening to the radio when "our song" came on the air. My eyes filled with tears and began to roll down my cheeks. I missed him so much. I went to my bedroom and cried myself to sleep.

The next day when I came home from work, Jack was sitting on the front porch talking with my dad! What in the world was going on? I couldn't believe that Jack was there, talking with my dad, after all the opposition. I didn't know what to say or do.

My folks told me that they had talked that night after I went to bed crying and agreed that if I loved Jack that much, they wouldn't stand in the way. My mom had called Jack that afternoon and told him it was all right with them if he came over, so he was there to greet me with their permission.

We started making wedding plans right away.

38

Jack and I were so happy to be together again. We were laughing and crying and hugging each other all at once. And Mom and Dad were happy for us. It was never that they didn't like Jack. You couldn't help but like him. Their only concern was his disability and being able to provide for a family.

I understood their point of view. When you dream of your baby girl getting married, that dream does not include her Prince Charming having a leg amputated. They considered that a huge obstacle. I never did. I never considered Jack to be handicapped.

My mom and dad, together with Jack and me, set the wedding date as January 18 of the new year. We wanted to get married as soon as possible, but Mom thought it would take at least that long to accomplish everything.

Jack's dad gave him some very good advice—get a job! That had been a thorn in my parent's sides and rightly so.

His dad wanted him to take over his barbershop someday, so to please his dad, Jack enrolled in Barber College. That pleased my parents to no end. Jack was at Barber College all day and doing homework at night, so he no longer kept me out to all hours of the morning. Everything was falling in place nicely, and everyone was happy about our plans to marry.

If I recall correctly, Barber College was about three months of intense education. It's not just get a pair of scissors and a set of clippers and hang a shingle out to cut hair. He had to learn much about diseases of the scalp, bone structure, and many other things you wouldn't think were related to cutting hair. One thing he had to do before graduating was shave a balloon with a straight razor without bursting the balloon. Jack made it through, got his license, and took the other chair in his dad's barbershop.

One of the first things Jack and I did as far as wedding plans was to decide which church to be married in. He was raised as a Baptist, and I was attending Oak Park Methodist Church. As is customary, the wedding generally takes place in the bride's church, so we made an appointment with Rev. Marshall Hoyt at Oak Park Methodist Church for counseling and to reserve the date.

Mom and I were busy every weekend taking care of the endless details involved with a wedding. Since one of the most important things is the bridal gown, we began shopping for that right away. I never dreamed it would be so difficult! There were no wedding gowns to be found! With all of the men coming home from the service, there was a great need for wedding gowns. As soon as the shops received a shipment, they were snapped up.

Mom and I went from store to store with no success. We went to all of the ladies shops that lined both sides of Saginaw Street to no avail. I left my name at the stores and asked them to call if they received any. One day, I got a call from Goodman's. They had received two gowns, and one was in my size. I asked them to hold it for me.

The dress fit perfectly—it required no alterations. It was a traditional gown, simple, but elegant. The fabric was brocaded taffeta. It was fashioned with a sweetheart neckline, and the shape of the fitted bodice echoed the cut of the neckline. Covered buttons marched in a solid column from the neckline to the bottom of the bodice. The sleeves were gathered at the cap, narrowed down to the wrist, and was held snugly in place with a single covered button. The train was chapel length and was detachable. There was a looped bow at the back waistline, so the gown looked nice from the back even when the train was detached. I was so thrilled to have found a dress that I loved, and of course, it went home with me. It cost $80.

One of the men I worked with did photography as a sideline business. He came to our house on Hamilton Avenue to take my picture to be in the society section of *The Flint Journal*. He hung a blanket up in the basement for a backdrop and seated me in front of it. That was my formal wedding photograph.

I asked my sister, Peg, to be my matron of honor. My sister, Edna, and my sister-in-law, Betty, were to be my bridesmaids. I would have loved to have my sister, Ag, too, but she was still in Florida.

The problem of dresses for them was the same as my gown—none available. So they ended up wearing gowns they had worn for previous weddings in our family. It worked out fine; they had only been worn once and had been stored in tissue after being dry-cleaned.

Jack asked a childhood friend of his Warren Harrison to be his best man. As groomsmen, he asked Peg's husband Sam and Edna's husband Frank to do the honors.

Since my dad hadn't been feeling well and not wanting to put stress on him, Mom and I thought it best if my brother, Don, walked me down the aisle and gave me away. Dad was pleased with that decision.

The invitations were chosen, the cake was ordered from Eastside Bakery, and the florist chosen. A sigh of relief.

Peg gave a wedding shower in my honor. The gift theme was miscellaneous. As with most showers, we played games, chatted with those we hadn't seen in a while, and discussed wedding details. Peg had decorated the refreshment table with a picturesque bride in the center and pink and white satin streamers the length of the table. Many family members, friends, and neighbors attended; and the gift table overflowed with lovely packages.

The very next night, Jack's mom gave a kitchen shower for me, and it was much the same as Peg's and just as nice. The dining room table was centered with wedding bells suspended from a rose-covered wedding arch. There were a lot of ladies in attendance at that shower too, and I received so many useful things needed for a kitchen.

When Mom and I got home from the shower that night, we found Dad not feeling well. He had pain in his chest. Mom rushed to get him some water with baking soda, but he said he already had taken some. Between the two of us, we got him to lay down and rest. I was so worried about him. The wedding was just around the corner.

CHAPTER 39

Our house was in a quandary. Before long, the holidays would be upon us, and the wedding soon after. Dad was having heart problems, but thankfully, he was on medication and was resting well.

Jack was working at the barbershop with his dad. There are many hours to be filled with talk in a two-chair shop. There just aren't customers there all the time, so Jack and his dad had plenty of time to talk. Dad suggested to Jack that he should sell his two new cars and buy a house. That was a revelation that Jack had never considered. He loved his cars. I did too. But the more he thought about it, the more sense it made. Renting a house or apartment was like throwing money away. At the end of the year, you would own nothing, and all that money would be gone. The seed was planted.

Jack started looking at houses, while I was at work. He could leave the barbershop anytime he didn't have a customer, and his dad encouraged him to follow-up on his suggestion. After work one day, Jack took me to look at a brand new house. It was almost dark by the time we got there, winter darkness falling early. We went around the house, looking in all the windows.

We made an appointment with the builder and went back to see it the following Saturday. It was on Pierson Road near Clio Road, right next door to the former Mayfair Bible Church. It was four rooms—living room, kitchen, two bedrooms, a bathroom, and a utility room on the back for laundry facilities. It had hardwood floors that I loved but had no garage, no driveway, and no sidewalk. It was very basic, but to us, it looked like a mansion. It cost $6,900.

Jack sold his two shiny new cars, and we bought the house. You'd have to know Jack's love for cars to realize what a sacrifice that must have been. He bought a 1938 brown Buick with no complaining, and we had our honeymoon house.

Our wedding invitations went out the week before Christmas. We were so in love and excited as any two kids anticipating the arrival of Christmas.

We shared part of Christmas with my family and part with Jack's mom and Bill. For my Christmas gift, Jack gave me a fur coat purchased from Ferris Brothers and a set of silverware in a beautiful pecan case. The pattern was "First Love."

The holidays went by in a flurry of activity, and soon, it was the New Year. We went to a party at Edna and Frank's house to celebrate the New Year along with Peg and Sam, Betty and Don, and other friends. At midnight after everyone had shared their New Year's kisses under the mistletoe, they sang "Happy Birthday" to me. It was my twentieth birthday.

For my birthday gift, Jack gave me a lovely string of graduated pearls, purchased at Wethered and Rice Jewelers, that I would wear on my wedding day.

Jack had told me once that growing up an only child, he worried that he would never be an uncle. Surrounded by my big family, I told him that when we were married, he would instantly be an uncle many times over.

We celebrated Jack's birthday on the 14th of January—he turned twenty-two.

I couldn't think of any wedding details left undone. My attendants had chosen the dresses they would wear. Peg was wearing a blue chiffon floor-length gown with a silk lace bodice and a matching hat of blue net. Edna and Betty chose pink and blue gowns, identical in style, with jersey eyelet bodices, cap sleeves, and double-net skirts. They would wear matching Juliet caps with brief veils. All of the girls were carrying colonial bouquets in lace baskets.

Jack was wearing a new blue suit. He bought his clothes from Buckingham's, an upscale men's store, downtown Flint. They gave him his suit as a wedding gift. Their thoughtfulness assured a future relationship, as well as being a wedding gift and a "thank you" for serving our country.

I had also chosen my "something old, something new…"

My "something old" was my mother's Bible. It meant so very much to her. For my wedding day, the florist covered it in white satin and placed an orchid on top with streamers cascading down. *I love you so very much, Mom. It is an honor for me to carry your Bible on my wedding day.*

My "something new" was my string of pearls that Jack had given me for my birthday.

My "something borrowed" was Edna's wedding veil. When we found it difficult to find a wedding veil, Edna graciously offered hers. It was lovely. I was thankful for it and pleased to wear it. The tiara was a crown of hearts encrusted with seed pearls. The veil was silk tulle edged in French lace.

My "something blue" was a family tradition—a blue satin ribbon tied in a small bow and pinned under my gown.

Our wedding was the following Saturday.

40

Our wedding day dawned bright and beautiful—a sunny day and unusually warm for January. The sidewalks were wet with melting snow.

The wedding hour was set for 3:00 p.m. My attendants and I met at the church at 2:00 p.m. and excitedly attended to last-minute details. The florist arrived with the altar flowers and lit the candelabra. Identical corsages were presented to my mom and Jack's mom, and they were gorgeous. She fastened the boutonnieres for Jack and his attendants, my dad, and Jack's dad. The girl's flower-filled lace baskets were beautiful, and I was so very pleased with my mom's Bible, covered with white satin, topped with a lovely orchid.

At precisely three o'clock, the music began, and my attendants, looking lovely in their long gowns, proceeded down the center aisle.

Don was waiting to escort me down the aisle. When I saw my beloved waiting for me at the front of the church, all the emotions of recent weeks caught up to me. My eyes started to mist over, and I said, "I think I'm going to cry." Don said, "You can't! There isn't time! They're playing the music now!" The organist had indeed begun the bridal processional, and Don took my arm, and down the aisle we went.

Our wedding reception was at Mom and Dad's home on East Hamilton Avenue. The newspaper article with all the details of the wedding and the reception, said that there were a hundred guests. No one counted, but there were a lot of people there.

January 18, 1947

Our four-tiered wedding cake was exceptionally beautiful, I thought. It was centered on the lace-covered dining room table. It was topped with a bride and groom standing under a floral arch. The florist had placed vases of chrysanthemums and gladioli throughout the house, giving it a festive flair.

It was about 6:00 p.m. when we left for our honeymoon trip. For going-away, I chose a chartreuse crepe dress, brown velvet hat, and brown leather sandals. The orchid I had carried for my wedding was pinned to my fur coat that Jack had given to me for Christmas.

Our destination was Niagara Falls, New York, but we were so exhausted from the past weeks we stayed overnight at Port Huron, Michigan, where we checked into the Harrington Inn. The young girl at the desk gave us the keys to a room on the second floor. A more mature woman behind the desk whispered in her ear, "Don't give them that room. It's got twin beds. Can't you see they just got married? She's wearing a corsage." I was embarrassed to no end, nothing like announcing to the whole world that it was our wedding night. Jack just chuckled; he thought it was pretty funny.

We were tired and hungry. We went to a nice restaurant for a great dinner, and I had my very first steak. I didn't even know what kind to order, so Jack ordered for me—a filet mignon. Delicious!

We were at Niagara four days before heading back home. The weather had changed dramatically, and we were caught up in a terrible blizzard. We could barely see the hood of the car. Jack got behind a semitruck, and we followed it most of the way home.

We stopped for lunch, and I didn't know our money was almost gone. I ordered fish and chips, and Jack had a hamburger. When we pulled in the driveway at our little honeymoon house, we had $2 left.

CHAPTER 41

We purchased basic needs furniture for our little house before we got married. When I say basic, it was minimal—a matching couch and chair for the living room, an area rug, and a table with a radio on it. The kitchen had a table and four chairs. The stove and refrigerator came with the house. Just a bed and chest for our bedroom, and the other bedroom was empty—so very spartan. We had a rug and no vacuum, but we had a broom. We had a laundry room, but no washing machine. I did our laundry at Mom's. And we couldn't have been happier. It was meant for us to be together.

I didn't know how to cook when we got married; it was a day-by-day learning experience. Good thing Jack knew how. I learned by trying recipes from my mom and Jack's mom and before long was fixing meals for company.

Jack was working at the barbershop, I had my job at GM's Chevrolet National Parts Division, and Jack had his $89.00 a month disability check from the government. We thought, *Oh boy! We'll have $89.00 a month for the rest of our lives.* We thought we really had it made.

We found out early on that I was pregnant and before long had to give up my job. Jack's earnings at the barbershop didn't amount to that much. Maybe $20.00 a week. We would have had a hard time getting by without that $89.00 a month for his disability.

Our honeymoon house, being constructed right after World War II, was built with green lumber; and before long, as the wood dried out, all kinds of things began to warp out of shape.

As the cold days of January closed in on us, the front door of our honeymoon house warped. The snow would blow right through the crack in the door and stay frozen on the living room rug. Our floor furnace was in the center of our house and didn't warm the house enough to melt the snow.

We survived the winter in our little house, and with the warmth of spring, we forgot about the snow frozen on the rug. We had emerald green and white-striped canvas awnings installed on the front of the house. It looked fresh and summery.

We were happy newlyweds, expecting a baby, and sharing our joy with others. There were several young married couples right in my own family to go out for dinner with, go to a movie together, or have over to play cards. Friends of ours also in that "newly married" group were always ready for weekend fun too, so we had a busy social life.

I thrived on pregnancy—almost glowed. Morning sickness was something that never bothered me. I felt great and was ready to go at a moment's notice, slipping into one of my cute maternity outfits. Back then, we wore dresses. I just purchased a few, knowing I would only need them for a short time. They had skirts that adjusted around the tummy and had swing jackets that were hip-length and very becoming.

Throughout my pregnancy, I craved chocolate fudgesicles and popcorn. Jack would go to the Nortown Theater on North Saginaw Street, and they would let him go into the lobby without a ticket and purchase a big box of popcorn to satisfy my craving.

The funniest thing happened one summer day. I was several months along in my pregnancy, and Jack and I were relaxing in bed one morning, in no rush to get up. It was a warm, sunny day, and we had the bedroom windows up. Of course, there were no screens. We had just started to doze off again when suddenly we heard the strangest sound—a horse neighing! There was a horse standing outside our house with his head sticking right through our bedroom window!

We learned later that several horses had escaped through an unlocked gate at a riding stable down the road from us.

~~~

It was the morning of August 16 that I began having contractions. Jack called his dad to let him know he wouldn't be to work that day—the baby was coming. I had Jack drive me over to Mom and Dad's house. First baby, I wanted my mom!

Mom had an appointment scheduled at the beauty shop to get a permanent, and I urged her to keep the appointment—the pains weren't that far along. She got home around 4:00 p.m., and the pains were progressing slowly. Around midnight, I thought I was wetting my pants, but Mom said, "No, your water broke. The baby can come any time." Jack, Mom, and I rushed to Hurley Hospital.

I thought the contractions were hard then—little did I know about childbirth! I had no idea what to expect, and the pains kept getting worse. I was so nauseated and began throwing up. That had happened three or four times when a kind nurse quietly said to me, "You're making it so hard on you and the baby. Every time you throw up, you suck the baby back up, and it has to travel all that way over again." Mercifully, I didn't throw up anymore, and things progressed pretty quickly after that.

Our baby girl made her debut on Sunday morning at 8:30 a.m. on August 17, delivered by Dr. C. P. Clark, the obstetrician who delivered my sister's babies. She weighed 6 lb 1 oz., and we named her Carol Ann. They didn't have ultrasound then, so you didn't know the gender of a baby until birth.

Of course, Carol Ann was the prettiest baby in the nursery and good beyond belief. We didn't get to have the babies in the room with us in those days, they were kept in the nursery, and we only had them with us for nursing. When they brought her to me, her dark hair was brushed into a little curl on top of her head. She had beautiful blue eyes, a pink blush on her cheeks, and a sweet little heart-shaped mouth.

After the ten-day hospital stay, we brought our tiny treasure home to our honeymoon house where we had the nursery ready and waiting for her. We had a new crib and chest for her, but for now, while she was so tiny, I had a woven basket with handles. It was soft and cozy around her tiny body when tucked in with the fluffy new baby blankets. I could carry her from room to room with me, and I wanted this little bundle of love with me every moment.

Carol Ann was such a beautiful baby and so good. I could take her anywhere to visit, and she never cried or made a fuss. She loved to be cuddled, but if we were visiting at someone else's house, I could wrap her in her little blanket and put pillows around her so she couldn't roll, and she would go right to sleep on their bed. Never any fuss.

Our little family of three was having the best time. I loved taking care of my baby and waiting for Jack to get home from work. I always took a few minutes to freshen up, put on makeup, and brush my hair before he came home.

Before long, winter was upon us, and the snow frozen on the rug again. I put Carol Ann to bed wearing a bonnet and mittens to make sure she was warm. The honeymoon house was listed for sale as soon as spring arrived. It sold right away for just what we had paid for it.

We purchased a darling home over on East Court Street.

I was expecting again.

CHAPTER 42

We loved our home on East Court Street. The East Court Street area was a lovely community of large homes. Ours was the first small home on the street that I considered lined with mansions.

Our home had a small front porch and a separate entrance way leading into a living room with a fireplace. A dining room and kitchen completed the rooms that faced the white picket fenced-in backyard. Facing the street were the two bedrooms. And it had a full basement with a furnace that could heat the whole house! No more snow on the carpet. We paid $7,500 for it, and it was a huge improvement.

Jack was not doing well in the barber trade. Most of the customers had been coming to his dad for years and wanted to continue on as his customer. That meant a lot of hours just sitting around for Jack and not earning much at all. One week, he brought home $9.00 for his paycheck, and that was the last straw. I remember dodging the milkman because I didn't have the money to pay our bill. It was during this time period that Jack made a foolish mistake. I sent him to the drug store one night to get a box of Band-Aids. He was gone about two hours. He not only bought Band-Aids but also had stopped by a furniture store and purchased a big console with a radio and phonograph. Needless to say, I was pretty upset with him. It did look beautiful in our living room, and eventually, we did get it paid for.

Jack decided he had to make a job change. His first love was cars, and he thought he would be good at selling them.

That job change was the best thing that could have happened to him. He got a job at a small dealership that sold Pontiacs. He was so happy with the change and so enthusiastic about selling a product he loved he couldn't help but be successful.

Jack was pleasant to have a conversation with because he knew how to put people at ease. He focused on the other person and was a good listener. All these natural abilities gave him a great deal of confidence, and he was successful right from the very beginning, and he was happy with his job. He was excited about going to work every day. Jack received no salary, just worked on commission, so if you didn't sell anything, you didn't get a paycheck. He never missed a paycheck.

<p style="text-align:center">~~~</p>

We were attending Central Methodist Church on Garland Street—a lovely old red brick building near downtown Flint, which was easy access from our home on East Court Street. It was at that church that I had my first salvation experience.

Even though I had attended church all my life, I didn't understand salvation. I'm sure I had heard the gospel presented many times, but for some reason, it just didn't penetrate my head. Anyway, one Sunday in church at the end of his sermon, the pastor prayed, and with all eyes closed, he said if you wanted to invite Jesus into your heart as Lord and Savior to take one step to the right. I thought that was very strange and must have been presented in that way to keep from embarrassing people. I took a step to the right. Nothing happened. I didn't feel any different, and I still didn't know what salvation was. If I was saved by taking that small step to the right, it was known to God alone.

<p style="text-align:center">~~~</p>

It wasn't long after that when our second baby was born. Jack and I were out on a Saturday night date. We went to Frankenmuth for one of their world famous chicken dinners. On the drive home, my stomach started feeling a little funny. The baby wasn't due for three more weeks. Still, Carol Ann had come early.

We went home and went to bed. I thought maybe I had eaten too much. I didn't really feel that bad and went to sleep right away. About 4:00 a.m., I felt warm water starting to flow. Jack called my sister, Peg, to come and stay with Carol Ann, and we went to the hospital. I thought probably I would have ten or twelve hours of hard labor ahead of me. I hardly made it to the hospital! Emergency put me in a wheelchair without even checking me in and rushed me straight to the delivery room. My obstetrician, Dr. Samuel Sorkin, made it just in the nick of time because he happened to be at his mother's house just a couple of doors from the hospital.

Husbands weren't allowed in the delivery room in those days. Dr. Sorkin's fee for delivering the baby was $75. When he stepped out of the delivery room to tell Jack that we had a beautiful baby girl, Jack was standing there with the $75 in his hand. Dr. Sorkin laughingly said that was a "first" for him.

Our precious little baby girl was born on July 12 at 6:11 a.m. on a Sunday morning and weighed 5 lb 7 oz. We named her Barbara Lee.

She was so very tiny it was an almost painless birth. I only felt a couple of hard pains—one with the head, one with the shoulders. After ten days of hospital care, we took our tiny bundle of love home. My mom came and stayed with us to help with the two babies. They were only eleven months apart. My mom slept on the sofa in the living room and held Barbie in her arms all night long.

Barbie was a darling little baby. She had platinum hair and her dad's sparkling blue eyes. Her complexion was so fair it almost looked translucent, and she had a tiny little rosebud mouth. She was happiest when she was being cuddled in my arms, and I loved to snuggle with her. She was nursing every two hours, so she got held a lot.

Barbie wasn't gaining weight. When her weight dropped to 5 lb 4 oz., the doctor said that we had to take her back to the hospital. They didn't put her in the nursery. She was put on a regular medical floor and was in a hospital bed, not a crib. That just tore my heart out; I couldn't bear seeing her there. I thought she would be in a bassinet with a nurse caring for her in with other babies, but here she was, all alone in that big hospital bed. She was there overnight.

When I went to the hospital the next day and saw her in that big bed, I just gathered her in my arms and held her close and cried and cried. I couldn't leave her there a moment longer; I was taking her home with me. They told me I couldn't, so I said, "Stop me!" And I took her home. I guess if she had been in the nursery with the other babies and a nurse in there with them, I would have left her. But to see that tiny bundle in that big bed, all alone, I just couldn't handle it.

The doctor put Barbie on formula, and she had to be fed with an eyedropper at the beginning. Soon, she progressed to nipples specially formulated for babies with small mouths. She started gaining weight right away, reaching all of the health goals, and over the next few weeks, she rounded out and had the little baby wrinkles in all the right places.

I was in my happy world—a husband who I loved with all my heart, two precious babies that I adored, and a house that I liked very much. Life was sweet.

⤳

A new phenomenon was taking place in America at that time. Television was just beginning to make an appearance in American households, and we purchased one. Ours was giant in comparison to the neighbors that lived behind us—the only other people we knew who owned a set. Their television was the size of a grapefruit. Ours was a whopping eleven inches, about the size of a soccer ball! We had a set of "rabbit ears" on top of our TV—two metal rods that you could position this way and that to get better reception. We also put a wadded-up ball of aluminum foil on the tips of the rabbit ears to enhance reception. I don't know if that helped or not, but someone came up with the idea, and everyone was doing it.

We were the first ones in my family to have a television. On Saturday nights now, our date night was at home watching television. We would line up folding chairs in our living room and dining room theater-style and invite the family over to watch. And they all came. Never mind that there were only about three stations, the entertainment was poor, and usually so much snowy interference you had difficulty seeing the program. At midnight, the stations signed off for the night with the playing of the national anthem and the American flag waving on the screen. Everyone loved television, and everyone wanted one. Our Saturday night get-togethers didn't last very long because everyone in the family purchased one. A new era was born.

It was spring of the next year, April 1949, that my beloved father passed away. I got a frantic call from my mother to "come right away." Mr. and Mrs. Carter, an elderly couple who lived next door to us, came over to watch the girls. When Jack and I arrived, my dad was already gone. He had passed away sitting right up in his easy chair. They transferred my dad to a hearse, and my mom was so upset they gave her a sedative and took her away in an ambulance. I thought I had lost both of them.

Gone was the one who moved heaven and earth to provide for his family during the hard times. Gone was my "go-to person" who I considered so wise and knew all the answers. Gone were the days when Dad would hold my little ones on his lap, cradling one in each arm. Dad was only fifty-six years old—so young. I love you, Dad.

I was so thankful that Dad knew before he passed away that Jack was a loving, generous, and caring husband, a great provider, and an awesome father to our two baby girls.

That summer, Carol Ann was two and Barbie one year old. We bought a huge wicker baby buggy with big rubber tires and spoked wheels. I was so very proud of my two beautiful little girls. I kept them dressed up like little dolls. They had clean outfits every morning, and after their naps, I would put clean dresses on them again, put on the shoes I had polished while they were napping, and stroll them up and down all the streets in the East Court Street area with the big beautiful homes.

My next-door neighbor Wanda told me she had seen me downstairs ironing at three o'clock in the morning while she was getting a bottle for her youngest. Yes, I was ironing twenty-eight outfits a week for my two girls. That was before wash and wear, but I wanted them looking perfect all the time.

On one of our Sunday afternoon rides, we saw a colonial home being built on Pierson Road near Detroit Street. We stopped to look at it and ended up buying it. It was about twice as big as the house we were living in. Three bedrooms and two bathrooms, all the rooms were large. I thought that would be lovely. I would use the third bedroom for a sewing room.

CHAPTER 43

Our colonial home on Pierson Road was one of seven homes lined up facing that busy street. As it turned out, it was a great place to raise youngsters. All the families there had kids near in age to ours, so there were lots of playmates. The parents were all young, and not only were we neighbors, but we also developed a social network. It was a great neighborhood.

We put up a swing set in our yard, and Jack's stepfather, Bill, built a kid-size log cabin and a sandbox in the backyard. The yard was fenced, and the neighborhood kids loved to come and play. There was a bathroom right inside our back door, and all the kids went in and out. I never knew how many kids would be eating lunch at our house. If they were there, they were welcome to eat. It was the same for my girls at the neighbor's houses. That neighborhood was like one big happy family.

I never did get my sewing room. Before I got a sewing machine, I was expecting again. We put a crib in the "sewing room" and were excited about having another baby.

With Dad gone, Mom spent quite a lot of time at our house, and she was there with us when the baby decided it was time to be born and my water broke. She stayed with the girls, while Jack took me to the hospital. Only two pains with Barbie, so this one would surely be a piece of cake.

I had my most difficult birth—ten hours of hard labor—so you just never know. Ronald Reed was born at 10:21 a.m. on Sunday morning, February 19, 1951. He weighed 6 lb 12 oz. Just as I roused from the anesthetic, I heard the church bells ringing for a service nearby and gave thanks to the Lord for my baby. When Dr. Sorkin told me I had a boy, I thought he was teasing, so he positioned him so I could see his genitals and make sure.

We wanted a boy to round out our family, but only prayed for a healthy baby. Our joy was pretty hard to contain when we found out it was a boy. Every father wants a son to carry on the family name, and Jack was so thrilled to have a boy. Ron looked a lot like Carol Ann. He had that sweet round face, beautiful blue eyes, just the right size ears, so important for a boy, and dark hair. He was perfect in every way—such a sweet little baby and so good-natured.

The Visiting Nurse came to call when Ron was about a month old. She proceeded to show me how to bathe him. I thought I was pretty well schooled in that since he was my third baby, but she was being helpful, doing her job, so I just let her go ahead. She didn't have his genitals covered, and suddenly, his pride and joy stood erect and sprayed all over her white apron. She took it in good stride, evidently not being the first time it happened. She said that it was "all in a day's work" and gave him a little hug.

⌣

Jack had made a job change and was working at Applegate Chevrolet on South Saginaw Street by the Fisher Body Plant. Again, it was a commission-only job, but Jack liked that. He felt that you never got complacent or lazy that way. If you didn't sell, you didn't make any money. He loved people, loved his job, and loved his product; and he was very successful. Mr. Applegate soon promoted him to used car manager.

An important part of our Christian walk had taken place. We started to tithe. We didn't tithe on our net income; we started right out tithing on gross income. I've heard that you can tell about people's lives by looking in their checkbook. I took care of our checkbook, and our tithe checks were the first that I wrote out every month. I always gave our tithe checks first place, never wanting to give God leftovers.

At that time, I was also in charge of the nursery. Central Methodist was a large church, and we had quite a lot of babies in the nursery. I contacted all the mothers and asked them to take a turn caring for the babies. Since we only had to do it once every four or five weeks, it worked out great, and everyone was willing to do their part.

It was a very happy time in my life. Having three babies so close together never seemed to bother me. I was young and full of energy. I kept my household schedule like my mom always did. Washing on Monday, Tuesday and Wednesday were ironing days, Thursday was grocery day, and Friday's I cleaned house and changed the bedding. Weekends were reserved for fun time and church on Sunday.

I can't say I never got off schedule. I tried to get things done while the kids were napping, and most times, it worked out. Jack was good about helping too. He thought nothing of helping with the supper dishes. He quite often gave the kids their baths at night and got them in their pajamas, giving me some time to relax. Their bedtime was eight o'clock, so we had a nice evening ahead to enjoy. Television had improved greatly; we also enjoyed putting a stack of records on the phonograph and listening to music or dancing.

Ron, our sweet baby boy, was only three months old when I missed a period. Yes, I was pregnant again! My brother, Don, teased me saying, "Don't you kids know what's causing this?" I was surprised to be expecting again, but none of our babies were planned. It just happened.

When I was pregnant, I always did well healthwise—never had morning sickness, full of energy, and happy as a lark. Before the actual birth, I always got a spurt of energy. I should have known the delivery time was near when I got the urge to clean out cupboards on January 26. Sure enough, my water broke that night.

A quick call was made to my sister, Peg, and her husband, Sam, to come to take care of our three little ones. There had been freezing rain during the night, and the roads were as slick as an ice skating rink. We cautiously made our way to the hospital.

We were blessed with another baby boy. Gerald Jack, weighing 6 lb 5 oz. made his debut at 1:06 p.m., on January 27, 1952. Jerry was such a darling little baby. He had sparkling blue eyes and platinum blond hair like Barbie. He was perfect in every way and such a little blessing. God knew just what we needed to fill that crib. Two girls and now two boys—my world was complete.

The following is a page from my family tree book:

Four Special Babies

A beautiful baby girl—there's something so wonderful about a first born child. The awe of a miracle of God. She had dark curly hair, a blush on her cheeks, a rosebud mouth. And a sweet disposition. The nurses at the hospital told me she was the best baby in the nursery, and I'm sure it was true. The first time they brought her to me, they had brushed her dark hair into waves. Just like a doll. We named her Carol Ann. So dear and precious to my heart. Loved from the moment of conception. She was like no other child. Surely we couldn't love anything on earth as much. My world was complete.

Soon I discovered I was expecting again. Barbara Lee arrived three weeks early—so tiny, so fragile—an almost painless birth. If she stayed at home, we had to feed her with an eye dropper—so she had a return trip to the hospital where she could receive special care. She was such a sweet baby. And what a joy! Platinum blonde hair, sparkling blue eyes—a busy bundle of dynamite right from the beginning. She loved being held and I loved to cuddle her, too. So dear and precious to my heart. Two beautiful baby girls. Yes, there's always plenty of love for another baby. And she was like no other child. My world was complete.

We were building a three bedroom home. I was going to have a sewing room. Before the home was ready to move into, I was expecting again and that sewing room was turned into a blue nursery. You could not believe the joy we felt when the doctor told me I had delivered a beautiful baby boy. When I came out of the anesthetic, the church bells were ringing for Sunday morning service. I thanked God for my healthy, beautiful baby—Ronald Reed—such a sweet baby—exceptionally good—brunette like Carol Ann. Two little girls to care for, now a baby boy. He was like no other child. Who could ever wish for more? My world was complete.

Yes, shortly after Ron was born, I was expecting again. Two cribs in the nursery would be fine. We were blessed with a beautiful baby boy—Gerald Jack. How wonderful. Two girls, two boys. The Lord knew just what we needed to fill that waiting crib. Jerry was such a good baby, special in every way. The girls loved to "mother" the boys. It was just like having two real live dolls of their own. Jerry had blonde hair and blue eyes, like Barb, and he was so sweet and loving. He matched Barb in the "busy" department, too. My youngest—so special—so loved. So precious and dear to my heart. Thank You, Lord. And do you know—he's like no other child.

I wonder if they know how much they're loved? My world *is* complete.

All four of our children were born within the first five years of our marriage, and they were four years and five months apart. We were married in January 1947, and Jerry, our youngest, was born in January 1952. There was also one miscarriage between Barb and

Ron. All four were born at Hurley Hospital, Flint, Michigan. All four came early, and all were born on Sunday.

The fact that they were all born on Sunday was a blessing from God. I was always concerned that I would be home alone with the little ones when my time for delivery came and that I wouldn't be able to get ahold of Jack. The Lord solved that in such a loving way by having them all arrive on Sunday, the only day Jack didn't work. Thank you, Father.

44

A horrific tornado struck Flint, Michigan, on June 8, 1953. After all these years, that tornado still ranks as one of the ten worst in our country's history.

It was a warm, humid day. The girls had dashed off to play with friends, and I was pulling the boys, who were one and two, down the street in their little red wagon. I noticed that everything was very quiet, almost like being in a vacuum. It even seemed the traffic on our normally busy street wasn't creating any noise. The atmosphere seemed to suddenly turn an eerie yellow. It was oddly frightening. I called for the girls to come, and we hurried home.

When we reached the house, our phone was ringing. It was my brother, Don. "Did you get hit?" he shouted. I didn't know what he meant. He exclaimed excitedly, "You just got missed then. Huge tornado just went down Coldwater Road. Took out a lot of houses!"

By then, I could hear the ambulances screaming past the corner near our house. Jack called to make sure we were all right and to tell me he wouldn't be home from work. The devastation was so immense that the police had asked the employees at Applegate Chevrolet to drive station wagons, trucks, or anything they could to the scene to pick up the dead and injured and transport them to the Flint hospitals. They worked throughout the night. It was like a war zone.

A path a mile wide and a mile long had destroyed almost 350 homes. The death toll was 116 and 844 injured. Victims ranged from five months to eighty years old.

Our entire city was in mourning. Everybody knew somebody who was killed or injured. Our next-door neighbor's sister lost both of her legs. A man that Jack drove to the hospital had gotten knocked unconscious when a beam struck him in the back of the head while he was going from his barn to his house. A lady had a board with a nail driven through it impaled in her knee. Jack drove people all night long, each with their own story to tell of the tornado.

One family told about their entire house, wood floors and all, being blown away just after they had gone to the basement. A young teenage couple were holding each other in their arms, and she was swept away. A baby was torn from her mother's arms, her little body later found in a creek near their home.

One mom lost all three of her children. A young couple was moving furniture into their new house when the house and everything in it was blown away. Their refrigerator was found up in a tree. One lady said that she had been downstairs ironing when the tornado hit. When she came upstairs, all of the houses across the street were gone. One family had nothing left of their home but the front steps.

Our governor, Mennen G. Williams, had been to a dinner; and he helped in the rescue effort still wearing his dress clothes.

Debris from Flint was blown all the way to Canada. The stories went on and on. The degree of tragedy was horrendous.

Just a mile away, our home was untouched, but our hearts and prayers went out to those who were hurting.

~~~

We lived in our colonial house on Pierson Road for five years. It was a wonderful time of togetherness for me and my four little ones. All four were born by the time I was twenty-five years old. I treasure the memories of dandelion bouquets, Mother's Day breakfast in bed, Easter egg hunts, and picnics under the dining room table—ice cream cones and Hershey bars—laying on a blanket in the sunshine with them finding shapes in the clouds—angels, bunnies, puppies—cocoa with marshmallows—catching fireflies at dusk. We had such fun together.

They were all preschoolers. In the morning, after breakfast, the girls would take the boys for a ride in the wagon, while I made the beds. It worked out really well; I only found the boys stranded and crying behind a neighbor's garage once where the girls had parked them and gone off to play with their friends.

Carol Ann and Barbie liked to play house and have Ron and Jerry be their little ones, but the boys didn't always cooperate with that. Sometimes, they would let the girls hug them or hold them, but most times, they just wriggled away, not knowing they were supposed to play a role.

Our dining room table often served as a tent. I would throw blankets over it, hanging down to the carpet, and they would play under it. At lunchtime, we would all have our sandwiches and chips in the semidarkness of the tent, Mom in the tent with them.

When the weather was nice, they liked eating their lunch on the front porch. I bought five little baskets and would pack a picnic lunch to enjoy on the front steps. Sometimes, our steps would be filled with neighbor kids too, joining in our little picnic.

Our fenced-in backyard was a favorite hangout for the neighborhood kids too. With the log cabin, swing set, sandbox and in the summer time a wading pool and the hose, there was lots to do.

The kids had a good-sized toy chest that we kept in the dining room. Carol Ann was a neatnik. She wanted all of those toys lined up just so in the toy chest. She would patiently straighten them all out; and Barb, my little bundle of dynamite, would go to the chest and toss them all out. So we had a few tears over that.

We had our own family streaker too. I had just given Jerry a bath and was drying him off when the phone rang. In that quick moment when I answered the phone, my two-year-old was out the door, buck-naked, running as fast as his little legs could carry him right down the sidewalk on that busy street. He didn't get very far; I was hot on his trail. He only made it to the house next door when I scooped him up in my arms, wrapped him in a fluffy towel, and carried him home.

Barbara Lee and Carol Ann

Ronald Reed and Gerald Jack

There were a lot of kids in that one block. There was an empty lot on the corner, and then came our house with four children. Next door to us were Parrs, with one child; Powells with two; Howlands with two; and Russells with two. There were eleven children in five homes, and all very much in the same age bracket.

There was a beautiful brick church at the west end of our block—St. Agnes Catholic Church. Their complex also included a rectory where Father Maurice Olk lived, a convent for the nuns, and a school. For some reason, the neighborhood kids thought the rectory was haunted, probably because they didn't see little kids there like all the other homes in the neighborhood. They used to dare each other to walk across the lawn.

⌇

They had contests at Applegate Chevrolet where the salesmen could win points and with those points choose prizes. One of those prizes was a Singer Sewing Machine in a nice wooden cabinet—I finally got my sewing machine! Another prize I remember was a hobby horse for the kids to ride on. It was large, covered with real fur, and stood on a platform that had springs. It was quite something, and the kids loved it. For a while, it was in the middle of the living room floor with someone riding it most of the time. When the children got older, we gave the horse away. I've regretted many times not keeping it for our grandchildren. It was unique and would have been a nice family heirloom.

They had one contest at Applegate's that I will never forget. We had a couple that we were friends with, Bob and Rose Gilchrist. They were wonderful Christian people, and we enjoyed their company very much. They were having guest musicians at their church one Sunday evening, and they invited us to join them at their church, so we did. It was a Baptist church out on Grand Blanc Road.

A special collection is always taken up for guests that come to a church. When it was time for the offering, Jack whispered in my ear, "How much money have you got in your wallet?"

I replied, "None. How much have you got?"

He said, "None. How much is in the checkbook?"

"Fifteen dollars," I responded.

"Write them a check for fifteen dollars," he said.

Jack got paid on Fridays, and we had a whole week to go, but I wrote out the check for $15. The next morning when he went to work, Mr. Applegate told him he had won the contest for the trip to Las Vegas—two tickets for us to fly out to Vegas and spend a week. Jack told him we really didn't want to go to Vegas. Mr. Applegate said, "Okay. We'll give you $500 in place of the trip!"

That was just one of many times when the Lord answered our need if we got in a bind. I can't proclaim enough how good the Lord is to His children when they are faithful to obey Him. Jack and I both considered it a privilege to tithe and always gave with joyful hearts.

Jack was doing really well in his job as a used car manager. It was not only his love for cars and people but also his honesty in all of his dealing. He estimated that 75% of his sales were return customers. His earnings had soared, and he was very generous. After having some lean times while he was barbering, Jack wanted to shower his family with good things.

We had dinner out about once a week. Oftentimes, we would ride over to Frankenmuth after church on Sunday for their famous chicken dinner. Another place the kids loved was Chris and Millie Panoff's Lighthouse that was right near downtown where Detroit Street and Saginaw Street join together. They got to sit at the counter and order their own meal, while Mom and Dad sat at a table next to them. Chris had his own secret recipe for his baked ham—they came out of the oven coal black on the outside and oh so delicious. The steak sandwiches and handmade milkshakes were also a favorite there.

And the Coney Island hot dogs! Many times, we would give the kids their baths, get them in their Dr. Denton footed pajamas, then drive downtown to the Original Coney Island, and get a bag of Coney's to take home. Sometimes, we'd swing by Freddy's Donuts on North Saginaw Street and take a dozen donuts home for dessert. We had such fun with our kids.

We all loved the drive-in theaters. I would pop a big bag full of popcorn, put some sodas in a cooler, and get the kids in their pajamas. They always fell asleep soon after the movie started, and when we got home, we could just put them in their beds.

It was during this time period on Pierson Road that Jack bought me my first car. I was thrilled to have my own wheels. We had a young girl who lived behind us that I could hire to babysit on the spur of the moment. Wow! What freedom, having a car right in our driveway ready to go anytime I was. I'd been in the habit of calling my mother every morning at eight thirty sharp, right on the mark. Now when I called her, I would ask if she had any errands to do, groceries to get, or maybe go downtown shopping. Mom didn't have a car, so it was a real blessing for her too, and I loved spending time with her.

Jack with our four beautiful children

My mother and I had a very close relationship. I had a great relationship with all of my siblings too and was blessed with many friends, but Mom was my best friend. She was the best mom in the whole world. She liked being at our house and would come at the drop of a hat to help with the children. She loved each one of her children equally; there was no partiality—I just needed her more, I guess, with the kids so close together.

We took Mom on vacations with us too. She lived alone now and had no opportunity to go on a vacation, so we always included her in our vacation plans.

All four of our children were baptized at Central Methodist Church. They ranged in age from infant to two years old when we dedicated their lives to Christ.

Our church had bought property on Ballenger Highway and was in a building program, raising money to pay for it. Jack and I were both deeply entrenched in activities at that church. My mom and my sisters attended there too, and we were all members of the Women's Society of Christian Service (WSCS).

Jack and I started early on saying grace before our meals. As the kids got older, they took turns thanking God for our meals too. We said grace before meals when we were eating out too. We taught the kids to give their thanks to the Lord whether at home or out. We also said bedtime prayers together. Sometimes, their eyes would droop sleepily, and they would be sound asleep before the "Amen" was said.

Carol Ann started kindergarten; where had the time flown? I took her picture the first day of school all dressed up in her new school outfit, and Barbie was right there with her, still in her Dr. Denton pajamas, wishing she could go too. My mom stayed with the other three kids, while I walked Carol Ann to school. There was a tear in my eye as I walked home, but Carol Ann loved school.

The "baby" years passed quickly and seem to be all wrapped up in gossamer and sunshine. Jack and I loved each other with a spontaneity that every young couple wasn't fortunate enough to have. We cherished each other with an unfailing love. We never fought. We had disagreements, but to fight, yell, or name call, we just didn't do it.

We loved our little ones with all of our hearts—as for me, they were my life. I always used to joke with Jack, saying that I loved them more, because I got a nine-month start. But I've always said that the happiest time of my life was when my children were under my wings—like a mother hen with her chicks. I wanted their childhood to be filled with love just like mine was, and I'm certain all of them would say we succeeded.

45

When we bought our house on Pierson Road, there was an empty lot next to our house on the east side. A brick building went up there, and it turned out to be a doctor's office. Dr. Joseph Guyon and his wife Marianne were both doctors. They lived there and also had their offices there. We became friends, and they were also our family doctors. They had four boys. That made fifteen kids in six houses.

On the northwest corner of Detroit Street and Pierson Road, an L-shaped shopping center was built named North Flint Shopping Center. It housed around sixteen shops. It was anchored by a drug store, Federal's Department Store and Kresge's Five and Ten Cent Store. It was really handy, and I enjoyed shopping there, but it brought in a lot of traffic.

The St. Agnes Catholic Church complex was there when we built our house. We loved having the church in our neighborhood and considered it a big plus. The doctor's office and the shopping center came later. We were beginning to feel enclosed with commercial buildings. We decided it was time for us to move on—time for one of our famous rides where we ended up buying a house!

We found a subdivision where they were just starting to build homes called Mary Gardens. It ran west off Clio Road between Carpenter and Coldwater roads. There was nothing around it but woods. When we decided to build there, we thought we were moving out in the country.

Alex Gaus was building in that subdivision, and we hired him to build our home with just a handshake. A contract was never signed, only a handshake and trust. Mr. Gaus delivered everything that he had promised. Imagine doing that nowadays. We built an all-brick ranch house. It was the first home where I had a built-in dishwasher.

A fun memory—the travelling pony

It was 1956. Elvis Presley made his first appearance on Ed Sullivan's television show.

"In God We Trust" was adopted as our national motto. I thought it had always been our national motto. I pray that it always is.

When living in the house on Martharose Court in Mary Gardens, I did my grocery shopping at the Hamady's Market on Clio and Pierson roads. My budget for the week was $12.00, and that included everything except milk, and that was delivered to our home.

We had just nicely gotten moved into our house in Mary Gardens when the man with the Shetland pony came to our neighborhood. You know what I'm talking about. The same man went to every neighborhood in America that had young kids. For a small amount of money, he would set the kids on the pony, walk them around the house, and then take their photo. I've heard that if a person passes gas and a match is lit to it, you can actually see a blue flame. True or not, I don't know. But if it is true and a match was lit behind that pony, our new house would have gone up in a big blue flame. That pony passed gas with every step he took! Fortunately, he didn't drop any biscuits, the kids loved the little ride, and I treasure the photo.

Soon after we were settled in our home in Mary Gardens, we took a vacation trip to Miami, Florida. We took my mom with us and were driving a Chevrolet convertible. That meant three adults in the front seat and four kids in the backseat. In a convertible, there is a canvas swing-type recess where the convertible top rests when not in use. When the top is up, the kids discovered that it made a very comfortable place to sleep, somewhat like a hammock. They all loved to get in it, and one of them was sleeping in it most of the way to Florida. Jack called that little recess a "fart sack" and seemed like every time we looked back there, one of the kids butts were flying over the backseat to get in it.

There wasn't any expressway back then, and we drove two-lane highways through every little town imaginable for those 1500 miles to Miami Beach. It didn't matter; we had a wonderful time.

We stayed in an ocean-front hotel. The day before we arrived, a woman staying at the same hotel had been bitten by a shark. Because of that, we stayed near the shore with the children, not going very far out into the ocean at all and spending most of our time in the pool. Carol Ann took diving lessons from a private instructor while we were there and learned to dive off the high board. I think she had a childhood crush on her instructor, but I know one thing for sure. We all fell in love with the pool!

We were eating all of our meals out and our little Barbie's favorite thing to eat was chicken. She would have eaten it three times a day if she could. We always teased her that her love for chicken stemmed from the fact that I had eaten a big chicken dinner at Frankenmuth the night before she was born. On our trip, Jack told her she could only order chicken once a day. I thought she might even order it for breakfast, but she held off every day for lunch or dinner.

We had a big scare at dinner one night when Ronnie got a chicken bone stuck in his throat and started choking. I jumped out of my chair and ran around the table to him. Our waitress shouted, "Feed him bread." We did, the bone slid down with the bread, and a crisis was averted. I was so thankful our waitress knew what to do and thankful to God for watching over our little family.

It's always fun to go on vacation, but fun to get home to your own bed too. Mom got her house keys out in Lansing and held them in her hand all the way to her little bungalow on Frank Street.

That trip was a revelation to us, because we loved being in the pool together. The next summer we had one put in at our home. It was lovely—twenty by forty feet in size and three to eight feet deep on a gradual slope. We had a concrete pad surrounding it with plenty of room at one end for lounge chairs. A diving board and two ladders were installed. A bathhouse to change into swimsuits completed it. We had it enclosed with a chain-link fence with a padlock on the gate. Even so, we were required to carry a $100,000 insurance policy on it. As far as entertainment and family fun, it's the best investment we ever made.

With a pool in our yard, I knew I had to learn how to swim. I was deathly afraid of water. Jack used to tease me about gripping the sides of the bathtub when bathing. None of my siblings knew how to swim either—we were all scared to death of the water. When Mom and Dad were a young married couple, they went on a camping trip to Houghton Lake with some friends. They were out on the lake fishing when a storm suddenly came up. Their small boat quickly filled with water, and Mom didn't know how to swim. Dad, being an excellent swimmer, was able to bring her to shore, but that experience frightened Mom so much that she didn't want any of us kids to go near the water.

I talked my three sisters, Peg, Ag, and Edna, into going with me to the YWCA for swimming lessons. For our first lesson, the male instructor put a brick on the floor of the pool and told us to go down and get it. I said, "I wouldn't go down for that brick if you offered me a thousand dollars." We all skedaddled out of the pool, and that ended that.

For safety's sake, I knew I had to learn how to swim in case a child ever needed help. I overcame the fear of water by myself. I filled our bathroom sink with water. With my feet firmly planted on the floor, where I knew I could lift my head out of the water any time, I taught myself how to immerse my face in the water, blow bubbles out, turn my head to the side, breathe in, and repeat. Overcoming that fear, I soon became an excellent swimmer and also went on to take classes to learn the Heimlich maneuver and how to expel water if someone has ingested it and CPR if someone is having a heart attack. My friend Metha Shew, who used to be a lifeguard, taught me how to dive. Everyone in our family became excellent swimmers.

Before the pool was completed, our youngest, Jerry, had a horrific accident. There were just open fields with high weeds across the street from our house. He was running through those fields barefoot, even though it was forbidden. There was a broken bottle nestled down in the weeds. He saw the bottle and jumped over it, but there was a stick in the neck of the bottle, and he came down on the stick. That in turn catapulted the bottle into the back of his leg at the ankle. How he got home was a miracle. His foot was almost severed.

I was in shock and don't know how I was able to hold it together, but I wrapped his leg in a towel and my neighbor, Mr. Kozal, took me to Emergency at Hurley Hospital.

Jerry was in surgery for several hours. He had completely severed the tendon in his leg. They are like elastic, and it had snapped up his leg. The doctor had to draw that back down. Then, it was held in place by a button—just a regular button about the size of a nickel—sewed to the bottom of Jerry's heel. His leg was enclosed in a cast up to his knee, just his toes peeking out. The doctor told me that he would probably be crippled.

I know I was in shock because I didn't cry until I got home; then, I broke down. The tears began to flow, and there was no stopping them. My baby boy.

It was a hard summer for Jerry because the pool was finished shortly after his accident, and all the other kids were swimming, and he was sitting in a wheelchair watching. I have to say that when the other kids weren't in the pool, they were very generous about giving their time to Jerry, rolling him around the block in his wheelchair.

Midsummer, Jerry got his cast off, and I asked the surgeon if it was okay for him to go in the pool. He said, "Absolutely! Underwater therapy is the best thing that could happen for him." So Jerry got christened in the pool right away, and in just a couple of days, he was swimming like a little tadpole. With that water therapy every day, it wasn't long before he was running. When the surgeon heard that, he was so amazed he stopped by our house to see Jerry just to make sure it was true. So when I say that the pool was the best investment we ever made, it was in many ways, but this was the very best reason. Our baby boy wasn't crippled. Thank you, Father, for taking care of my youngest. Our family keeps you busy. Later on, in high school, our son who the surgeon said would probably be crippled earned a varsity letter in track.

We had so much fun with that pool. Our neighborhood in Mary Gardens was peppered with kids just like our neighborhood on Pierson Road. I opened the pool every afternoon at one o'clock. Every neighborhood child was welcome to join us if their mom would come to watch them and if they obeyed the "no running" rule. Of course, all the kids wanted to come, and they were made welcome. We had a pool full of kids every day, and we enjoyed sharing it. It was a very nice way to get acquainted with all of our neighbors.

~⁓

The kids were enrolled at Westwood Heights School on Jennings Road, and this would be Jerry's kindergarten year. All four of our kids in school—the years were flying by so fast!

The bus stop to pick the kids up for school was two blocks away, so I would walk down to meet the kindergarten bus at noon to meet Jerry. One day, our neighbor's boy took a condom to school for Show and Tell. I have no idea what he "told" about it, but when the kindergarten bus pulled up, he had that condom out the window, and it was stretched out almost as long as the bus. His mother, who was at the bus stop also, was speechless, but we had lots of laughs about it over the years.

Barbie was in the second grade when we moved there. She had a secret admirer. One day, Mr. Gaus' son, Butchie (Lee), who was in her class at school, brought her his mother's diamond engagement ring. He told Barbie, very seriously, that his mom had lots of diamond rings and she wouldn't miss it. When Barbie got home from school that day, we walked together to the Gaus home where she returned the ring to Mrs. Gaus. Young love thwarted!

CHAPTER 46

We had only lived in Mary Gardens a short time when my sister, Edna, and her husband, Frank, bought the lot across the street from us and built a home. They had three daughters, Linda, Louise, and Kathy. They were very close in age to our girls, and we were so happy to have them living near us. They went to school and all the school functions together. Best friends.

Dr. Guyon and his wife Marianne also built a home in Mary Gardens one block over from us. They were still our family physicians.

There was quite a lot of building going on in our subdivision, and it was filling up fast. Mr. Gaus and his brother were building another home on our street just around the curve. They were putting some fancy brick trim on the house for added curb appeal. The process was to put extra mortar under the bricks and then squish it down, giving the appearance more texture. Ronnie and Jerry thought they had made a mistake; it didn't look like the brick at our house. So after the workmen went home, they "fixed it" for them. They took sticks and scraped all the excess mortar off. It had to be done all over the next day.

We had a procession of pets while the kids were living at home. We had Prince, a German shepherd; Ginger, a Collie; and Duchess, another German shepherd. We also had Myrtle the Turtle amble into our yard one day. I let the kids dig a hole in our backyard about five feet across, a foot deep, and fill it with water for Myrtle. We went out one day to find broken shells by her little pool. Myrtle and the babies were gone.

Our summer fun always centered on the pool. Carol Ann and Barbie had summer birthdays, so pool parties were always popular. I still opened the pool up every day at one o'clock, and the same rules applied—all are welcome to come if Mom will come to oversee you and no running.

In the summer, I also coached the Little League team. All the neighborhood boys wanted to play, but their dads all worked, so I said I would do it. My brother, Don, owned Crane's Furniture on Clio Road. I called him and asked if he would sponsor our team, which he was pleased to do. All the boys got black shirts and baseball caps with the Crane's Furniture name and logo embroidered in white. We had a wonderful time together and won about half of our games. I made sure every boy got time on the field no matter what their age or ability was. Winning is not the most important thing—being part of the team is. The baseball diamond backed up to the A&W on Clio Road, so after the game, we would go to their window, and I would treat them to an icy cold Root Beer.

Jerry continued to be my little bundle of busy dynamite. He and Ron were tossing a soft football around in the living room when Jerry fell, hitting his forehead on the marble window sill and splitting his forehead open. We had to rush him to Dr. Guyon's for stitches. Not long after that, he was running to go out the front door, missed the door handle, and his arm went through the glass storm door, cutting his wrist. It was back to the doctor's for stitches. Dr. Guyon told me that when you have several children, it seems like there's always one who takes the bumps for all of them. In our case, it was Jerry.

When it came time to get the stitches out, my little bundle of busy dynamite didn't want to take time to go to the doctor's. He pleaded with me to remove the stitches myself. I told him that I would if he would stay still and not move. I sterilized my manicuring scissors, he laid very still, and I removed the stitches. I did the same when the stitches on his wrist were healed.

Late August turned our thoughts to shopping for school clothes. Ron and Jerry were usually pleased with what I chose for them and would rather stay home and play. Carol Ann and Barb looked forward to a day downtown choosing their own outfits. It was an end of summer ritual.

Their favorite store was Smith-Bridgman's. At noontime, we'd take a break and have lunch at the mezzanine counter where we enjoyed watching all the people riding the escalator. Our goal was to finish the shopping in one trip, but sometimes, we had to make a return trip. Smith-Bridgman's had a huge variety in styles and a wide price range, making it a fun place to shop.

Before we knew it, Labor Day had passed, and the first day of school had arrived. I set the alarm clock early and was the first one to get up. There were always a few bumps in the road the first day with nervous excitement. There were lunches to be packed, and I thought the world would end if the kids didn't have a hot breakfast and then a sigh of relief when they left for the bus stop.

We always bought "sensible" shoes for our girls to wear to school—loafers or saddle shoes. They left the house in them, but when they got on the bus, they changed out to their patent leather dress shoes or tennies. No way were they wearing those dorky shoes to school. And I always made sure all the kids had their coats buttoned when the weather called for it, but as soon as they got around the curve at the corner, the buttons and zippers were undone. Little did Mom and Dad know.

They had a dress code at Westwood Heights School. The girls had to wear dresses, and they had to be a certain length. If they looked too short, they had to kneel down on the floor. If their dress didn't touch the floor, they were sent home.

There wasn't any Internet, tablets, or iPhones for kids to spend their time on. The girls would hurry home from school, and the three of us would watch *General Hospital* to hear the latest drama taking place with Luke and Laura. But what they were really waiting for was the program that followed when the announcer would proclaim, "This is American Bandstand *Live* from Philadelphia with Dick Clark!" The boys just wanted to be outside.

Central Methodist Church had completed their building fund and were now in their new facility on Ballenger Highway. My mother, my sisters, and I continued to be involved in the church activities. There were ten circles of ladies in the WSCS. Edna and I were chair-ladies of two of the circles, and Peg was president over all ten. I also served as a greeter once a month and helped with the annual bazaar. Mom was always there too, serving in many different capacities. We all worked in the kitchen when a dinner was being served.

We often went out for dinner after church, and we all loved going to the Bavarian Inn at Frankenmuth for family-style chicken dinner. We were on our way there one Sunday when Jack got pulled over by the police while passing through the little village of Clio. At the traffic light, the car ahead of us was turning left, so Jack pulled around them and continued on. Apparently, this is against the law in Clio. Soon, we heard the siren behind us. The police officer came up, got Jack's information, explained what he had done wrong, and proceeded to write out a ticket. The police officer had a bandolier around his waist that held his bullets. Ron, who was about four at that time, put his little hand out the window, carefully ran his finger over the top of the bullets, and in awestruck admiration asked, "Are these real bullets?" With that, the police officer looked in the back-seat, saw the four kids, and said to Jack, "You need the money more than I do, mister! Just count this as a warning!" With that, he put his book of tickets away and said, "Have a nice day." Nice save, Ron.

Just as much fun for us was to get fast food at the McDonald's that opened up on Clio Road near Pasadena. That may have been the first location that opened in Flint. I'm not sure about that, but McDonald's were just beginning to appear around the nation. Jack could stop on the way home from work and bring dinner with him. He worked until 9:00 p.m. on Mondays and Fridays, but McDonald's was a quick midweek dinner, and the kids loved it. The hamburgers were 15¢, and the fries were 10¢—family dinner for six served up hot and delicious for $1.50. We had milk with it instead of buying soda.

I loved being a Mom

Jack always had a dream of opening up a small restaurant called Curnsburgers. That dream never materialized, but the kids did love it when Dad cooked the Curnsburgers at home and served them with homemade milkshakes.

Our family loved milk—everyone except me, that is. We had six gallons of milk delivered every other day by McDonald Dairy. They didn't have a box big enough to hold six gallons, so they made one for us that we kept on our back porch. After a while, the delivery man just started carrying the milk in the house and put it in the refrigerator for me.

~~~

I was so happy being a stay-at-home mom. We no longer made tents out of the dining room table, but we often had lunch on the picnic table out by the pool. Jack and I loved to dance, and we would dance for the kids. We'd put a stack of records on and dance in the family room. All four of the kids would line up on the sofa and bounce. They would sit there and bounce as long as we danced.

Christmas at our house was always spectacular. Jack and I wanted to "wow" the kids with a mountain of presents. That was another aspect of my life that was a holdover from the depression years when there wasn't much under our tree.

I enjoyed decorating the house for Christmas, the pungent aroma of pine throughout the house. The tinsel on the tree had to be smoothed out to perfection before it went on the tree, just like my mom always did it. Many of the decorations were handmade. I had a large Bible that was too big for daily use, but on Christmas, it came out of its box, was placed on our coffee table, opened to the birth of Jesus in the Gospel of Luke, and marked with a big burgundy velvet bookmark.

Our nativity scene was large and played a prominent role in our Christmas celebration. The stable was made of wood taken from a one-hundred-year-old barn. The holy family and the animals were probably ten or twelve inches high. The little baby Jesus was separate from the manger, and over the years, all of our kids carried Him around in their little baby fingers, and He survived all those years without so much as a chip.

I baked dozens and dozens of cookies and made many different kinds of handmade chocolates. I made magic cookie bars, chocolate chip cookies, peanut butter cookies, chocolate cookies with chocolate frosting, oatmeal cookies with chocolate chips and nuts, coconut macaroons, and one of the kids favorites—thimble or thumbprint cookies where you press your thumb into the cookie dough before baking and fill the thumbprint with strawberry or raspberry jam.

For our candy treats, I made buckeyes, turtles, coconut bonbons, chocolate-covered cherries, truffles, cashew clusters, chocolate creams, and chocolate-covered caramels, Jack's favorite. The handmade chocolates are easy to make, just time-consuming, but they look so impressive. Cookie and candy trays made delightful gifts.

I never learned how to make fudge. I tried several recipes, but never mastered that skill. It never set up so you could pick a piece up—just came out too soft. My candy and cookie recipes have been used so many years; some of them are barely legible anymore.

We had a few Christmas traditions that just kind of fell in place. For one thing, we always had Sara Lee Pecan Coffee Cake with our breakfast on Christmas morning. Another tradition was watching the movie *Miracle on 34th Street*— the old version with Maureen O'Hara, John Payne, and Natalie Wood.

On Christmas Eve, we would let the kids choose one thing from the wrapped gifts under the tree. After they went to bed, Jack and I would put out the things that weren't wrapped. I would put dresses for Carol Ann and Barb across the back of the sofa, and things like tricycles for Ron and Jerry were hidden at my mom's house until after they went to bed. Then, Jack would retrieve the items secreted away at Mom's, and she would come with him to have Christmas at our house.

We put Hershey bars with almonds out for Santa in case he got too many cookies. One Christmas Eve, the kids were in bed, not sleeping, but all four of them chattering away, so excited about Christmas. Suddenly, Carol Ann shouted, "Santa's here! I just heard him bite into a nut!" I heard eight feet hit the floor, but we had to quickly get them settled down in bed again so Jack and I could finish putting the gifts out.

The year the girls got full-sized bikes for their big gift, we thought they would be so thrilled to see them standing by the tree. I was poised with my camera, just waiting to capture their excited expression—that moment of joy. Still groggy with sleep, they didn't even go near them, just kind of stumbled to the sofa and sat down in a daze. I never did get that photo, but they loved the bikes, after they woke up. No Kodak moment for memories.

47

The years were disbursing quickly like a fog disappears when the sun breaks through—time going by way too fast.

It was 1960 and John F. Kennedy was elected president of the United States of America. Our kids were growing up. Slow down the earth, Lord. Let me enjoy their childhood years. Don't let the days fly by so fast.

In our family room, along one wall, we had four built-in desks and a cabinet for my sewing machine. I was sewing one evening when an announcement came on the television about Russia launching the "Sputnik." The Sputnik was an artificial satellite placed in space to orbit the world. I had no idea what that was all about or what the purpose might be, but the race for space dominance had begun. A bit of fear tugged at my heart.

America's answer to Russia's "Sputnik" was to put our own shuttle in space. John Glenn and his team of astronauts were the first to orbit the earth, circling it three times.

But to teen America, nothing compared to the invasion of the Beatles when they came to our country—no, not bugs, but the best-selling band in history. They were famous in England and were coming here to make an appearance on the *Ed Sullivan Show* on black-and-white television. Their fame and music preceded them, and they were welcomed to America by thousands of screaming teen girls.

Jack wouldn't let Carol Ann and Barb watch them on our television because he wanted to watch Sunday night football, so they went across the street to their Aunt Edna and Uncle Frank's house and watched the Beatles' performance with their cousins, Linda, Louise, and Kathy. The Beatles appeared in their Edwardian-style suits and mop-top haircuts with the girls in the live audience screaming so loud you could barely hear their music. Newscasts revealed that almost half of the people in America who owned television sets were tuned in to watch the Beatles that night.

We had quite a few television programs that we enjoyed watching as a family. We loved Jackie Gleason and Red Skelton—their shows were comedy at its finest—back when comedy shows were funny and not off-color or political. Other programs that we enjoyed included *The Lone Ranger, The Gene Autry Show, Death Valley Days, Gunsmoke, Adventures of Superman, Bonanza, The Waltons,* and *Little House on the Prairie.*

They're growing up

As for Jack and me, our marriage was blessed in every way. Jack was everything a woman could want in a husband. He was loving, caring, gentle, and a great provider. We seemed to bring out the best in each other. We thought alike and had the same values and goals. We were spontaneously affectionate with each other—completely devoted to each other. We rarely had a disagreement, but if we did, it was quickly healed. We never went to bed angry with each other.

Jack had a great sense of humor and a cute way of expressing himself. He called a dollop of whipped cream a "dolly-pop." A cul-de-sac to him was a "cuddlesack." And when the Kia automobiles came out, he called them "Kita." I asked him why he did that because there was no "t" in their name, and he said because he liked his word better than theirs. I think he was right!

Jack did things to express his love that probably not one husband in a million would do. He came home one day with his arms filled with mink coats. He spread them out on the back of the couch and said, "Take your pick!" I was surprised, to say the least. He would surprise me in the same way by bringing home suits and dresses for me to choose from.

I honored Jack too by taking time to be attractive when he came home after a busy day at work—things as simple as putting on lipstick and brushing my hair and having dinner ready on the table. That was family time when all six of us would sit down at the table, thank the Lord for our meal, and tell about our day.

After the newness of television wore off, we resumed going out on our Saturday night dates. It kept our love for each other fresh and new. No matter what the week had brought, we both looked forward to going out on Saturday night. Usually, it was dinner and a movie and sometimes dancing.

One Saturday night, we had been to the Capitol Theater for a movie and afterward went across Harrison Street to get a dessert at Uncle Bob's Diner. We were sitting at the counter, and a gentleman approached us. He introduced himself and told us he was a dentist. He said that I had the most beautiful smile he had ever seen and that he would like me to come to work for him. I told him I was a stay-at-home mom to four children, but thanked him for the very nice compliment. If Jack hadn't been sitting right there beside me,

I would have thought this very strange, but evidently, the man was sincere, asking right in front of my husband.

We were still attending Central Methodist Church. With Jack being raised in the Baptist faith, he wasn't in agreement with some of the teaching at that church. I didn't realize it was eating away at him—he never said much about it. He knew that I enjoyed going there because my mom and my sisters went there, and we were active in everything that went on at that church. So I guess he didn't want to rock the boat.

~⁓

I called my mother faithfully every morning at eight thirty to see if she needed anything or wanted to go anywhere. She was my dearest mom. I would do anything for her, and I loved her so much. She was as close to an angel as anyone can be on this earth.

One afternoon, I was at Dr. Sorkin's office on Beach Street for my annual gynecology checkup. My mom was with me, because we were going to do some shopping downtown. Suddenly, the receptionist started screaming, "President Kennedy has been shot!" Everyone present in that office was absolutely stunned, no one knowing what to say or do. Needless to say, Mom and I went home to find out more on the television.

At the kids' school, they announced that President Kennedy had been shot. When Walter Cronkite announced that the president was dead over the loud speakers in the rooms, the kids were all excused for the day. The buses were being lined up to take them home. Barb said that her teacher laid her head down on her desk and sobbed. Most of the kids were crying, too.

We learned later that President Kennedy was fatally shot by Lee Harvey Oswald, a former U.S. Marine. The president was riding in a motorcade in Dallas when Oswald fired a rifle from a window of a book depository, hitting the president in the head.

The entire nation was shocked; the whole world stunned. People wept openly. Everyone was glued to their television sets, hoping to learn more about what happened. Some simply prayed.

Anyone who was alive when this tragic event occurred can tell you exactly where they were at that given time. It's something you never forget.

CHAPTER 48

I search among earth's lovely words to find
The meaning of a word loved by mankind:
The brief word "Mother", yet no pens express
A definition for her tenderness,
Her constancy, her selfless love, her care
I search for words for her—they are not there.
For one might quite as well strive to define
The sun's gold warmth, the night skies' silver shine,
The earthy fragrance of the furrowed loam,
The dear, essential things that make a home:
Fire and lamplight and a table spread,
The waiting comfort of a clean, smooth bed,
And a mother teaching a kneeling child to pray,
Thus guiding a dear one on his upward way.
Ah, where are the scholarly wise ones on our earth
Who can estimate a good, true mother's worth
(Author Unknown)

December 9, 1964, was one of the darkest days of my life. My beloved mom went home to be with the Lord. Nothing compared to it except the day my dad passed away.

Mom had developed a health problem known as congestive heart failure. That heart problem causes a buildup of fluid in your lungs, making it difficult to breathe. Mom would call me when she had an attack, and day or night, I would drop everything to go to her. Sometimes, at two or three o'clock in the morning, she would call, and Jack and I would rush to her. More than once, we found her with her bedroom window raised, her head resting on the window sill, gasping for air. A few days in the hospital would usually get her feeling better.

But not this time. It was a cold, snowy, dark winter day. She was in Flint Osteopathic Hospital on Ballenger Highway. I went to the hospital every day to spend the afternoon. Mom seemed to be responding, and I thought she would be home in a day or two. On the Saturday before her death, I fed her what turned out to be her last meal for she was in a coma the next morning.

When I came to visit the afternoon of December 9, she was resting quietly, still in the coma. She had a stack of get-well cards on her bedside table from family members and friends. I began reading the cards—the messages so sweet and tender. My heart overflowed with love for my mom, reading all of these loving messages, and I began to weep. I didn't want Mom to hear me crying, so I went out in the hall. I was standing outside of Mom's door when a kind nurse put her arms around me and said, "Why don't you go home. You've been here all afternoon. I promise we'll call you if there's any change." I will forever regret that I left, but I kissed my mom goodbye and whispered, "I love you, Mom," and went home.

It was dinnertime when I got home. The kids were all home from school. I made a quick supper of Lipton chicken noodle soup. Before we sat down to eat, the phone rang. It was the hospital calling to say I should come. When I arrived, all of my siblings were there too. They didn't take us to Mom's room. They took us to the chapel. That's when I knew she was gone. We didn't get to see Mom.

On the way out of the hospital, we walked past the delivery rooms, and I heard a newborn baby utter its first cry. My mom taking her last breath and a newborn taking its first. The world will go on, but I didn't know how I could go on without my mom. How would I live without my dearest mom, my best friend, my confidant who I could share anything with and know that the bond of love would never be broken? All of her life, she gave me (all of us kids) the richest gift anyone can give—unconditional love.

My mother was an amazing woman. I always marveled that she did so much and did everything well. She was an excellent housekeeper. Our home was always immaculate. I remember going to sleep to the hum of the vacuum cleaner because Mom cleaned house every night after we went to bed. She was an outstanding cook, seldom using a recipe. Just a pinch of this and a pinch of that, but everything always came out perfect. She was an accomplished seamstress and made most of our clothes.

Another thing that always impressed me about my mother was her impeccable appearance. She was always neat and attractive. One of the most incredible things about her—I never saw my mom without nylons and midhigh heels. It didn't matter what she was doing, whether cleaning the house, doing the washing, scrubbing a floor, or on vacation, whatever. I never saw her without heels and nylons.

Oh, Mom, I love you so much. How can I live without you?

CHAPTER 49

The eight thirty time period when I had called my mom every day were now times of weeping, missing my mom and missing making our plans for the day. I moved my Bible study time up to eight thirty, and that helped a little bit. For my family's sake, I tried to keep our home life like it was before, but it was difficult.

Mom passed away in December, and Jack and I were having our eighteenth wedding anniversary on January 17, about six weeks after Mom passed away. Our anniversary fell on a Sunday that year, and I took the kids to church alone. Jack didn't go that day. So the kids were all in their Sunday school classes, and I was sitting by myself, quite near the front of the church.

I've mentioned before that they seldom gave an altar call in that church, but that Sunday, Rev. Harold Nessel preached a beautiful sermon and gave an altar call at the conclusion. The church was filled to capacity. I went forward to accept Christ as my Savior. I was the only person in that packed church who went forward. And I tell you truly, I did not walk that aisle under my own power. Someone (the Holy Spirit) literally propelled me out of my seat and down that aisle. It's difficult to express what happened. I felt as though I was floating. I knew something wonderful had happened, but I stood at that altar all alone; no one came to counsel me or to explain salvation. No one put their arm around my shoulders to rejoice with me—not the pastor, nor deacon, an usher, or layperson. Church was dismissed, and everyone went their own way as I just stood there in front of the altar all alone. I went home as clueless about salvation as I was before, but the joy in my heart was amazing. I was simply bubbling over with happiness, having a feeling of ecstasy that I never wanted to end.

In retrospect, I believe I was saved that day, even though I didn't understand it. I believe that if I had died that night, I would have gone to heaven because I took that step of inviting Jesus into my heart as Lord and Savior.

My mom had been in heaven just a short time, and I can just imagine her at Jesus's feet pleading with Him to "get my baby saved."

～～

Where had the years flown? The years go by so fast. It seems like just yesterday the kids were babies; now, they were all in their teens. Carol Ann was in her senior year at Hamady High School, and my baby boy was thirteen years old.

We were pretty strict with the girls. They were allowed to date, but they had a midnight curfew. They were good about obeying it, but they felt if they were in the driveway, that was "home." If they didn't come right in, Jack would start flashing the porch light. They knew that if he had to get up a second time and had to flash it again, he would start down the steps; so when the second flash occurred, they came right in.

Carol Ann was dating her high school sweetheart Jim Lusk. They started going together when she was fifteen and started talking about marriage pretty quickly into their relationship. Jim gave Carol Ann an engagement ring, and Jack and I just about flipped out. Our little girl wanting to get married? We liked Jim very much, he was a nice polite young man, but just like most parents, we thought they were way too young and wanted them to wait. I drove Carol Ann over to Jim's home and made her return the ring.

You just can't stop young love—especially when it's true love. I peeked in Carol Ann's bedroom one night when I thought she was doing homework, and she was gone! I hadn't seen her go out the door and was really alarmed. I sent the boys out to look for her, but they knew where to find her. She had gone out her bedroom window, right over the top of the window box filled with geraniums, to meet her sweetheart.

Like my parents consenting to let me marry Jack, we gave our blessing to Carol Ann and Jim. We agreed that they could get married after she graduated from high school. Carol Ann was voted homecoming princess, graduated with honor cords, and was salutatorian of her senior class. They were married later that summer.

CHAPTER 50

I continued with my Bible study period at that early morning hour after the kids got on the school bus, and the house was quiet. For my study guide at that time, I was using a book entitled *Streams in the Desert* by Mrs. Charles E. Cowman. For each day in the year, there is a Bible verse followed by an appropriate lesson or discussion. Then, I would spend time with the Lord in prayer.

It was December 9, exactly one year after my mom had passed away. The Bible verse for that day was Luke 8:52, "She is not dead, but sleepeth." Sleepeth, in the Bible, symbolizes peace, rest, and the promise of an awakening.

I only remember reading the Bible verse that day; I recall absolutely nothing of what the lesson may have been about. I missed my mother so much, and it was the one-year date of her death. I started crying. With tears coursing down my face, I began to tell Jesus how much I missed her. Then, I had the most beautiful thing happen that anyone could imagine. I had an out-of-body experience!

I was floating through space, over endless fields of beautiful pastel-colored flowers, like wild flowers—for as far as I could see, fields of flowers. The sun was shining brightly, and it was so peaceful there. A feeling of euphoria surrounded me—a joy that I cannot explain. I was happy to be there.

It wasn't like some out-of-body experiences that I've heard about. I didn't see Jesus, any family members, or a tunnel with a light at the end of it. Nothing like that—just the fields of flowers, the peace, joy, and feeling of euphoria. And I was floating over the top of it, slowly passing over these fields of flowers.

How long a period of time that passed, I cannot say. After a time, I was back at home, sitting again at my kitchen table with my devotional book opened, my heart exploding with great joy.

That intense joy and feeling of euphoria remained in my heart. So on December 13, the one-year anniversary of my mom's burial, I decided to read once again the December 9 lesson, hoping to have that phenomenal, beautiful spiritual experience again. Imagine my surprise to discover that Luke 8:52 was not there in that book on December 9! I thumbed through the pages of that book, and it's not in there anywhere. It was a gift from God on that particular day just for me. It was a miracle from God to comfort me and reassure me that my mother was in heaven.

Thank you, Lord. You are more than wonderful to me. I will never forget the beautiful miracle You gave me. You changed the printing in a book for just one day. You gave me a glimpse of heaven. I felt the presence of God. The joy in my heart, the beauty of heaven, the peace that I felt will be remembered forever. I would have been content to stay. Someday, I will stay, and I will see Jesus face to face and be reunited with all my loved ones.

I still have that book; I keep it in my desk, near at hand. My visit to heaven happened fifty-three years ago, but I remember it as though it happened yesterday. Before retelling this experience again, I went through that book once more page by page just to make certain I did not make a mistake. That verse is not there on December 9 or on any other page in the entire book.

51

Bob Hope was coming to Flint! Bob Hope was a famous Hollywood comedian, actor, singer, and dancer. He had made countless movies; probably, most people would recall his "road" shows filmed with Bing Crosby, another famous Hollywood star. However, this legendary comedian is best remembered and loved for the USO performances he put on for American military personnel. For almost fifty years, Bob Hope traveled the world putting on these shows to lift the morale of our service men and women.

Because of Bob Hope's unique connection with the military and Jack being disabled Navy, Jack was asked if we would like to pick Bob Hope up at Bishop Airport and take him to the IMA where his show was to be held. Would we? It would be an honor.

Bob Hope arrived at Bishop Airport in his own private jet. We (and another couple we didn't know) drove Bob Hope and his business manager, who was traveling with him, to the IMA and back to Bishop after his performance. I was a little intimidated by his presence, but not Jack. After all, he had met a president!

The IMA was packed out with admirers who were looking forward to being entertained by this American icon. Bob Hope was famous for his witty one-liner jokes and always made people laugh. He didn't disappoint. The audience roared with laughter time after time by his humorous comments. He kept them in stitches for almost two hours.

When Bob Hope was ready to leave, we were chatting on the tarmac while his pilot readied the plane for takeoff. Jack was presented with a small black jewelry box. Inside was a pair of gold cufflinks made in the shape of Bob Hope's famous "ski nose" profile. We were told that they could not be purchased anywhere; they could only be obtained directly from the star himself. What a nice gift—a rare piece of memorabilia, a great conversation piece, and maybe of value to collectors.

Soon, the conversation turned to golf. Bob Hope had a tournament named after him, the Bob Hope Classic, that was played in Palm Springs, California, every year. We told him how very much we would enjoy seeing this tournament. Bob Hope had his manager write our name and address in a little spiral notebook he carried with him, and we were promised tickets. The tickets never did arrive, and we ended up watching it on television. But we felt very honored to have even a small part in Bob Hope's visit to Flint.

~⁀ɔ

After church one Sunday, while we were still attending Central Methodist Church, we stopped to chat with the pastor in the vestibule. That was not unusual, and I thought nothing of it until Jack asked the pastor, "Why don't you ever give an altar call?" When Pastor Lloyd Nixon answered, "Oh, that's old fashioned. We don't do that anymore," I thought Jack was going to explode. I knew this had been building up inside of him for a long time. Jack continued, "If you don't ever ask people to accept Christ, how will they ever get saved?" Alluding to his background in the car business, Jack said, "I would never sell a car if I didn't ask people if they wanted to buy it. There might be just one person in the congregation that doesn't know Christ, maybe a visitor who has never been asked that question." When the pastor didn't respond, Jack blurted out, "Well, you can take our names off the roll. We'll never be back!" And we never did.

I was stunned, shocked, speechless, devastated, and felt betrayed. I didn't want to leave that church. A good-sized part of my life centered on the work I did in that church. We had been members there for eighteen years. Our children were all baptized there. We had learned the privilege of tithing there. I had been in charge of the nursery when the kids were little. I was a greeter at the door to welcome people and knew just about everybody who attended there. I was chairlady of a circle for years. I worked on the bazaar every year and helped in the kitchen when dinners were being served. And I still didn't understand salvation.

Jack was firm in his decision, and true to his word, we never set foot in that church again. The sad part was we didn't go anywhere. We visited here and there, searching for a church home. I remember visiting North Baptist Church where Dr. Cedric Sears was pastor. He gave an altar call at the end of his sermon, and one of his ushers physically took hold of me and tried to pull me down to the altar. That embarrassed me and drove me even further away from the church. We continued to tithe and put our money in where we were visiting. For several years, we sent our tithe money to John Hagee Ministries that we watched on television.

Those seemed like lost years to me. I don't know how long we went without a home church, but it was a few years. I missed the music, the preaching, the fellowship, and the "being together" of a real church service.

～

America was deeply involved in the Vietnam War during this time period. Some had the audacity to call it a "conflict," but when almost 60,000 American service members died, I call that war. Those who were over there in those rain-soaked jungles getting shot at knew it wasn't just a conflict—it was war, and war is hell.

Many Americans didn't approve of the war and didn't support the soldiers when they returned home, which was a travesty. We heard about them getting cursed at and spit on. Some of those boys went to school with our kids. They weren't over there because they wanted to be. They were young men who just wanted to be home, living their lives. They went because their country called.

Both of our boys had to register for the draft. Ron's number was so high, he never got called to service, and Jerry was deferred because of the injury suffered when he was a child and his foot was almost severed. There was a big knot on the back of his heel, and the medical doctors said that he would never be able to wear Army boots. Jerry also had a broken eardrum that we didn't even know about. So thank God our sons were spared, but my heart goes out to those who did go. To me, they are American heroes.

～

Barb graduated the year after Carol Ann. She had been honored throughout high school. She was voted Prom Princess in her freshman year. Her senior year, she was voted Princess on the Homecoming Court and the Prom Court. She and her date, O. D. Edmonds, who she later married, were voted the Cutest Couple.

When it came to cars, Jack was more than generous with our boys. In their senior year in high school, Ron got a Corvette, and Jerry got a Buick convertible.

Cars had always flowed through our family like a stream going downhill. With Jack in the business, I never knew what I'd be driving, but they were always new. Over the years, we had forty-one just red convertibles, not including other colors. And that was just convertibles.

Jack came in the beauty shop one day when I was getting my hair done, tapped on the hair drier, and said, "I just sold your car." He handed me a set of keys and said, "There's a new car in the same spot you were parked in." Or he would stop by work, exchange keys with me, and there would be a different car in the spot where I had parked that morning. It wasn't uncommon for him to do that.

We had one car that we held onto for quite a few years. Mrs. Sloan (Sloan Museum) traded her car in for a new model. Jack jumped at the opportunity to buy the trade-in. It was a 1965 baby blue Buick convertible with white leather interior and white top. We called it our "ice cream car" and only took it out on beautiful sunny days. Jack displayed it at the Sloan Museum Auto Fair that is held each summer on the lawn at the Sloan Museum.

～

Oh, what hopes we have for our children. What dreams. Our kids were hilarious, brilliant, loving, and kind. Sometimes when you feel they are making a mistake, you want so much to step in—to change their path, or help them make a different decision. We did our best for them and were so very proud of them. We raised them in a Christian home, prayed over them, provided for them, and set a good example for them.

Over time, our children got married, moved on with their lives, and created their own homes. Carol Ann, Barb, and Ron all married their high school sweethearts. Jerry was a little longer finding his soul mate, but all of our kids were out on their own.

Empty nest syndrome just didn't work for me. I was so lost with all the kids gone. I needed more to fill my days.

I decided to brush up on my shorthand and typing and look for a job. I went to the Flint Public Library and checked out records that dictated correspondence to me, gradually building up my shorthand speed. We rented a typewriter, and I transcribed my notes. That skill learned in high school came back to me very quickly after all those years.

I had been out of the work-force for eighteen years. I heard about an opening at Michigan National Bank and went for an interview with Mr. Cyrus Truran, vice president of the mortgage department, for a position as his secretary. I got hired on the spot and started the following Monday.

Michigan National Bank was located in the Mott Foundation Building on S. Saginaw Street. When you walked into the street level of that huge building, there was an escalator straight ahead and a bank of elevators to the right. The escalator ran to the second floor where Michigan National Bank took up the entire floor. My desk faced the escalator. I enjoyed very much being in the workforce again, interacting with people every day. It was very enjoyable working with the public and being a small part of helping people acquire a home.

My niece Margie and her husband John wanted to buy a one-hundred-year-old farm in Linden. They had tried several places but weren't able to get a mortgage because the property was so old. I spoke to Mr. Truran about them and helped secure a mortgage for them. John was on supervision at Buick, and there should never have been a question with the other places they tried; they were as good as gold.

While I was working there, the auditors came in one day. Everyone was on pins and needles, including me. Being in the mortgage department, I worked with figures in the millions of dollars. The auditors worked an entire day in our department alone. I was called into the conference room where they were working. They informed me that my figure was off 10¢. I didn't think that was a big deal, and I said, "How about I buy you guys a cup of coffee, and we forget the dime." The auditors replied rather sternly, "No, we're going over these figures until we find the dime." And that's what we did—started over at the beginning, a tedious job, but we searched until we found the 10¢ error.

Jack came downtown often and stopped in at the bank to take me out for lunch. We went to the Masonic Temple one day—great food at a great price. We were seated a couple of tables away from C. S. Mott, Flint's famous philanthropist. He was by himself, and I've always regretted that when he was finished dining, I didn't go over and introduce myself and tell him how very much I enjoyed the Mott Foundation classes that were offered each year.

When the class opportunities were listed in *The Flint Journal* every fall, I always signed up for something. I took sewing classes at Doyle School. At Durant School, I learned how to knit—first a simple scarf and then advancing to socks and mittens. I took classes in Bridge, too, but over the years, my favorite was the class where I learned how to make petit fours and many other exotic desserts. Our instructor in that class shared a recipe with us that she called the Hundred-Dollar Cake. She and her husband were vacationing in New York, staying at the Waldorf Astoria. After enjoying a slice of moist, dense chocolate cake for dessert one evening, she requested a copy of the recipe, and the chef presented it to her. When they checked out, there was a charge on their bill for $100 for the cake recipe. That's where it got the name, and it is a wonderful cake!

Over the years, I signed up for so many classes. I wish I had thanked Mr. Mott that day.

⌒

After a period of time working at Michigan National Bank, I decided to see if I could get a job with General Motors. There was no place to advance at the bank; I would always have the same position, and the salary wasn't that much. It couldn't hurt to try. I made an appointment with the personnel department at General Motors Parts Division on Bristol Road, went in, and took the tests and passed. I was hired to work in the stenographic pool. Some thought I would regret making that move, but I never did. I met many girls there who ended up being lifetime friends.

Grandma

We're
grandparents!

CHAPTER 52

I enjoyed my job at General Motors Parts Division tremendously. Where I had started out in the stenographic pool, in three years' time, I had advanced to private secretary to Carl Madsen, director of Marketing and Research. He had a huge office with a private bathroom. My office was outside his door—Mahogany Row.

I advanced quickly because I was a perfectionist and always willing to go the extra mile. If they needed me for anything, I would go in early, stay late, or work through my lunch hour. I loved and appreciated my job and the abundance of friends I had in the workplace.

Grandchildren were arriving on the scene too. They were so precious to our hearts, and we loved spending time with them. They loved to come visit too and spend the night with Grandma and Grandpa.

Barb and Ron came over one day to tell us that Jack Van Impe was coming to Flint, and they wanted Jack and me to join them to go see him. Jack told them we would go.

Jack Van Impe was well-known for his hell and brimstone preaching. I didn't want to go, but didn't say anything. I thought by the time the designated day arrived, they would forget all about it, but they didn't. When that Sunday arrived and Barb, Ron, and Jack were still planning on going, I said that I didn't want to go. Jack said, "Yes, we're going. I promised the kids." So we did.

I would never be the same after that day. What a sermon Van Impe preached! He was at the IMA, and it was filled with excited people anticipating his sermon. He was in great form preaching the hell and brimstone he was famous for. It was enough to scare you to death. I knew I had sin in my life, and I thought I was going to hell for sure. Ron wanted me to go down front and even said that he would go with me, but I wouldn't be budged out of my seat. I regret disappointing my husband, my son, and my daughter that day.

But that's not the end of the story. When I went to bed that night, I couldn't sleep. I got out of bed and paced the floors, got back in bed, couldn't sleep, got up again, and paced the floors. Five times! The Holy Spirit had ahold of me, and He wasn't letting go. A battle was being fought for my soul. At five o'clock that morning, after being up all night, I got down on my knees in our family room and pleaded for God's forgiveness. I knew I had sin in my life and was not living a Christlike life. I repented and begged Jesus to come into my heart and save me. Oh, what a feeling of relief flooded my soul and my heart. I had to go to work that day, but I was so happy my heart was singing.

After being out of church for several years, our search for a home church started in earnest. The Lord led us to Gilead Baptist Church on Carpenter Road where Pastor Richard Slaght lovingly answered all my questions and calmed all my fears.

He explained to me that Jesus died on the cross to pay for our sins and that if we asked forgiveness for our sins and turned from our sinful ways and invited Jesus into our hearts as Lord and Savior, we would be saved—now and forever, eternally. When I protested that I "wasn't good enough to be saved," Pastor Slaght said that none of us are good enough and quoted Romans 3:23, "All have sinned and come short of the glory of God," and that Jesus wants us to come to Him just as we are.

I prayed the sinner's prayer right there, right then. I repeated after the pastor a simple prayer, confessing my sin and asking God for my forgiveness, in faith believing that Jesus died on the cross for my sin, that God raised Him from the dead, and that He now sits at the right hand of God. Then, I asked Him to come into my heart and be my Lord and Savior.

Baptism followed on a Sunday shortly thereafter, and Jack was so thrilled that I finally "got it" he called and invited our whole family to visit our church to share in my newfound joy. I was immersed and thankful that I wasn't afraid to go underwater. God was preparing me all those years ago.

I'm not saying that I learned everything and understood everything right then, but the Bible held new meaning for me. It was like a light bulb had been turned on in my brain, and knowledge started to come to me. The Bible was revealed to me in a new way. I grew under the teaching of Pastor Slaght. And he gave an altar call every Sunday, which made Jack very happy.

I'm so grateful to my heavenly Father for giving His one and only Son so that we can be saved. I'm so in awe of His plan for mankind; the scope of it is difficult to comprehend.

I'm so thankful to Jesus, who loved me so much that He died on the cross for me. Praise His Holy Name. He's my Savior, my Redeemer, Rose of Sharon, sweet Lily of the Valley, my Bright Morning Star. He's my Caring Counselor, Great Physician, Divine Healer, Loving Shepherd, Mighty Warrior, King of Kings, and Lord of Lords. He fills my every need.

I can never thank Him enough for what He did for me. I look forward to the day when it will be my privilege to kneel at His feet, my tears washing over the wounds He bore for my sake, and tell Him how grateful I am.

I'm so thankful for the Holy Spirit who lives within me—my Comforter. He gives me the strength day by day to try and live a life that glorifies my heavenly Father. I know I'm still not living a "perfect" life. I have lots of shortcomings and failures. It grieves me when I hurt my Lord. It's so good to know that He will forgive us if only we will confess our sins and ask for forgiveness.

Salvation had finally been revealed to my heart and my understanding. I truly "was blind, but now I see." It seems impossible that I was blind for so long even though I attended church faithfully most of my life. I love You, Lord.

53

Just Jack and me now rattling around in our house. We did just what you would expect. We built a bigger one!

We bought three acres of land out on Seymour Road that used to be a nursery. It was covered with blue spruce trees; it looked like a Christmas tree forest. We called all of our friends and invited them to come and help themselves to as many trees as they wanted. With their help, we got space for our house and the front yard cleared out. The back acreage had a big pond, and we had sand hauled in to create a nice bottom and a little area to sit out there.

We built an all-brick three-bedroom and two and a half bath home with a front and back porch. It was 2350 square feet, so all of the rooms were big. The guest bath was 10 x 12 feet with a sunken tub. There was no retirement plan of any kind selling cars, so we decided to invest in this house for a retirement nest egg and put the best of everything in it.

⌒

I was enjoying church again. Jack and I jumped in with both feet, attending Bible Study and church on Sundays and the midweek service. We were really soaking up the gospel. Pastor Slaght had us memorize Bible verses, and I still remember the one from our very first class, 1 John 1:9:

> If we confess our sins, He is faithful and
> just to forgive our sins, and cleanse us from all
> unrighteousness.

That verse may have been chosen because of my protests that "I wasn't good enough to be saved."

There wasn't anyone cleaning the church on a regular basis, so Jack and I volunteered for that. We cleaned both levels of the church, including all of the Sunday school rooms and bathroom stalls. We wanted it to look nice and neat, like our home. We felt we were honoring God by cleaning His home. The pastor said that the church hadn't looked that good in a long time.

～

One of Jack's coworker's owned an airplane, and I wanted so much to fly. I had never been in a plane. Jack made arrangements for me to meet his friend, Randy at Dalton Airport on Pierson Road where he kept his plane hangared. When I saw the plane, I was shocked. It was a little two-seater made of canvas. I didn't know whether to say I didn't want to go or what to do. It didn't look very safe. *Well*, I thought, *Randy wouldn't go up in it if it wasn't safe*, so off we went. I couldn't believe it when I looked down, and there was a hole in the canvas between my feet! But I have to say that was one of the most exciting, enjoyable times I've ever experienced. He flew me over our house and pointed out other landmarks that I would recognize. I absolutely loved it and was hooked on flying!

We joined a Travel Club and went to France, Monaco, Italy, Hawaii, and the Bahamas. We had tickets to visit Spain, but Jack fell and broke his hip, so that trip didn't materialize. All of this, across both oceans, before Jack confided in me that he didn't like to fly, so we stopped taking trips.

25th Wedding Anniversary

We had a very special experience while in France. We were shopping one day in Roquebrune-Cap-Martin and were in a candy shop when a school bus pulled up at that very corner. About forty boys piled off the bus. We asked the shop owner about them, and he told us that they were orphans and that they lived in the orphanage at the top of the hill. We called out to them and motioned for them to come into the candy shop. We told the shopkeeper to tell them they could all choose a treat costing $1 American as a gift from us. I wish you could have seen the excitement in that shop as they each chose their favorite. They said that no one had ever done anything for them like that. The shopkeeper translated their thanks to us. We took a group photo of them in front of the shop, and with a lot of hugs exchanged, they happily started the climb up the hill.

A treasured souvenir was brought home from that same little village of Roquebrune—a small nativity scene. The shop where we purchased it was unique in that it seemed to be carved right out of the side of a mountain and was very much cave-like. The man who created the nativity scene was also the owner of the little shop and he autographed it for me.

The set was made of ceramic and hand-painted. Jesus, Mary, and Joseph were in a small stable with a thatched roof. The three wise men, an angel, and a cow completed the set. To make sure it didn't get broken in my luggage, I carried it home on the plane in my lap. It's always been one of my favorite things to display at Christmas and a sweet reminder of the orphan boys we were blessed to meet that day.

We took a cruise and toured some of the Caribbean Islands. Jack said that he had seen all the water he cared to see while he was in the Navy, so that was our only cruise.

～⌒～

Carol Ann and Barb were attending a small church on Red Arrow Road named People's Full Gospel that was pastored by Phillip Bowlin. It was built right in with the neighborhood houses in that area. They were having a mid-week guest speaker and my daughters asked me to join them.

I invited some of my friends at GMPD to go with me, and my long-time friend Lori MacNeil, said that she would like to go. We had seen an ad in the newspaper where Italia Gardens was serving mushroomburgers as a special that night. That sounded good, so after work, Lori and I went there for a delicious burger and then drove out to the church for the 7:00 p.m. service.

The guest speaker gave a great sermon. At the conclusion, he invited anyone who wanted a closer walk with God to come down front to be anointed with oil. Who wouldn't want a closer walk with God? The whole congregation got up; I did too. Folks were lined up all around the perimeter of the church. How I got to be first in line is a mystery to me to this day. It sure wasn't something I wanted; I would have preferred to be last. But somehow there I was, first in line, standing before this pastor. It had to be divine intervention that put me first because if I had any idea of what was going to happen, this lady would have run for the hills and I would have missed a marvelous spiritual blessing. Before the pastor even got to me, I was falling back, gently, down on the carpet, a catcher behind me—someone covering me with a sheet! I was down for the count! Down under the power of the Holy Spirit!

Now, nothing like that had ever happened to me before, and I really didn't understand it. I rested on the floor a minute or two as others went down around me. I was giddy—absolutely drunk on the Holy Spirit.

After the service, I drove Lori to her home, from Red Arrow Road to Lavender Street, which is near the corner of Ballenger Highway and Flushing Road. From there, I was driving on Flushing Road to my house when I saw the dreaded flashers of a police cruiser in my rearview mirror. I pulled over and lowered the window. I swear I was as drunk on the Spirit as a person drunk on alcohol. I looked up at that huge police officer and said in a stupor, "Have you ever been slain in the Spirit?" "No-o-o," he slowly drawled out. "But I know what you're talking about. Do you know you're driving with no headlights?" Of course, I didn't! But Lori didn't know it either! He gave me the ticket anyway and told me to drive safely home.

Lori told me the next day at work that she would go to church with me again sometime if I promised not to lay down on the floor.

Fun with some of my friends from GMPD. I'm far right

When the kids were younger, I always teased them that when they were old enough to make their own peanut butter and jelly sandwiches, I wanted to learn to play golf. There was an old set of men's golf clubs in a storage room at Applegate's that they found in the trunk of a car that someone had turned in. Jack brought them home, and I called my sister, Peg, and made plans to go golfing with her and her husband, Sam. They golfed almost every day, and both were great golfers.

The score for that first round of golf must have been close to three digits, and that was only for nine holes. It was a Saturday, and the course was busy. The clubs were too long for me, being men's clubs, and I didn't know how to hit the ball. After three or four holes,

I said that I would pick up my ball and just walk along while Peg and Sam finished their round. Sam said, "Don't do it. If you quit now, you'll never come back." So I finished the round, and as bad as my game was, I had fun.

We purchased a set of ladies clubs; I took some lessons and loved playing the game. I played three times a week. After work, I played on a league with girls I worked with at Genesee Valley Meadows, right across the street from GMPD. Another night, I played with girls from Buick at Mott Park Golf Course. On the weekends, Jack and I played together, usually with Peg and Sam. It was more than just the game of golf that I enjoyed. It was the camaraderie of being with friends and enjoying the great outdoors.

We joined Davison Country Club and enjoyed many activities there, not just golf. I took lessons from the golf pro at the club and got my golf score down where it was respectable. Dance lessons were offered there too, and we signed up for those. We danced every chance we got, and knowing the various dances only made it more fun.

So between work, church, the grandkids, and golf, our empty nest syndrome was filled with many things, and the time passed by quickly.

~⁓

For many years, the Buick Open Golf Tournament was held at Warwick Hills Country Club in Grand Blanc, Michigan, a suburb of Flint. It was such a pleasure to go there and see all of the professional golfers play. I enjoyed it so much that I took vacation days from work so I wouldn't miss a day of the five-day event.

Of all the great players, Arnold Palmer was my favorite, and one year, I had the chance to meet him. I wanted to get his autograph. When he came off the eighteenth green, Jack and I tried to catch him; but "Arnie's army," as his fans were called, were hot on his trail too. We had been in a good place to catch him, but soon, his "army" started to flood by us. Jack exclaimed, "Oh, I'll never be able to catch him with this wooden leg of mine." Arnie stopped in his tracks.

"Who has a wooden leg?" he asked. When Jack replied, "I do," Arnie turned around and came back to us. He asked Jack if he played golf. Jack responded that he did and added that I would really like his autograph. Arnie said, "I'll do better than that." Turning to his caddy, he said, "After I sign my score card, get a copy of it and give it to her." With a handshake for both of us, he was off, with his admiring "army" following him. Sure to his word, his caddy brought a copy of Arnie's score card out of the building where they verify the cards and gave it to us. Arnie was such a nice man—a true gentleman.

My favorite golf tournament to watch on television is the Masters. It's played every April at Augusta National Golf Club in Augusta, Georgia; it's the only major tournament that is played at the same course every year. In April, the flowers at Augusta are a riot of blossoms, glorious to behold.

One year on our way home from Florida, we decided to take a side trip to Augusta to visit the course, have lunch in the club house, and play a round of golf. We didn't realize how difficult that was! Of course, it's gated, and we were stopped by a uniformed guard at the gatehouse. He was very kind, very polite, but he explained that we couldn't play golf or have lunch in the clubhouse because Mamie Eisenhower, the widow of former president Dwight D. Eisenhower, was in residence on the grounds at that time in their cottage. Eisenhower was a member at Augusta National, and when he was elected president in 1952, the club's membership built a cabin for him—one of ten on the property. It was built by Secret Service security guidelines and has an eagle above the front porch.

The guard said that the only way we could get on the grounds was to play a round with their golf professional, and it would cost $100. We passed our only opportunity. It wasn't the $100—we were both too embarrassed to play with the pro! So our chance was forever lost. That was almost forty years ago; I doubt very much that it's possible to get on the course that way at any cost anymore.

The guard gave us a pamphlet listing all the members at Augusta National for a souvenir. He said that you have to be a millionaire to become a member and be sponsored by another member. According to the guard, many members have never been to the course and that some live overseas. It's just a status symbol to be a member at the most exclusive golf course in the world.

～

We pulled in the church parking lot, and everyone was standing outside, all abuzz. As soon as we got out of our car, we learned that the church doors were locked, the pastor not there. It was later when we learned that he had left his wife and taken up with one of the ladies of our church. Eventually, pastor divorced his wife, and he and our church piano player got married and moved to Florida.

That shook my faith. Pastor Slaght had led me to the Lord, explained salvation to me, and baptized me. I looked up to him as a man of God only to learn that he had feet of clay. Well, it may have shaken my faith, but it didn't break it. I had to keep my eyes on Jesus. People, after all, are human, and as the Bible says, all have sinned and fallen short of the glory of God.

Of course, that broke the church up, with the members all scattering in different directions. We had to find another church home. Again.

CHAPTER 54

The doctor told Jack that he should retire. All those years of standing on pavement selling cars for thirty years had taken their toll. Jack had arthritis all through his body, including his spine. The hip that he had broken when we were preparing for our trip to Spain was making it more difficult and painful to walk. Jack had suffered a great deal of pain throughout the years with his leg. Many times, I've seen pressure boils on the stump of the leg that was amputated. He would still put on his prosthesis and go to work. It's hard to imagine how painful that had to be, but he never complained. Even when he broke his hip, he went to work on crutches. You can't help but admire a man like that.

Farewell party—saying goodbye
to my friends at GMPD

So Jack retired, and soon after, I gave up my job at GMPD. I only had fourteen years of service, so couldn't retire; I just had to walk away. I was given a farewell party and was told that I was the only person ever to be given a party that didn't retire. I had so many friends there and had a huge crowd attend the dinner to celebrate my departure. They had also taken up a collection for me and presented me with a money tree. I had mixed feelings about leaving that night, but was soon enjoying being at home.

We had to find a new church home, and after visiting different churches, we found our heart's desire at Trinity Assembly of God with Pastor David Krist. God's people there just praised the Lord with such joy—it was truly a beautiful thing to be a part of the services there. The presence of the Lord was so evident in that assembly. We continued to grow under the anointed leadership of Pastor Krist.

⌣⌣⌐

A growth about the size of a marble grew on the palm of my right hand. Our family physician told me it was a ganglion and needed surgery. He said that he wouldn't touch it because of all the nerves, tendons, and arteries whirling around it. He made an appointment for me with a surgeon who specialized in such things. Before the surgery date came, I got concerned about the seriousness of the surgery and canceled the appointment. I was afraid I might lose the use of my hand.

As time progressed, the size of the growth enlarged a bit and was becoming troublesome in doing the simplest of tasks. I decided to go ahead with the surgery and rescheduled the appointment.

It was about midnight, Jack had already gone to bed, and I was watching *The 700 Club* on Trinity Broadcasting Network. Ben Kinchlow was going to pray at the end of the program for anyone who needed a healing. In faith, I held my hand outstretched toward the television while Ben prayed. When I got up in the morning, the growth was gone. Thank you, Jesus! It has never come back. That's how quickly God can perform a miracle. It just takes the blink of an eye. He blessed me with a miraculous healing. No wonder I love Him so.

~~~

With some extra time on my hands, I started looking into our family history. My sister, Ag, was interested in genealogy too, so we did a lot of research together.

We went everywhere we could think of that would have family records—court houses, libraries, the Mormon's records, cemeteries, and also quizzed family members. We went through city directories and tracked down and photographed every house related to our family that we could find. It was very time-consuming and somewhat expensive too, because we got all legal documents with seals on them.

I wanted to do Jack's side of the family too, but he wouldn't let me. He said, "My mother and dad didn't want me. They kept all five of the other kids and gave me away." So he forbade me to research his past. I came from a family with five kids and told him it would drive me crazy to know I had five brothers and sisters out there and not know them. I insisted that they probably didn't even know he was born and would be overjoyed to know about him. He wasn't having any of it, and I wouldn't go against his will. If we had pursued the search then, Jack would have learned the truth about his adoption, and it would have meant so much to him. But it was not to be. It was many more years before we found out the truth.

We stayed in our big, retirement investment home, five more years after Jack retired. We had been vacationing in Florida and decided we would like to spend our winters there. So our retirement nest egg home was sold. We purchased a home in Lakeland, Florida, for the winters. I could never totally give up Michigan; it would always be my "home." To spend the summers, we purchased a home on Thomas Street in Mott Park. Mott Park was well known as a community of homes built for all the General Motors employees when GM built their automobile plants in Flint. Thousands of people moved to Michigan to work in the GM plants, and they needed housing.

We were enjoying the best of both worlds—Michigan in the summer and Florida in the winter. Everyone in Florida is from somewhere else it seems and eager to make friends. A conversation opener was always, "Where are you from?" and friendships were quickly made.

When we made our plans to buy a winter home in Florida, I started right away praying for a church. We found one immediately that completely met our needs at Edgewood Baptist Church pastored by Dick Moore. It was quite a bit smaller than our church in Flint.

We were active in the Senior Saints. Jack and I cooked a roast pork dinner for our senior group of about thirty people—complete with dessert. Following the dinner, Jack shared his experience about cooking a meal for President Roosevelt, and they all got a kick out of that. Many of them were veterans too.

On our way to church, we had to pass a strip mall that had a Publix Grocery store in it. The KKK was picketing on the sidewalk out front—something about the pay scale at Publix, according to what we heard. They were in full Klan dress with the cone hats that covered their faces, only exposing their eyes, and long white robes. We had to stop at the traffic light, and they were close enough to reach out and touch us. I have to admit it was scary. Guess I didn't think the KKK was still out there. Not what you expect to see on a quiet Sunday morning on your way to church anyway.

⤳

We saw new neighbors moving in across the street from us and were very surprised to find out it was George Jones and his wife Nancy. George Jones was world-famous, internationally known for his country music. He was often called the greatest of all country singers; he was a country music legend, a superstar. And they were moving in right across the street.

By the time they moved by us, George Jones had married his fourth wife Nancy. He had battled alcoholism for years, and Nancy seemed to possess the magic—whatever it took—to keep George from drinking. She was largely credited for getting him off alcohol.

Jack and I had seen a movie about George Jones' life when he was married to Tammy Wynette. George and Tammy had a home in south Lakeland that had some acreage. There was a big barn on the property, and we were told that George and Tammy held concerts there, but that was before we knew George. Anyway, in the movie, it showed George shooting up that house with a rifle and riding into town on a lawn mower to get beer. Jack asked him about that, and George told him he didn't shoot the house up, but that he did ride the lawn mower to town for beer.

Both George and Nancy were down-to-earth, just good everyday people. If you went to Morrison's cafeteria in North Lakeland, you would see an autographed photo of George Jones on the wall near the cash register—another testimony of their humility—their love for people. They were not too proud to dine in a cafeteria with ordinary folks.

They were riding their bikes around the neighborhood one day when Nancy challenged George to a race to see who could get home first. George played it straight and stayed on the road. Nancy, who had fallen behind, took a shortcut through our yard and was waiting in their driveway when George came around the corner of our street. They had a good laugh over that.

Nancy and George lived across the street from us for three years. Each Christmas morning of those three years, a gift from them appeared on our porch outside our front door. The first year, it was a potted Norfolk pine that we planted in the yard beside our house. The second Christmas, they gave us a replica vintage radio. The third Christmas, they gave us a footbath. It would heat the water and make your feet feel so good. Jack used to tease them, saying that he only felt half as good because he only had one foot. Nancy and George moved soon after that—built a big home in Franklin, Tennessee. My memories of them are fond.

55

Flint was rocked to the core when in 1986, a fifty-five-year-old Flint socialite was brutally murdered.

Margarette Eby was a professor and provost at the University of Michigan-Flint. She lived in the gate house at Applewood, the estate of Charles S. Mott and his wife, Ruth.

Jeffery Wayne Gorton attended Flint Southwestern and was a standout member of the chess team. He developed a fetish for stealing women's underwear while still in high school and served two years in prison for that offense.

He met his first wife at a Flint roller rink in 1981. Gorton was described as a meek suburban dad who rarely raised his voice, helped his two children with their homework, and attended a Baptist church in Mt. Morris, Michigan. Lurking inside this seemingly harmless man was a serial killer.

In September 1986, Jeffery Gorton bound and gagged Margarette Eby, raped her, and slit her throat, nearly decapitating her. He wasn't arrested for fifteen years when a fingerprint that had been lifted from a faucet at the gatehouse when Margarette was murdered was traced to him. Semen taken from Ms. Eby matched a sample that was taken from an airline stewardess murdered in the same manner at a Detroit motel linking the two murders to Gorton.

Justin Weathers, who is married to my granddaughter, Stephanie, worked with Gorton at the Gorton family's sprinkler company in Flint. Justin remembers that the police got further DNA from a cup

Gorton was drinking from at the workplace. Justin recalled Gorton as being soft-spoken and talking about religion a lot.

Gorton had a lengthy criminal record and received two life terms for the two murders he committed.

〜

Our family had grown with marriages that had taken place and grandchildren and those children's marriages. When we got together as a family, it was a big group. Jack would glance over at me, smile, and say, "We sure started something."

Looking back on the last decade, the years just seemed to have melted away. We spent the summer months in Michigan and the winter months in Florida.

Our son, Ron, his wife Paula, and their two children had moved to Florida before we bought a home there; so we were blessed to have a part of our family in Florida. In Michigan, we had the support of a huge loving and caring family.

During that decade, we sold our place in Mott Park and bought a cottage at Houghton Lake. It reminded me of my dad—buying the general store in Henderson and going back home again. Houghton Lake had played a big part in Jack's life when he was growing up. Maybe he was "going back home again" too.

On our first fourth of July at the lake, twenty-seven people came up to spend a week with us—family and friends. Ron and Paula and their kids drove up from Florida. There weren't many times anymore when all four of our kids were together. We rented two other cabins to sleep everyone and some of the grandkids slept in a tent in our front yard.

We had the best time that week. It was one of my favorite times at the lake and holds so many sweet memories. The guys enjoyed fishing, and everyone loved our speedboat. There's no telling how many tanks of gas went through the boat that week, but a lot. Our grandson Michael caught the biggest fish, and I think everyone had their picture taken holding Michael's fish. Then, there was all the laughter the night a skunk let a stink bomb under one of the cabins.

It was really pungent, and the aroma brought all of us out of our cabins in the middle of the night. On the fourth, Jack and I cooked steaks with all the trimmings for all twenty-seven. Great memories.

Enjoying life at Houghton Lake

It was while spending a summer at the cabin that an incident happened at Walmart that could have easily killed me.

There's a Walmart Super Center at Houghton Lake now, but back when this incident happened, it was one of their small stores. At that location, the grocery carts were kept inside the store. You just walked in the entry aisle, turned to the left, and the carts were right there by the checkout lanes.

It was September 1, and Walmart was preparing for the Labor Day holiday. Along the left side of the entry aisle parallel with the carts, they had cartons of soda pop stacked up six or seven feet high— quite a bit taller than me. I went behind that display to get my shopping cart, and Jack was getting in a riding cart when suddenly, that display of soda pop crashed down all over me.

Pepsi-Cola cartons exploded all around me. They hit me from my head to my toes and everywhere in between, down my back, since I was facing away from them. They came down with great force; one carton flew over my shoulder and landed in my cart. If you could have seen all of those cartons on the floor right where I was standing, I think God must have had me encircled with angels because it's a miracle I was still standing. Thank God it didn't happen to a little child; they probably would have been killed.

The accident was caused by the Pepsi-Cola delivery man. He brought his product in to stack it and found that the Coca-Cola delivery person had edged over on his space. That angered him, and he shoved his cartons to get them in the allotted space, causing them to come down forcefully. He heard me cry out and came around the back of the display to see if I was all right, told us what he had done, and apologized.

Lisa, the store manager, filled out all of the necessary papers recording what had happened. An ambulance pulled up to the front of the store, but no one ever mentioned it or asked me about going to get checked. I was crying like crazy, hurting all over, and just wanted to go home.

Lisa called in the afternoon to see how I was doing and said the young man who caused the accident had later denied everything—very likely after he called his company and told them what happened.

I couldn't stop crying. I had an appointment with my hairdresser the next day, and when I called her to cancel, I burst out crying again. I couldn't believe what was happening to me. I hurt all over, but this was emotional.

At the urging of Jack, our children, and our pastor, I finally went to Emergency. Everyone at the hospital was very kind and sympathetic. I was crying uncontrollably as I talked with the young girl who filled out my papers, the triage nurse, and the doctor. The doctor was very understanding, saying the accident must have scared me half to death. He also said that it could have easily killed me. I told the doctor there was a guardian angel behind me or it would have broken my back. He said, "Yes, or worse."

The diagnosis was posttraumatic syndrome, concussion, cephalgia (headaches), and depression. Posttraumatic syndrome is hard to explain, but the incident kept replaying over and over in my mind, and every time, I would weep again—not sobbing, but quietly crying, the tears just running down my face. They did so many tests and found evidence of a ministroke deep down in my brain. The doctor prescribed medication for pain and another for anxiety.

When Jack went to get my prescriptions filled, he bought a carton of Pepsi-Cola that was the same size that had fallen on me. They contained twelve 16.9-ounce bottles, and the carton weighed over thirteen pounds—about the weight of a bowling ball. We estimated that twenty to twenty-five cartons fell on me. So imagine someone throwing twenty to twenty-five bowling balls at you as hard as they could.

When Jack picked my records up from the hospital, we thought we should talk to a lawyer. We called two of the lawyers that advertise on television all the time. Neither one would take the case. We called our personal lawyer, our friend and neighbor who used to live across the street from us, and he wouldn't take the case either. He said, "You won't get anyone to go against Walmart. They have the best—a big legal department. They never pay for anything." So we didn't call anyone else.

We have some wonderful friends, Mary and Jim Keating, who have a son who is a lawyer. Mary and Jim came to visit. Mary burst through our back door at the cottage, gave me a big hug, and excitedly exclaimed, "Guess what! Our son's law firm will take your case!" Their son has the largest law firm in northern Michigan; he's located in Saginaw.

My case was assigned to a very kind and caring lawyer named Greg. He called on the phone and asked all kinds of questions about my accident, and quite unexpectedly, I started to cry. Again. This was twenty-three days after it happened. I just couldn't get over how traumatized I still was.

I had an appointment with my doctor, Dr. Jeffery Strickler, on a Friday. Vacation Bible School was starting at our church the following Monday, and I was scheduled to be a teacher in one of the classes.

When I went to the doctor that previous Friday, he had unsettling news for me. He said that one of the head x-rays clearly showed that I had multiple myeloma (a form of cancer). He said that he was 95% sure. I was stunned, but told him, "I'm going to continue with my plans to teach at VBS. My life is in God's hands. Whether I have it or don't, I'm in God's care."

When the next CT scan of my head was taken, there was no evidence of it, and the doctor was the one stunned. He couldn't believe it. He said that the evidence shows up as perfect round circles, kind of clear like a bubble, the way I understood it. He said that they were clearly evident, but now gone. I thank You, heavenly Father. You are my everything.

It took a long time to get this case settled—more than three years. There were so many appointments with doctors, specialists, and tests at hospitals in Florida as well as Michigan. It just seemed to go on forever with someone asking for one more test, one more CT scan of my head, one more x-ray. Finally, I was called to the lawyer's office to give a deposition. Greg set up a conference call where Jack and I, Greg, and the other lawyer could all hear the conversation. I gave all of my answers clearly and didn't cry! Greg said that I did a good job.

Our family lawyer was correct when he said that Walmart wouldn't pay anything. The responsibility for the accident was put on the vendor, Pepsi-Cola, not Walmart. I guess that was fair, because their employee admitted he had caused the accident, even though he later denied it. He had told us the truth right when it happened. In the end, they offered to settle out of court for $30,000. Greg said, "You don't have to accept that, Arlene. If you go to court, a jury will award you a lot more." Three long years of test after test. I just wanted it to be over, so accepted their offer. The law office only charged me ten percent of my settlement; they could have lawfully charged much more; so I netted $27,000. That covered all of my medical expenses, and that's all I cared about.

Snowbirds

56

I truly believe that God causes people to cross our path for a certain reason and at a certain time—divine appointments—like the time in France when we were in the candy shop when the busload of orphan boys pulled up. A world away, but I believe we were there at that particular time to bless those boys in a small way.

Another instance of what I call divine appointments happened in church down in Florida on Mother's Day. All churches are packed out on Mother's Day, and that day was no exception. Jack wasn't with me that day.

Our pastor was well into his sermon when the lady sitting directly in front of me stood up. She was a stranger to me, and I knew most of the people in that church, but on Mother's Day, some people come that only show up on Easter, Mother's Day, and Christmas. The lady had a little girl with her about eight years old. The lady boldly stood up and clearly called out—interrupting pastor's sermon. "I need help!" she shouted out. The pastor was stunned into silence, and everyone turned to look at her. I doubt if anyone had experienced this in church before; I know I hadn't.

We were sitting about halfway down in the center section. She called out that their family was homeless. The pastor asked where her husband was. She replied that he was at a gas station cleaning their baby up. The pastor asked what their needs were. She said that they needed everything—food, clothing, and diapers. The pastor had the gentleman in charge of those things at our church stand up so she could identify him and make plans after church for help.

I knew in my heart that the Lord had placed her in that seat directly in front of me. My heart went out to this dear mother who braved the stares of strangers to seek help for her family. I admired her so much for the courage she had to ask. I gave her everything I had in my wallet, even the $20 I hide away in my wallet for emergencies; I had sixty-some dollars with me and folded it up and handed it to her. I didn't identify myself in any way to her.

When I was walking to my car, I heard someone behind me calling out my name. I turned around, and it was the lady that had been setting in front of me. She wanted to thank me for the gift. How did she know my name? I've wondered many times if she was an angel and God wanted to know how the people of our church would respond to her cry for help. She was supposed to be meeting with the man who handled food distribution, yet here she was in the parking lot with me. The Bible says that sometimes, we entertain angels unaware. I'll find out when I get to heaven.

Jack and I had another incredible experience while attending the same church in Florida. Our Bible Study class had a dinner meeting once a month at the church. On this particular night, a new couple sat directly across the table from Jack and me. One of our class members had invited them to come to the dinner. We introduced ourselves and learned that their names were Margaret and Jack Worden. We enjoyed their company throughout the dinner.

When the meal was finished, Margaret went to the front of our group and quite unexpectedly began to tell their story. She and Jack were homeless, living in an old car. Here again, they were placed directly across from us. If they had been at the end of one of the long tables, we might not have been so involved.

Margaret and Jack came to our Bible Study class the next Sunday, and we became better acquainted with their situation. Long story short, the Lord spoke to my heart. He said that we were to buy them a home. And we did. It was a mobile home of Margaret's choosing. Jack and I had found one that we thought suitable; it was more money, a nicer home, but Margaret said that they couldn't pay for lot rent in that location. She knew right where she wanted to be.

It was located close enough to a shopping center where she could walk to Walmart.

We didn't tell anyone about buying Margaret and Jack their home—not even our children, and certainly no one in our church. No one knew except the four of us, and God.

We were friends with Margaret and Jack for many years. They continued to attend our Bible Study class, and Margaret would regale our class from time to time about how she went dumpster-diving and found the nicest things. We would take groceries to their home from time to time, and when I gave her cash, she would roll it up and stuff it down her bra. Margaret could really stretch a dollar, and her husband never got his hands on any of the cash.

Their mobile home park backed right up to the water, and after some years, a company bought that park to acquire the waterfront property. The mobile homes were bought by the new owner and torn down for a big new building of some kind. Margaret and Jack were afraid when their house was purchased by that company, we might want the money from the sale. Not to worry, dear friends, the home was yours, and the money yours to keep to buy another home.

Divine appointment? We'll find out someday.

CHAPTER 57

Over the years, I've written in journals that I named "My Ordinary Days." Reading back through them, I am amazed at the steady stream of company—both family and friends—that we entertained in our home. Whether in Michigan or Florida, there was a procession of folks in our homes—such a grand reminder of how blessed we were.

We had hundreds, probably thousands, of meals cooked and shared; family for the holidays and vacations; friends for dinner, card games, or board games; groups to go dancing; and friends to play golf with. And we were invited to their homes just as often. Sweet memories.

Another thing that Jack and I enjoyed through the years were our "day trips." We would get in the car on a sunny day with no destination planned—just head off east, west, north, or south, just start off in any direction. We would find a village, town, or city and see what they had to offer. We found that every place had something of interest.

Sometimes, we would discover a historical home to tour, a museum, or antique shop. Once, we discovered an antique doll museum that was in a private home. Some towns might have a lovely Victorian downtown area or maybe a farmer's market. We searched for local eateries, shunning the fast-food places. Sometimes, it was as simple as finding a café with homemade pies or a new flavor of ice cream. We always had our golf clubs in the trunk and sometimes ended up playing a round of golf. It always turned into a delightful day.

Another enjoyable pastime was seeing stage plays. When in Flint, we always purchased season tickets to Whiting Auditorium. We had the same seats every year, seven rows back, center. In Florida, we had the Tampa Bay Performing Arts Center where we could see stage shows direct from New York City. Fabulous.

One November day when we were in Michigan, Jack said, "How would you like to go golfing tomorrow?" Right! Golfing in Michigan in November! We played golf the next day!

We got in the car, no destination in mind, but packed for the weekend and headed south. We ended up at Corbin, Kentucky, which happens to be the home of Kentucky Fried Chicken. We checked into a Holiday Inn perched high on a mountaintop. The next day, we had lunch at the original restaurant where the colonel started his business and went to a golf course in the afternoon where we were paired up with the mayor of that little city. We just never knew where our little jaunts would end up, and they were all fun, but that's the only time we ever played golf with a mayor.

We stayed at the Grand Hotel on Mackinac Island on two different occasions. The second time, our room was directly across from the Presidential Suite. I had commented that I would sure like to see what that was like. The next morning when we headed out for breakfast, Jack went straight across the hall and knocked on the door. I was standing there, probably with my mouth still hanging open in shock, when a lady opened the door. After pleasantries were exchanged, Jack very calmly said, "My wife has always wanted to see what the Presidential Suite is like." The friendly couple invited us in and gave us a tour of the whole suite, which was lovely, of course. With their kindness, I recovered from my embarrassment. But, I swear, if the president had been in residence, that husband of mine probably would have done the same thing!

⌣⌢

When your old wedding ring was new,
And each dream that I dreamed came true,
I remember with pride how you stood by my side

What a beautiful picture you made as my bride.
Even though silver crowns your hair,
I can still see the gold ringlets there;
Love's old flame is the same
As the day I changed your name,
When your old wedding ring was new.

Jack was in the car one day, when he heard this song played on the radio. He loved the words and special meaning. He called the radio station to find out more about it. They told him the title of the song was "When Your Old Wedding Ring Was New," and the vocalist was Jimmy Roselli.

Jack went to a local music store and bought a tape by Jimmy Roselli that included that song. He placed it in the tape deck of our car and set it so that every time I got in the car, he could press just one button, and that song would play. I thought that was pretty romantic for a guy seventy-five years old that had already celebrated his golden wedding anniversary. I loved the song as much as he did, and it became "our" song. We played it over and over.

We were in the car one day with our granddaughter, Laura, and a friend of hers. As always, Jack pressed the button, and "our" song came on. I turned around to say something to Laura, and her eyes were filled with tears—so full they were ready to spill down her cheeks. I said, "What's the matter, honey?" She replied, "I don't know, Grandma. I've just never known anyone who has been married as long as you and Grandpa that still love and respect each other." My heart went out to her. It's true—there aren't that many of us out there.

⌣⌣

I was in my late seventies when I entered the world of electronic technology. I had wanted a computer for quite some time, but Jack didn't want me to get one. "They're a tool of the Devil," he exclaimed. "Not if you don't touch the wrong key," I stated my case. "I'm not going to be searching for wrong things."

Jack finally gave in to my pleas and I was thrilled with my new computer. Barb and Ron both used computers in their work place and they were instrumental in teaching me how to navigate the internet.

My computer has been a source of joy to me. I wonder now how I ever got along without one. When I left the work-force in 1978 at General Motors, we didn't have computers. Soon after, they would be on everyone's desks.

~⁓

Over time, changes in Jack's health had been creeping into our daily life. Little by little, subtle changes were taking place. He wasn't eating as much as normal and was nauseated much of the time.

He had a series of episodes where he fell down. When he was stronger, and I was younger, I was able to grab ahold of his belt in the back and with his help get him up on his feet, but now that he was growing weaker and unable to help, it was problematic.

Sometimes, there were outbursts of anger. Frustration, maybe, but it was so unlike Jack, who always had such a positive outlook on everything. Was it the beginning of dementia?

Cancer developed on his cheek and the top of his head. Surgery was required, and they had to take him back in the operating room three times before they were satisfied that they had gotten all of it.

One night, he woke me up six times during the night—four times to use the urinal and twice because he thought he heard someone talking. The next morning, he stopped up the toilet, and it overflowed. That's all part of being a caregiver. You are on call around the clock.

We had our son Ron and his wife, Paula, for dinner. I had prepared a roast with all the trimmings. Jack lost everything right at the table. The nausea was escalating. From then on, he ate with a wastebasket beside his chair.

50th Wedding Anniversary

He had difficulty swallowing his food and often had choking episodes. I would do the Heimlich maneuver or pound on his back to dislodge the food.

He suffered hearing loss too, which is not uncommon. Sometimes, the comments he made were pretty funny, because he didn't hear me correctly. Making conversation with him one day, I said, "When I took the garbage out, the raindrops were this big around," and with my thumb and forefinger indicated that the raindrops were the size of a 50¢ piece. Really alarmed, he shouted back, "You killed an armadillo?" Don't ask me where it came from, but sometimes, it was really hilarious.

The funniest one ever was about a commercial we saw on television about a new medication. I commented, "With all of those side effects, who would want to take it?" Jack asked, "What's it for?" I replied, "Psoriasis." He shouted back, "Sore asses?" That one really cracked me up. Laughter is good medicine.

We had purchased a lift chair for Jack that almost raised him up to a standing position. Even with that help, I had to call 911 twice in one day. He collapsed when trying to get up. I tried and tried to get him up from the floor, but he was too weak to help, and I had to call 911. The two men easily raised him up. A few hours later, he was unable to get up from the commode. I had to call them again, and the same attendants came. When 911 has to make two calls in one day, they are required to transport to the hospital.

There was a follow-up visit with our primary care doctor when he was released from the hospital. After Jack's examination and he had returned to the waiting room, the doctor asked me if we had living wills. I said, "Yes." She said, "Where's my copy?" I thought I had already given her a copy and apologized for not doing so. I told her I had an appointment with her in April and would mark my calendar to bring a copy. She replied, "Don't wait. Bring it right away. His heart is very weak, and something could happen at any time."

I was devastated. I knew Jack had a lot of problems, but to have the doctor come right out and say that really upset me. That night, I started having chest pains about 8:00 p.m. We were on our way to the Emergency Room when the pains subsided, and I had Jack turn around and take me back home. Evidently, it was an anxiety attack. The stress was getting to me.

These changes took place over time, but it was one thing after another and was so incredibly sad. I didn't mind taking care of him at all. There was no doubt in my mind that if the situation was reversed, he would do the same for me.

CHAPTER 58

Time slipped quietly by. Sometimes, we were able to attend church, or accept an invitation to a friend's home to play cards. Those times became less and less frequent.

I became a full-time caregiver, only leaving Jack long enough to get groceries. He had grown totally dependent on walking with his cane, crutches, or walker or walking behind me with his hands on my shoulders for support.

The doctor scheduled yet another test for Jack—a barium swallow—to see if they could figure out why he was so nauseated, coughing, and choking at mealtime. It was so difficult for him to eat. Consequently, he was eating very little, and I could see him growing weaker. There were no helpful results from the test.

His condition continued to deteriorate. Just a week later, his blood sugar tested high, in the mid 240s. I called the doctor to see if I should take him to Emergency. She said to keep track of his sugar and I did, but things continued to get worse. That night, he was unable to get up from his chair at the supper table without help. It was just a few steps with his walker to get to his lift chair, but when he reached it, he just stood there looking at it, couldn't figure out how to get turned around to sit down. He looked at me with such pleading in his eyes; he didn't know what to do. It just broke my heart. He had said all day he didn't want to go to the hospital, but when he couldn't get into his chair, I gently said, "Jack, you need help." His eyes were filled with sadness, and he said, "Yes, I need help." I immediately called 911, and they transported him to Emergency.

We're in our 80's!

They scheduled a barium swallow test for Jack even though he had been given one two weeks before. This time, the test revealed that his throat muscles had weakened and was allowing food and liquids to pass into his lungs. He had pneumonia and bronchitis. They put a feeding tube up his nose and down into his stomach. Very painful!

After two days, they did a procedure to insert a feeding tube directly into his stomach. He had been on liquid food ever since the first tube was inserted. They told me that one bite of food or one sip of water could jeopardize his life. I felt so hopeless when I left the hospital that night. I really didn't think he would be leaving the hospital. I was sobbing before I even made it to the elevator.

I called all the kids as soon as I got home to tell them everything that had taken place and the changes in their dad. Both of our daughters, Carol Ann and Barb, made plans to fly to Florida right away. Ron just lived twenty miles away from us, and Jerry was on his way down from Michigan.

Jack was transferred to a nursing home, and it seemed as if he was making progress for a time. They even had him doing exercises for a few days, and that raised my hopes tremendously even though I knew he was still very weak and still had the feeding tube.

I went to the hospital and nursing home every day without fail. No way was I going to disappoint him. At the nursing home, the aids would dress him in the morning and put him in a wheelchair. He would sit in the doorway of his room, and when he saw me coming down the hall, he would roll out and come to me. I would give him a kiss and take him out to the big front porch. He enjoyed the fresh air and watching the cars go by.

One morning when I went in, I noticed immediately that something was wrong. He was hallucinating and seeing all kinds of strange things in his room. He saw the ceiling and walls moving, cobwebs hanging down, a yellow truck, lots of motorcycles, cowboys, buffaloes, a zebra, an elephant, rabbits, ducks, and many more things—all in his room. "Can't you see them?" he asked repeatedly.

The hallucinations continued, and I couldn't get an answer as to what might be causing this to happen. It was very painful for me to see this happening because I couldn't do anything to help him. I never did get an answer from any of the staff at the nursing home. Both of our sons, Ron and Jerry, thought maybe pain medication could be causing it. It was very difficult to imagine what all of that looked like to Jack and how he could ever understand what was going on. He must have been so bewildered and confused.

Carol Ann and Barb left for home after a week, and both of the boys came to stay with me at my house. Jack recognized all the children and was so very pleased that they came to visit. He was lucid right up until the end.

When Ron, Jerry, and I left the nursing home on the night of November 11, 2008, Jack was sleeping peacefully—more peacefully than I had seen him in a long time. Very early the next morning, our phone rang. Jerry grabbed the phone before I could get to it. It was the nursing home. They called to say that Jack had passed away at 5:57 a.m.

59

Jack's body was laid to rest at Great Lakes National Cemetery in Holly, Michigan, with full military honors. We had decided together many years ago the epitaph we wanted inscribed on our headstones. It would say, "Gone to thank Jesus."

His whole home-going service was awesome. I asked our pastor to give a strong Christian message with an altar call. He did, and two of our great-grandchildren invited Jesus into their heart as Lord and Savior, and four family members rededicated their lives to Christ. I'm sure Jack was rejoicing in heaven about that.

A family friend, Pastor Sheri McCrandall, sang a beautiful song, "If You Could See Me Now," about being in heaven, standing straight and tall, and walking on streets of gold. It's a real tearjerker, but was so appropriate for Jack. Whole at last with two good legs, a clear mind, and a healthy body—thank you, Lord.

At the cemetery, all of the military men were in full dress uniforms. Jack's casket was draped with an American flag. Two Navy men folded the flag and handed it to my granddaughter Stephanie's husband, who is a Marine. Justin presented the flag to me. Then, there was a 21-gun salute followed by "Taps." That just about tears your heart out. A fallen hero. The tears were running down my cheeks then, just as they are now as I relive it.

One of the service men brought me three shell casings to commemorate Jack's life. Ron and Jerry collected the rest of them so they could be shared with the family. It was a moving, emotional service. Jack would have been pleased with the military honors.

60

Other ladies who have lost their husbands tell me that "time heals everything." Others tell me my life will never be the same. One thing is for certain—my life is forever changed.

My immediate family, my extended family, and my church family surrounded me with their love. There was so much paperwork to take care of. My granddaughter Natalie went with me to the Social Security office and the Veterans Affairs department, which was so helpful, since my head still seemed to be in a fog at times.

There were so many "firsts" it was mind-boggling. Soon, Thanksgiving, Christmas, my birthday, Jack's birthday, and our anniversary were right around the corner—all in the next two months, things that Jack and I had celebrated together for almost sixty-two years.

Our friends still continued to invite me to their homes when they were having a group over. It was always couples and me, being an extra. I appreciated their kindness, but it was uncomfortable being the odd one.

My lady friends invited me out for lunch or an afternoon of games, which I enjoyed very much. Being a caregiver for the past three years, I had dropped out of every social contact I had, and I found that I craved companionship. Over time, I joined three lunch clubs and three card groups and went out for lunch after church with lady friends. In a one-week period, I counted twenty-nine ladies who I had contact with in one way or another. I needed that friendship.

After a period of time, I got back into my church activities. I was asked to assist in our Bible Study class, and I accepted. A friend, Naomi Gee, asked me if I would help with a Bible Study at a local nursing home on Friday mornings. I said yes. We had an outreach program at our church where we went out on Tuesday afternoons, called on people in their homes, and presented the gospel. We went out in groups of three. I did that for three seasons and became a leader.

Believe it or not, before Jack passed away, I had never pumped gas, and I'd been driving over sixty years. When Jack was in the hospital or in the nursing home, I would get one of my kids or grandkids to do it for me. Then came the day when I was driving on fumes, pressing my luck, and none of them were nearby. I prayed a simple prayer asking God to send me an angel and pulled up to a pump. I waited until a man pulled up beside me who had his wife with him. When I walked toward him, he smiled and said, "What do you need?" I told him that my husband had passed away, and I didn't have a clue how to pump gas. He very kindly showed me how easy it was, and I told him he was an answer to prayer. Don't ask me why I hadn't ever had one of the kids show me. Just wasn't on my mind, and probably all of them thought I knew how.

After a while, I cleaned out Jack's closet and donated his clothes. It was a hard thing to do, and I got pretty choked up. But the memories aren't in the clothes—the memories are in my heart.

The days passed swiftly, and before long, one year had passed, then two, and then three. I continued to spend the summers in Michigan and the winters in Florida. When it was time for me to travel, whoever was available in the family would fly to get me and drive me back in my car. Most times, it was Jerry, but my grandson, Michael, drove me a time or two. One time, my granddaughter Michelle volunteered, so she and her mom, Carol Ann, came. Another year, Carol Ann and Barb came. There was always someone who could come.

When Jack and I traveled, I would always put the tip for the maid in the Gideon's Bible that you find in every motel room. I'd open the Bible to Acts 16:31, circle that verse, and leave the Bible open so the maid would see it with the money lying right there. That verse reads, "Believe on the Lord Jesus, and you will be saved, you and your household."

The year I was traveling with Carol Ann and Michelle, I was going through my ritual with the Bible, tucking my tip for the maid by Acts 16:31. I said to the girls, "It's so sad. No one ever reads these Bibles. They're always just like new." Just then, a leaf dropped into my lap. "Oh, someone read this one," I exclaimed. "They dried a leaf in it!"

"Mom," Carol Ann shouted. "That's marijuana!"

With that, Michelle began clicking photos of me, gray-haired grandma with the Holy Bible in one hand and the marijuana leaf in the other. Barb was working for the Genesee County Sheriff's Department at that time. She took the photos to work and showed them to all the detectives, who got quite a kick out of the old lady with the Bible and the leaf.

Then, there was the year Carol Ann and Barb drove me home. We had a miraculous trip.

On the evening before our departure, I purchased takeout dinners from Boston Market, and we went over to share dinner with Ron and Paula. When Ron hugged me goodbye, he looked me square in the eyes and said, "Mom, if you ever have a blowout on your car, don't hit the brakes." He went on to explain that it could turn your car sideways, causing it to roll over. He had never said anything even remotely close to that to me before.

The first day of travel was uneventful, and the second day started out well too. We took a side trip in the morning to the little village of Juliette, Georgia, where they filmed the movie *Fried Green Tomatoes*. The Whistle Stop Café that the movie centered around didn't open until lunchtime, and the shops were only open in the afternoon, but we had fun looking around and taking pictures. We got back on the expressway about 10:30 a.m. Soon, we ran into a fierce rainstorm, and it lasted all day, making visibility very poor and travel slow. We were running late, and around nine thirty that night, and only about ten minutes from our motel, my car blew a tire on the right front! First time ever.

I happened to be driving at that moment with Barb in the passenger seat. When the blowout happened, Ron's face appeared before me just like he was there, and I heard him say, "Don't hit the brakes, Mom." Your natural instinct is to hit the brakes, but heeding this warning, I let the car drift to the shoulder of the road under its own power and come to a safe stop. I don't recall this, but Barb told me there was a semitruck on my right and a car on my left. God only knows what would have happened if I had hit the brakes.

I believe the Holy Spirit prompted Ron to make that comment to me and brought his face before me at that crucial time. God used Ron to save our lives. What a caring and loving God we serve. I believe in miracles. Do you?

CHAPTER

61

It started out with a twinge in the roof of my mouth, hardly noticeable at first. I thought maybe it was a canker sore. It didn't go away and kept getting bigger. Before long, it was a hole big enough to put the tip of my tongue in. That hole kept getting bigger; then, a second hole appeared behind the first one. The skin on the roof of my mouth was disappearing.

My granddaughter, Laura, took a flashlight and shined it onto the roof of my mouth. She gasped when she saw it. "Grandma," she said. "You've got to go to the doctor right away." Carol Ann and Barb rushed me to the doctor that very day.

My doctor is my granddaughter, Michelle, who is a physician's assistant. She was pretty shocked when she viewed it and said that she had never seen anything like it. She called two other doctors in to see it. Same thing—they had never seen anything like it either.

Michelle arranged an appointment with an oral surgeon for me that very day. I think "cancer" was on everyone's mind. Dr. Mark Medel assured me it was not cancer. That was the good news. The bad news was that it was osteonecrosis. Osteo means bone, and necrosis means death. As the name indicates, the bone begins to weaken and die.

Osteonecrosis is caused by taking Fosamax, a prescription medication that was prescribed to me for osteoporosis. It's supposed to strengthen bones, but osteonecrosis can be a side effect. I believe it states that now in small print on their packaging. That information was not there when I was taking it. Over the next months, my primary care doctor and three oral surgeons would tell me that my condition was caused by Fosamax.

It was near time for my return to Florida, so Dr. Medel recommended an oral surgeon in Florida. Dr. Medel's written report to Dr. Mark Mitchell stated that two thirds of the roof of my mouth was gone, leaving exposed bone. I wasn't able to continue with Dr. Mitchell because he didn't take my insurance.

I tried not to think about my situation too much, but honestly, it was on my mind all the time. It was very difficult to eat and impossible to keep food away from the open area, so it would become irritated. To further complicate things, my throat and back of my mouth were swollen. More discomfort. I was now in my eighth month of living with this.

My primary care, Dr. Sunjic, recommended another specialist. Dr. Chuong took full x-rays around my head but said that he couldn't see enough, so he requested a CT scan. He explained to me that the floor of the nose and roof of the mouth are connected. That makes perfect sense, although I had not thought of it that way before. That makes surgery on the roof of the mouth very risky. A mistake, and I could end up eating through a tube.

The CT scan was performed and showed Dr. Chuong nothing except that I didn't have an opening into my nose from my mouth. He wanted to get surgery going right away. That would entail debriding (grinding) the dead bone from the roof of my mouth. This condition is very rare and surgery very risky. I asked him how many of these surgeries he had performed. He said that he had only seen "maybe" ten situations like this in his medical career. He didn't say that he had done surgery on any of them. He said that he could not guarantee any outcome—couldn't even say if the skin would grow back.

This was all very upsetting to me. I talked it over with my primary care, Dr. Sunjic. She said that Dr. Chuong's answers were all vague because this is so rare and there are no answers. After talking with Dr. Sunjic and discussing all of this with my children, I decided to put the surgery on hold for ninety days.

Carol Ann was hosting a family get-together. It's a big gathering when our family gets together, with an abundance of food, including homemade noodles, of course, and everyone talking at once. I was eating my dinner when the bone from the roof of my mouth fell on my tongue. I was so surprised I didn't say anything to anyone. I went to a quiet place and put my napkin up to my mouth and removed it. It was about the size of a 50¢ piece. There was also just a small amount of blood. I disposed of it and cautiously put my tongue up there. There was fresh, new skin covering the roof of my mouth! Praise the Lord! I shared my news with the family, and we celebrated!

It had been seventeen months. The loving heavenly Father that created me healed me. No wonder I love Him so much.

When my next appointment came up with my primary care doctor, I went in and very excitedly exclaimed, "I'm going to make your day!" I showed her the roof of my mouth, and she couldn't believe it. She was ecstatic. In her South American accent, she exclaimed, "I'm going to write a paper on theese. Theese will never happen again!" Whether or not she ever wrote that paper, I can't say, but I can say there was a lot of excitement in Dr. Sunjic's office that day.

62

I cannot end my story without sharing Jack's adoption papers with you. Do you remember that his adoptive parents told him that his parents were getting a divorce, that they had five children and his mother couldn't take care of another child, so she put him up for adoption?

When I came into the family and asked questions, I was told the same fairytale. The truth of Jack's birth and his adoption was so very different from what we were told. Jack lived his whole life believing a total untruth.

It was about three years after Jack passed away that I decided to file for his adoption papers. Even though we had been married almost sixty-two years, I couldn't get them because I wasn't a blood relative. Ridiculous! So I asked my eldest child Carol Ann to file for them. A copy of those official adoption documents follows:

**Child and Family
Services of Michigan, Inc.**

The Family . . .
our concern
Since 1891

2157 University Park Drive
Okemos, Michigan 48864

517/349-6226
517/349-0969 Fax
cfsm@cfsm.org
www.cfsm.org

Member of:

Local United Ways

Child Welfare
League of America

Michigan Federation for
Children and Families

Member Agencies:

Family Counseling & Children's
Services of Lenawee County
Adrian

Child & Family Services of
Northeast Michigan, Inc.
Alpena

Child & Family Services of
Southwestern Michigan, Inc.
Benton Harbor

Pathways, MI
Holland

Family Service &
Children's Aid
Jackson

Child & Family Services,
Capital Area
Lansing

Child & Family Services of
the Upper Peninsula, Inc.
Marquette

Family & Children's Service
of Midland, Inc.
Midland

Child & Family Services of
Northwestern Michigan, Inc.
Traverse City

February 7, 2011

Ms. Carol A. Lusk
8318 N. Linden Rd.
Mt. Morris, MI 48458

Dear Ms. Lusk:

In response to your request for identifying information regarding your father's birth family, we have accessed the Central Adoption Registry (C.A.R.) in Lansing. As of December 13, 2010, there were no statements filed by any birth family members. Since parental rights were terminated before May 28, 1945 and no denial statements are on file with the C.A.R., we are authorized to release identifying information to you.

Your father's birth name was Howard Frederick Barnes.

His birth mother's name was Mary Barnes. Her address was recorded as 198 Gilbert Street, Kalamazoo, Michigan.

His alleged birth father's name was recorded as Frank L. Cornish. His address was 524 Monroe Street, Kalamazoo, Michigan.

Enclosed is the non-identifying information available from our records. Also enclosed is the Central Adoption Registry Clearance form which assists adult adoptees in obtaining their original birth certificates from the Michigan Department of Community Health (MDCH). It is my understanding that the MDCH has determined that direct descendents of deceased adoptees are not entitled to receive a copy of the sealed original birth certificate of the adoptee, but I have included an application with their telephone number on the back in the event you have questions about filing a request.

Should you have any questions or concerns regarding the above or enclosed information provided by this agency, please do not hesitate to contact me at 1-800-878-6587. You may leave a message if I am not immediately available and I will return your call as soon as possible.

February 7, 2011
Page 02

Sincerely,

Christina McGregor
Post-Adoption Social Worker

Enclosures

Child and Family Services of Michigan, Inc.
Non-Identifying Information
Manly Jack Curns

Manly Jack Curns was born January 14, 1925 in the University Hospital of Ann Arbor, Washtenaw County, Michigan. At birth he weighed 6 lbs., 2 oz. He was in good physical condition, had been circumcised, and a Wassermann was negative at birth.

The status of termination of parental rights was voluntary. The birth mother signed a release of her parental rights on January 28, 1925.

He was placed with the Michigan Children's Aid Society on 02/24/1925. On 02/25/1925, he was placed in a temporary boarding home. He was transferred to the Receiving Home at St. Joseph on 02/28/1925 and remained there until he was transferred to the Receiving Home in Lansing on 05/18/1925. He was placed with his adoptive family on 05/20/1925 and his adoption was confirmed on 07/21/1926 by the Genesee County Probate Court.

The birth mother was born April 29, 1903 in Decatur, Michigan. She was described as a very pretty girl with golden hair, blue eyes, and a fair freckled complexion. She stood 5'2½" tall and had a slender build. She dressed well and made a very good impression. She started school at age 6 and finished at the Grant School in Chicago, 9th grade at age 16. She liked reading, spelling, and arithmetic and disliked geography. Her mother was a hotel worker and the birth mother lived with her until age 10. While visiting with relatives on a farm near Decatur, they met a family named Mitchell who lived in Chicago and had a summer home in the community. Mr. Mitchell was an insurance man. The Mitchell's became very fond of the birth mother and took her to Chicago, keeping her for six years. The birth mother liked the family but when Mrs. Mitchell became dissatisfied with her attitude, she was returned to her mother. Her mother had remarried and lived in Marshall where they stayed about a year before moving to Kalamazoo. The birth mother then went to live with a girlfriend. She became employed as a clerical worker for the Grace Corset Company at age 17 and earned $15.40 a week. She was a very charming, delicate, fragile type girl. She was said to have fair habits. She was of American nationality and preferred the Methodist Episcopal faith; although church had not been a factor in her life. Her health history was negative. She had been a breast fed, full term, normally delivered child. She reached puberty at age 13. Her home was in a rather poor district and they lived in the lower flat of an old fashioned house. It was very neat and clean and everything was in perfect order. The birth mother was anticipating marriage to a young man she had been dating and while she wished very much to have her baby, the man did not seem willing for her to keep him due to his resentment toward the alleged birth father.

The maternal grandparents separated in the birth mother's early childhood. The maternal grandfather was last heard from 10 years earlier. He was a blacksmith. He was of medium height and slender with very sandy hair and blue eyes. His relatives had similar fair coloring. It was believed that his parents were born in Ireland and he was born in the United States. His mother was thought to be about 85 years of age when she died. He had one sister and one brother who was the owner of a meat market.

ARLENE CURNS

The maternal grandmother's mother died when she was a girl and she had married very young, a man a great deal older than she who was the father of her three children. He was reportedly very cruel to her and she left him and was divorced a good many years ago. Eight years earlier she had come to Kalamazoo with her two children. She later sent her son to his father. She was of Irish and Dutch descent. She gave the impression as being rather coarse and common but the life she had lived would somewhat account for this. She had hardly any education, an unhappy marriage, and had to work hard all of her life. Her mother was born in Illinois and died in 1904. The cause of death was unknown. Her father was born in New York. He was a farmer and mechanic. She had one brother, age 41, who was a factory mechanic.

The birth mother had a brother, age 22, who was in the Navy. Another brother died at 4½ years of pneumonia or whooping cough.

The alleged birth father was born in Allegan County, Michigan. He was 35 years of age. He was described as having dark brown hair and eyes. He was of medium height and had a rather stocky build. He graduated from high school and entered the army shortly after. He was in France during the war. He returned to the United States with his nerves in very poor condition. He went south and was working there when his wife came down to see him and they were married. She became sick and they returned to Kalamazoo. His home life had not been very happy. He and his wife loved one another but her people were continually interfering and causing dissension between them. His wife's parents moved away and they had been very happy together since they had gone. He felt his wife would leave him if she heard about the situation with the birth mother. He owned and managed the Flint Auto Agency in Kalamazoo and earned approximately $5000 a year. He smoked and drank a little. He followed the Protestant faith and was of American nationality.

The birth father was reported to have been a young married man with a very sweet wife and baby. He initially denied paternity and claimed he never had sexual relations with the birth mother, but gave the birth mother's step-father $100 because he was afraid his wife would hear the story, and the step-father threatened to take the matter into Court. Later, when interviewed with the birth mother he still did not feel he could be the father of the baby but did admit he had relations with the birth mother. They first met and became acquainted by flirting on the street and he took her home from the factory several evenings, and their relations occurred on an evening in May. He called her up and asked her to go with him later in the evening for a ride. He admitted that he had been drinking but both said that he was not drunk. He agreed that he did not know of anyone with whom the birth mother had been going at that time, except a young man who was light complexioned and had gray eyes that she was still keeping company with. The social worker who interviewed the couple was convinced the birth mother was telling the truth and he was the father, however there were suspicions that both had had other relations. During one of the birth mother's initial interviews, the worker noted shifting eyes and a lack of straightforwardness. She was not going to tell anything more than she had to when asked.

Medical History
Of
Manly Jack Curns

02/25/1925   Inguinal and axillary glands enlarged.

03/14/1925   Child has eczema. Is undernourished. Weighs 7 lbs., 9 oz.

04/17/1925   Rather a sour looking baby and hasn't a very good disposition. Has long sandy hair and deep blue eyes.

08/24/1925   Child has a very good disposition and had been very well during the summer.

01/04/1926   The baby was a bright, attractive little fellow with a winsome smile. His eye was slightly crossed and he had been taken to an eye specialist who said that he was too young for anything to be done. He had cut four teeth and there were others breaking through. He crept backwards but was having difficulty going forward.

03/26/1926   Child in good physical condition. He had pneumonia last month but had recovered. He walked by holding onto furniture.

05/21/1926   Jack was developing splendidly. He had all of his teeth, walked alone, and was in very good physical condition. He was a very attractive child with light brown hair, hazel eyes, and rosy cheeks.

I love you and miss you, Howard Frederick Barnes. I do so wish you had known how very much your birth mom loved you and wanted to keep you. I pray that you have met her in heaven and know the truth now.

EPILOGUE

It seems as though my life has flown by. Looking back to my childhood when the block of ice for our ice box was delivered by a man driving a horse-drawn cart, how could I have dreamed of seeing men land on the moon, being able to have access to the whole world by a device held in the palm of my hand, or seeing cars zooming down the expressway with no driver. It's an amazing world that God has given us.

I've lived for almost a century and what a journey it has been. I'm the matriarch of a loving and caring family of forty-three that mean the world to me. I live at Houghton Lake in a little cottage. I'm content no matter my circumstances. God has blessed me richly. I'm as content in this little home as I was in our big retirement nest egg home that is worth over half a million dollars now. Jesus is preparing a mansion for me in heaven—that's a promise in the Bible. When the last chandelier is hung, He will take me home.

Now, I have great-grandchildren and great-greats that come to visit. We feed the ducks and go for walks. They lift every rock that surrounds the base of the two fairy trees in my front yard, checking for bugs, worms, and anything creepy-crawly. They draw pictures on my driveway with colored chalk. We do jigsaw puzzles and if they don't get completed, I store them on a foam board until their next visit. We play games together. There are always lots of high fives and fist bumps going on when we score a win on Candy Crush. Maybe there's a shriek of dismay as someone buys both Park Place and Boardwalk in the Monopoly game, but it's all in good fun. I have a "picture wall" on my refrigerator that is covered with carefully colored pictures from my great-grandchildren. Neatly printed on the back "I love you a lot" is inscribed. When my four great-greats are old enough to color, their artwork will be displayed too. They are so delightful—they fill my heart. Nine decades span our lives, but we enjoy each others' company. The love is mutual.

And I cook homemade noodles for them. They're still a family favorite, and mothers have taught daughters how to make them throughout the generations in our family.

We always end up looking at the old photographs in the metal bread box that belonged to my mother. My mom and I used to look at the pictures with the faded names scrawled on the back. I'd ask endless questions, and my mom would tell the stories. Now, the metal box belongs to me, and I tell the stories.

I enjoy viewing nature at my little place. I recently learned that ducks mate for life and stay together as long as they live. When they leave here for warmer climates, it's most likely grandpa leading the vee.

One year, I had robins build a nest, and I was able to enjoy that phenomenon of birth just like my mom did so many years ago. They built their nest in the eaves above my garage door, and I had a front-row seat from my bedroom window.

This past summer, doves built a nest over my front door. The view wasn't as good; they were too high, but I would wake up to activity and cooing. Soon, I saw the babies' little heads peeking over the top of the nest.

There are three white Himalayan rabbits that visit my yard. I don't know who they belong to or how they got to this area, but I enjoy having them come to call.

The squirrels are real clowns. They do a fine ballet jumping from tree limb to tree limb. Then, they perform on the telephone pole wires where they do a spectacular high-wire act.

The sunrises and sunsets are magnificent to behold. God sure knows how to paint masterpieces.

All of this nature and grandeur causes me to reflect on what an awesome God we serve.

I ponder about the birth of a baby—how miraculous it is. Only God! Consider our bodies, how unique and complex they are, but function perfectly. There are over two million working parts in the eye! Just imagine! Only God! Then, I look up to the heavens. The sun, the moon, and the thousands of stars and planets—all in place. There are 400 billion stars in the Milky Way alone! The earth is spinning completely around every twenty-four hours, and miraculously none of these are crashing into each other. Who but God could orchestrate that? Every snowflake is unique and individual. No two alike. And fingerprints! With the millions of people in this world, each fingerprint is different. That seems impossible, but with God, nothing is impossible. It will take forever, Lord, to absorb Your greatness.

But just because you're a Christian doesn't mean that you don't know heartache too. The blessing of a long life does not come without consequences and great sorrow.

Besides my mom and dad, I have lost all of my siblings and all of their spouses, save one—my sister Edna's husband, Frank. I have lost my beloved husband, Jack; a darling son, Ron; two precious granddaughters, Laura and Stephanie; a very special grandson, Kyle; three dear great-grandsons Mark, Neal, and baby Isaac; and a dearly loved daughter-in-law, Clariesse. My comfort is that when I go home, they will be there waiting for me, and we will rejoice together, praising God forever.

More than anything, I would love to know that you will be in heaven with me too and ask that you would pray a little prayer with me to invite Jesus into your heart,

Dear heavenly Father, I ask You to forgive my sins. I repent of my sins and give my life to You. I believe that Jesus is Your Son. I believe that He died on the cross to bear my sins, was buried, and rose from the dead and is living in heaven with You now. I ask You, Jesus, to come into my heart right now and be my Lord and Savior. Amen.

God knows your heart. If you said that prayer and meant it in your heart, you are now saved and will spend eternity in heaven with

Jesus. The gospel is simple, yet complex in its entirety, but God wanted it simple enough so even a child's mind and heart could grasp it.

So I pray that I'll see you in heaven. Until then, I'll continue to live in my little cottage at Houghton Lake and wait for Jack to ask me to dance once again.

⌇

It's been ten years, three months, eight days, eleven hours, and sixteen minutes since Jack passed away. I have missed him every one of those minutes. He was the love of my life—my soulmate—the one who could cause me to smile, make my heart beat faster, comfort me if I was blue.

Bon voyage, dear one, 'til we're together again

Beside my bed is a memory box holding certain mementoes. I carefully lift a Hallmark birthday card from the box—a card Jack gave me many years ago. Inside the cover, in faded, barely legible handwriting, the message is tender,

> I love you because you are all a wife should be. I love you because you show warmth and joy and kindness…because you understand my moods…because you make me happy and soothe away my cares with a smile or a touch or a word. I love you because you make our home a place of joy and true contentment. I love you because you are gentle and thoughtful and considerate. I love you because you have never lost your magic, your charm, your sweetness. I love you because you're my wife…my everything.

Ah, I miss you so.

Some night when the mist of sleep overtakes me, my beloved will come for me. "Well, look at you," I'll say. "You look as handsome as you did all those years ago when you wanted to take me for a ride in your Model A. Dressed all in white! You look wonderful, honey."

And he will say, "You look beautiful, sweetheart. Just like you did on our wedding day."

He will offer his hand and whisper in my ear, "Come, dance with me."

I will put my hand in his. As we dance away in the mist, I will softly say, "The music is heavenly. It's so good to be going home."

REFERENCES

Scripture verses taken from the New International Version Bible (Copyright 1978)

Arlene Curns, mother of four and matriarch of a family of 43, wrote her memoir when she was 92 years old. She experienced everything from having ice delivered to their house by horse and wagon to seeing driverless cars on the expressway—from keeping in touch with penny postcards to the internet highway—and remembers when gas was 10c a gallon.

When Arlene was three years old, her family moved to Flint, Michigan, also known as "The Vehicle City." Her career in Flint evolved from being a theater usherette at 35c an hour to mahogany row.

Arlene is enjoying her "Golden Years" with family and friends while residing in northern Michigan.

CPSIA information can be obtained
at www.ICGtesting.com
Printed in the USA
BVHW091956270519
549348BV00030BA/2751/P